BAYLEY-III CLINICAL USE AND INTERPRETATION

BAYLEY-III
CLINICAL USE
AND
INTERPRETATION

Edited by

LAWRENCE G. WEISS
Pearson Assessment, San Antonio, Texas, USA

THOMAS OAKLAND
University of Florida, Gainesville, Florida, USA

GLEN P. AYLWARD
Southern Illinois University School of Medicine, Springfield, Illinois, USA

AMSTERDAM • BOSTON • HEIDELBERG • LONDON
NEW YORK • OXFORD • PARIS • SAN DIEGO
SAN FRANCISCO • SINGAPORE • SYDNEY • TOKYO

Academic Press is an imprint of Elsevier

Academic Press is an imprint of Elsevier
32 Jamestown Road, London NW1 7BY, UK
30 Corporate Drive, Suite 400, Burlington, MA 01803, USA
525 B Street, Suite 1800, San Diego, CA 92101-4495, USA

First edition 2010

Notice
No responsibility is assumed by the publisher for any injury and/or damage to
persons or property as a matter of products liability, negligence or otherwise, or
from any use or operation of any methods, products, instructions or ideas
contained in the material herein. Because of rapid advances in the medical
sciences, in particular, independent verification of diagnoses and drug dosages
should be made

British Library Cataloguing-in-Publication Data
A catalogue record for this book is available from the British Library

Library of Congress Cataloging-in-Publication Data
A catalog record for this book is available from the Library of Congress

ISBN: 978-0-12-374177-6

For information on all Academic Press publications
visit our website at elsevierdirect.com

Typeset by TNQ Books and Journals Pvt Ltd.
www.tnq.co.in

Printed and bound in United States of America
10 11 12 13 14 15 10 9 8 7 6 5 4 3 2 1

Working together to grow
libraries in developing countries

www.elsevier.com | www.bookaid.org | www.sabre.org

ELSEVIER   BOOK AID
            International   Sabre Foundation

Contents

4.   The Bayley-III Motor Scale

JANE CASE-SMITH AND HELEN ALEXANDER

5.   The Bayley-III Social-Emotional Scale

CECILIA BREINBAUER, TWYLA L. MANCIL AND STANLEY GREENSPAN

6.   The Bayley-III Adaptive Behavior Scale

JENNIFER L. HARMAN AND TINA M. SMITH-BONAHUE

Preface

Following birth, an infant's first 4 years are recognized as critical in the establishment of a solid foundation for later development. Most infants exhibit a normal developmental course, and thus typically need only routine attention from pediatric specialists. However, the early development of a sizable number of infants is punctuated by delays that, if allowed to continue, can chart a course for later difficulties. These infants and young children need specialized attention from one or more professionals prepared to address these developmental concerns.

Professionals generally begin their work by acquiring a thorough understanding of a young child's development, one that leads to an accurate description of his or her behaviors. The Bayley Scales of Infant and Toddler Development, Third Edition (Bayley-III; Bayley, 2006) can assist importantly in this effort.

The Bayley-III provides an individual assessment of the developmental functioning of infants and young children between 1 and 42 months of age. The Bayley-III is one of few measures designed specifically for use with this population. It enables assessment of the following five behavior domains important to the provision of professional services in light of legal and professional standards: cognitive, language, motor, social-emotional, and adaptive functioning. The Bayley-III is likely to be the most widely used instrument to assess infants and toddlers, and many consider it to be the reference standard in that regard.

This book's individual chapters introduce professionals who use the Bayley-III to its test content, and includes important scholarship regarding the foundations from which the test content is derived. The chapters also help guide practitioners in the administration, scoring, and interpretation of the scale. The test's strengths and areas of concerns are discussed. Clinicians, other practitioners, and students are also likely to benefit from discussions of each scale's use with clinical groups, as well as from the inclusion of actual case studies of children who display delays in one or more of the five developmental domains.

Excellent introductory and concluding chapters surround the five chapters that focus on each of the individual scales. The book begins with an overview of the Bayley-III by the research director responsible for leading the test development project. This chapter illuminates the impact of advances in theory and clinical research that informed the revision of Bayley-II to become the Bayley-III. The book concludes with a scholarly chapter on research related to neurodevelopmental screening procedures in pediatric settings, using a related but distinct test, the Bayley Infant Neurodevelopmental Screener. Practical, reliable, and valid methods for screening in pediatric settings are offered. This chapter provides an excellent compendium of research for those making decisions about instituting screening programs for infants and toddlers.

A wide range of pediatric professionals, especially those who use the Bayley-III to evaluate development from multiple perspectives, is likely to be informed by the book's breadth of content, including its literature reviews. These include educational diagnostic specialists; developmental, clinical child, pediatric, and school psychologists; occupational and physical therapists; speech/language pathologists; and other members of the medical community. Psychologists may be most interested in the assessment of cognitive and adaptive functioning, speech/language pathologists in assessing language development, occupational and physical therapists in assessing fine and gross motor development, and early childhood specialists and others in evaluating social and emotional functioning. This book is particularly well suited as a text for new examiners learning to administer, score, and interpret the Bayley-III in a standardized and clinically appropriate manner.

The book's editors and authors recognize that evaluation of infant and toddler development requires teamwork that includes parents and professionals – often from more than one discipline. The book's organization enables professionals to focus on their area of specialty by reading the chapter or chapters most germane to their work. We also believe an understanding of all content within the book helps to develop perspectives that assist in providing a quality, multidisciplinary assessment that truly addresses the needs of infants and toddlers who display developmental concerns.

January 2010

Lawrence G. Weiss
Thomas Oakland
Glen P. Aylward

List of Contributors

Heather C. Agazzi   University of South Florida, Tampa, FL

Helen Alexander   Ohio State University, Columbus, OH

Kathleen H. Armstrong   University of South Florida, Tampa, FL

Glen P. Aylward   Southern Illinois University School of Medicine, Springfield, IL

Cecilia Breinbauer   Interdisciplinary Council on Developmental and Learning Disorders, Bethesda, MD

Jane Case-Smith   Ohio State University, Columbus, OH

Elizabeth R. Crais   University of North Carolina at Chapel Hill, Chapel Hill, NC

Stanley Greenspan   Interdisciplinary Council on Developmental and Learning Disorders, Bethesda, MD

Jennifer L. Harman   Yale University Child Study Center, New Haven, CT

Twyla L. Mancil   University of Florida, Gainesville, FL

Marites Piñon   Walden University, Minneapolis, MN

Tina M. Smith-Bonahue   University of Florida, Gainesville, FL

1

Theoretical Background and Structure of the Bayley Scales of Infant and Toddler Development, Third Edition

Marites Piñon

Walden University, Northbrook, IL

INTRODUCTION

The Bayley Scales of Infant and Toddler Development, Third Edition (Bayley-III; Bayley, 2006) is an individually adminis-tered instrument that assesses developmental functioning of children between 1 month and 42 months of age. It is used to identify suspected developmental delay in children consistent with current scholarship on child development, to assist in intervention planning and other important clinical services, as well as to be consistent with federal (e.g., Individuals With Disabilities Education Improvement Act of 2004, Public Law 108-446 [IDEIA], 2004; No Child Left Behind Act, 2001) and professional (e.g., American Educational Research Association, American Psychological Association, & National Council on Measurement in Education, 1999; National Research Council and Institute of Medicine, 2000) standards. Additionally, the Bayley-III is designed to promote an understanding of a child's strengths and weaknesses in relation to five developmental domains: cognitive, language, motor, social-emotional, and adaptive behavior.

RATIONALE FOR THE BAYLEY-III

Changes in the US population and evaluation needs prompt test revisions. Since the 1993 publication of the Bayley Scales of Infant Development-II (BSID-II; Bayley, 1993), characteristics of young children in the US have changed. For example, the proportion of children from parents with lower education levels (grade 12 or lower) has decreased (Pearson Education, 2008). Additionally, changes in infant cognitive development based on such characteristics as race/ethnicity and maternal education (Halle *et al.*, 2009) warranted a need for normative data that are representative of the current population. Normative data for the Bayley-III are representative of the US population for infants 1 month to 42 months of age in reference to race/ethnicity, sex, parent education level, and geographic region.

Guidelines from national and professional organizations for practitioners and clinicians reiterate the need to provide assessment instruments that both are valid for the assessment's intended goals and facilitate clinical utility. For example, the National Research Council (2008) recommends that assessments should match the stated purpose of the assessment needs in terms of frequency of administration, length of assessment, domains measured, and method used to assess the children or programs. Additionally, assessments should be conducted efficiently while obtaining valid results.

The National Association of School Psychologists (NASP, 2009) emphasizes the need for early childhood assessment that is fair, useful, and leads to informed decisions related to intervention. NASP underscores the importance of acquiring a comprehensive understanding of a young child's development through an assessment that includes multiple behaviors displayed in various environments.

The following goals for the Bayley-III were established and met: (a) update the normative data, (b) develop scales that assess distinct and important domains, (c) ensure the scale's high psychometric quality, (d) facilitate the scale's clinical utility, and (e) enhance its administrative features. These issues are reviewed below.

The Normative Data

Bayley-III normative data were collected in the US between January and October 2004. The norm sample was stratified on key demographic variables that include age, sex, parent education level, and geographic location. Approximately 10 percent of the norm group included children who displayed specific clinical diagnoses (i.e., children with Down syndrome, cerebral palsy, pervasive developmental disorder, premature birth, specific language impairment, prenatal alcohol exposure, asphyxiation at birth, small for gestational age, and at risk for developmental delay) to ensure the representativeness of the normative sample and to conduct needed clinical studies.

Neonatal development is rapid and varied. Thus, the acquisition of data from newborns that track their development precisely was emphasized by acquiring norm data from standardization age groups in 1-month intervals between 1 and 6 months of age, and in 2-month intervals between 6 and 12 months of age. Standardization age groups were in 3-month intervals between 12 and 30 months of age, and in 6-month intervals between 30 and 42 months of age. The method of inferential norming was used to derive subtest scores for the Cognitive, Language, and Motor Scales in 10-day intervals for ages 16 days to 5 months 15 days, and in 1-month intervals for ages 5 months 16 days to 36 months 15 days. Subtest scores were derived in 3-month intervals for ages 36 months 16 days to 42 months 15 days. Cognitive, Language, and Motor subtest scaled scores by age are located in Table A.1 of the *Bayley-III Administration Manual* (Bayley, 2006).

The scaled scores for the Social-Emotional Scale are reported according to the age ranges that represent the stages of social-emotional development identified by Greenspan (2004); they are found in Table A.2 of the *Bayley-III Administration Manual*. Scaled scores for the Adaptive Behavior skill areas, found in Table A.3, are reported in 1-month intervals for 0–11 months, then 2-month intervals for 12–23 months, and 3-month intervals for 24–42 months.

The Bayley-III assesses five domains: cognitive, language, motor, social-emotional, and adaptive skills. These domains reflect current federal, state, and professional standards for early childhood assessment. For example, clinicians working with children from birth to age 3 years are required to consider possible delays in cognitive, communication, physical, social or emotional, and adaptive development (IDEIA).

Psychometric Quality

During the revision of the BSID-II to the Bayley-III, all BSID-II items were reviewed for their appropriateness, and either retained or updated, or eliminated. New items were added to each scale to provide more depth and breadth in measuring young children's development. For example, items that are both easier and more demanding were added to the Cognitive, Language, and Motor Scales, thus providing a more accurate measure of early and later development, especially at the scales' floor and ceiling. Additionally, cognitive and language abilities are assessed separately. Language skills are measured more precisely by providing information on children's receptive language and expressive language skills. Motor skills are measured more precisely by providing information on children's fine motor and gross motor development. These qualities expand and strengthen content coverage and facilitate clinical utility.

The scale's psychometric qualities typically are evaluated by examining its reliability and validity (American Educational Research Association *et al.*, 1999). The scale's reliability was evaluated for both normative and clinical samples through studies that examined its internal consistency, inter-rater agreement, and test–retest stability. These results indicate the Bayley-III scales are reliable and maintain an acceptable degree of precision.

The scale's validity was evaluated through studies that examined the intercorrelations of its subtests, its internal structure through factor analysis, and its relationship with other measures (e.g., *Wechsler Preschool and Primary Scales of Intelligence*, Wechsler, 2002; *Preschool Language Scale – Fourth edition*, Zimmerman, Steiner, & Pond, 2002). The profiles of scores from nine clinical groups and matched non-clinical control groups also were compared.

Support for the validity of the individual scales and subtests is found in data that show subtests that form each scale correlate more strongly with their intended scale than with other scales. Factor analyses confirm a three-factor structure, thus supporting the inclusion of Motor, Language, and Cognitive Scales. Although, as expected, the three scales share some common variance, they are sufficiently independent of one another to warrant their separate measurement.

Clinical Utility

The scale's clinical utility is facilitated by data from special group studies, the use of growth scores and charts, details on ways to accommodate those with physical or cognitive limitations while maintaining standardized administrative methods, and the identification of developmental risk factors. These four topics are discussed below.

Special Group Studies

The Bayley-III is designed to be used as part of a comprehensive diagnostic assessment of young children referred for possible and various disorders and disabilities. Thus, studies were conducted to compare the score profiles of young children who are developing normally with those who display Down syndrome, pervasive developmental disorder, cerebral palsy, specific language impairment, prenatal alcohol exposure, asphyxiation at birth, small for gestational age, premature or low birth weight, or are at risk for developmental delay. Although membership in a given group increases the risk of developmental problems, not all members of any group necessarily will have delays, perhaps with the exception of Down syndrome or pervasive developmental disorder (PDD). Also, there is some overlap between groups as well as heterogeneity within groups (e.g., SGA, CP, asphyxia). Further, these clinical groups may not be representative of the populations they represent due to their relatively small size and the use of convenience rather than random sampling procedures. Nevertheless, the results indicate that the score profiles are consistent with expectations. Detailed descriptions of the studies are included in the *Technical Manual*.

DOWN SYNDROME

Children with Down syndrome are likely to experience mild to moderate intellectual disability as well as motor and language delay (Davis, 2008). Longitudinal research has indicated declines in IQ over time, with greater verbal deficits than visual processing deficits present as early as childhood (Carr, 2005). Various motor deficits, including hypertonia, hyperflexia, and motor planning and coordination delays, are also common among children with Down syndrome (Davis, 2008).

The Bayley-III was administered to 90 children diagnosed with Down syndrome. Children ranged in age from 5 to 42 months. Children with an IQ (measured or estimated) between 55 and 75 met the inclusion criteria for the study. Compared with a non-clinical matched control group, these children scored 2.5–3 standard deviations lower as well as showed less variability among subtest and composite scores.

PERVASIVE DEVELOPMENTAL DISORDER

Pervasive developmental disorder (PDD) is characterized by severe and pervasive impairment in social development, particularly communication (American Psychiatric Association, 2000). The presence of stereotyped behavior is another distinguishing feature. The degree to which social interaction, communication, and idiosyncratic behaviors are present distinguishes the types of PDD. Young children diagnosed with PDD are likely to exhibit impairment in joint attention, adaptive skills, expressive and receptive language, and fine motor skills (Ventola et al., 2007).

Children previously identified as meeting the *Diagnostic and Statistical Manual of Mental Disorders*, Fourth Edition, Text Revision (DSM-IV-TR; American Psychiatric Association, 2000) criteria for pervasive developmental disorder qualified for inclusion in this study, including those diagnosed with autism, Asperger's disorder, Rett's syndrome, childhood disintegrative disorder, and PPD not otherwise specified. The study consisted of 70 children, ages 16–42 months. As expected, Bayley-III scores were depressed for the PDD group: all subtests and composite scores were significantly lower for the sample with PDD than the matched control group. In particular, the mean scores for the Receptive Communication and Expressive

Communication subtests as well as the Social-Emotional subtest were markedly lower for the PDD group than the non-clinical matched control group; a common hallmark of PDD is severe and pervasive impairment in social interaction and communication skill.

CEREBRAL PALSY

Cerebral palsy (CP) describes a set of chronic, non-progressive conditions of posture and motor impairment (Koman, Smith, & Shilt, 2004). Individuals with CP cannot control movement and posture adequately. Intellectual functioning can vary from normal development to severe intellectual disability (Vargha-Khadem, Isaacs, van der Werf, Robb, & Wilson, 1992). Among children with CP who exhibit intellectual delay, behavioral problems also may be present (Eisenhower, Baker, & Blacher, 2005).

The test performance of children diagnosed with CP was expected to be depressed on the Bayley-III, particularly in the Motor Scale. The Bayley-III was administered to 73 children diagnosed with CP, ages 5–42 months. All subtest and composite scores for the CP group were significantly lower than those for the matched control. Both Fine Motor and Gross Motor scaled scores were significantly lower for the CP group than the control group, with gross motor performance relatively more impaired than fine motor. The low Cognitive mean score for the CP group is notable. Although intellectual deficiency is not a hallmark of CP, it sometimes is present. Practitioners should use caution in generalizing conclusions about intellectual functioning to all children diagnosed with CP.

SPECIFIC LANGUAGE IMPAIRMENT OR SUSPECTED IMPAIRMENT

A diagnosis of specific language impairment (SLI) typically indicates a substantial discrepancy between non-verbal intellectual performance and language ability (Bishop, 1997).

The Bayley-III was administered to 94 children, ages 13–42 months, diagnosed with SLI or receiving language services with or without diagnosis. Children with more global neurological impairment or developmental delay were excluded from the study, as were children whose sole language impairment diagnosis was an articulation disorder.

The mean performance of the SLI group was significantly lower on all Bayley-III subtests and composites than that of the match control group. Co-morbid cognitive delay was apparent in this sample, indicating the interdependence of language and cognition in development (Goorhuis-Brouwer & Knijff, 2002). The Social-Emotional mean score difference between the two groups also was large, indicating the role of language in social-emotional development.

AT RISK FOR DEVELOPMENTAL DELAY

Children may be identified as at risk for developmental delay for a variety of conditions, including genetic or congenital disorders, central nervous system disturbances, severe attachment disorders, respiratory distress as a newborn, brain hemorrhage, chronic infection, nutritional deprivation, mental or physical conditions, and biological or environmental factors. Children who were diagnosed formally with a developmental delay were not included in this study.

Children who were reported by a caregiver to meet the criteria for being at risk qualified for inclusion in the study. Children meeting criteria for inclusion in other special groups were excluded from this sample. The Bayley-III was administered to the sample of 75 children ages 4–42 months. The results showed the at-risk group scored significantly lower performance than the matched control group across all subtests and composites, with the largest differences evident for the Language and Motor Scales. The results emphasize the depressed performance of children who are at risk and the range of deficits present within the group.

ASPHYXIATION AT BIRTH

Studies suggest that intrapartum asphyxia beyond a critical threshold is associated with significantly lower cognitive, language, and motor performance than in children in the general population (Patel & Edwards, 1997; Porter-Stevens, Raz, & Sander, 1999). A sample of 43 children, ages 3–38 months, was identified by caregivers as experiencing oxygen deprivation during the birth process. Following administration of the Bayley-III, subtest and composite scaled scores for the asphyxia group were compared with scores of the non-clinical matched control group. With the exception of Expressive Communication, all subtest scores were significantly lower than those of the matched controls. Significantly poorer performance was also evident in the Language and Motor composites. The results support the general findings of developmental outcomes for children with intrapartum asphyxiation.

PRENATAL ALCOHOL EXPOSURE

The results of research on the effects of alcohol exposure on young children's development is mixed: motor impairment, cognitive, language, and visual–motor integration have been identified as possible deficits associated with prenatal alcohol exposure, particularly with diagnoses of fetal alcohol syndrome (e.g., Phelps, 2005). Other studies report effects of prenatal exposure to alcohol are minimal (e.g., Ernhart et al., 1995).

The Bayley-III was administered to a sample of 48 children, ages 4–42 months, whose birth mothers reported alcohol use during pregnancy. Mothers who reported abuse of other substances in addition to alcohol also were included. Cognitive, Language, and Social-Emotional mean scaled scores were found to be significantly lower for the clinical group than for the matched control group. Fine Motor and Gross Motor subtest scores (and the Motor Composite score) did not differ from those for the matched control group. The results are consistent with studies indicating language deficits for children diagnosed with prenatal exposure to alcohol and cocaine (Cone-Wesson, 2005).

SMALL FOR GESTATIONAL AGE

Infants small for gestational age (SGA) may be born full term or pre-term, yet are smaller than their gestational age-mates. Research results are mixed, with a general association between mental abnormalities and SGA (e.g., Ounsted, Moar, & Scott, 1983; Kahn-D'Angelo, 1987). However, many studies are confounded with other characteristics, such as exposure to neurotoxins before birth, or mothers who were malnourished during pregnancy.

A sample of 44 children, ages 4–42 months, were identified by caregivers as being born small for gestational age. Both term and pre-term children were included in the study, as long as their weight and size at birth were below that of 90 percent of gestational age-mates.

Significant differences in mean scores were found between the SGA group and the matched control group for the Receptive Communication and Gross Motor subtest scaled scores and the Motor Composite score. The mean scores of the SGA group generally were within the normal range, with the scores of the matched control group slightly higher than normal. These scores likely reflect a disproportionate number of children in the SGA sample (and therefore the matched control group) whose parents had high education levels (i.e., more than 12 years of school).

PREMATURE OR LOW BIRTH WEIGHT

Historically, the clinical literature on children born premature (i.e., before the 37th week of gestation) has contained sampling parameters that varied widely among studies, thus making general predictions about effects of prematurity on developmental outcomes difficult. While most children born prematurely with low birth weight have normal outcomes, this population is at higher risk for neuropsychological, cognitive, and physiological difficulties (Hack, Klein, & Taylor, 1995). Low birth weight children are at higher risk for learning disabilities and academic difficulties at school age (Xu & Filler, 2005). Given the increased risk of developmental delay, early assessment of developmental and functional capabilities of children born prematurely with low birth weight is especially important.

Pre-term children born no later than the 36th week of gestation qualified for the Bayley-III special groups study. In addition, these children may have met criteria for low birth weight (i.e., ≤ 2500 grams, or 5.51 pounds). The Bayley-III allows examiners to adjust an infant's age for prematurity (see below). The test was administered to 85 children with adjusted ages of 2–42 months who were identified by their caregivers as having been born prematurely. With the exception of less-developed fine motor skills, children born prematurely tended to be indistinguishable on average from children born at or near term. However, the adjustment for prematurity prior to administering the Bayley-III may have put premature children on a par with children younger in chronological age.

Adjusting for Prematurity

The Bayley-III provides examiners with the ability to adjust scores for prematurity up to 24 months. This constitutes one of the scale's most noteworthy features. The clinician may decide to adjust the age – and thus start point on the Bayley-III – of an infant born prematurely. Although not unanimously endorsed in the literature, the corrected age is typically used. The adjustment corrects for the child's expected chronological age had he or she been born at full term. For example, if a clinician were testing a child who is now 9 months old but was born 4 weeks premature, the clinician can adjust the child's age to 8 months (subtracting 1 month for prematurity), thus changing the start point and the normative tables that are used to derive the scaled scores. Clinicians are encouraged to compare the scaled scores derived using the child's adjusted age with the scores derived using the child's chronological age. In this way, the examiner can help the parents understand the child's developmental level from two important perspectives; compared to age peers, and taking into account their prematurity.

Growth Scores and Charts Provided to Monitor Growth

The IDEIA requires early intervention together with the monitoring of resulting changes in development. The Bayley-III provides a method to track performance in relation to same-age peers as well to compare an individual's performance at two or more times. Growth scores are provided for the Cognitive, Language, and Motor subtests. In contrast to developmental age equivalents, the Bayley-III growth scores are on an equal-interval scale and calibrated for each subtest. Thus, a change in 10 growth score points on the Fine Motor subtest represents the same relative amount of growth whether it is present at age 6 months or 16 months. In contrast, developmental age equivalents do not signify equal intervals of growth. Thus, when using them, a small change in a raw score may result in a large change in the developmental age equivalent.

The use of growth scores allows practitioners to plot the amount of an individual child's progress, including whether the child falls within a percentile range similar to same-age peers. In contrast, scaled scores are age-corrected and allow practitioners to compare the performance of a child only with his or her peers at one given time. For example, assume a 4-month, 5-day-old child obtains a scaled score of 8 on the cognitive domain and thus performs at the 25th percentile. One year later, at 16 months of age, the child is retested and continues to obtain a scaled score of 8 and thus performs at the 25th percentile. Although the child's scaled and percentile scores have not changed, he or she has acquired additional skills during the year, albeit comparable to those of age peers. However, these scores do not reflect the child's growth. The Bayley-III growth scores can be used to supplement normative scores and developmental age scores to better understand a child's development relative to his or her growth patterns as well as to peers. The use of growth scores enables clinicians to assess a child's ability in the cognitive, language, and motor domains, and track the trajectory of that child's growth. The use of periodic testing permits an examination of the child's growth over time and can be used consistent with Response to Intervention methods. In addition, growth scores can be very useful when describing for parents the progress that their child has made.

Accommodations and Modifications Guidelines

Some adaptations to standardized testing may be necessary when assessing a child with physical or neurological limitations. Directions for administering Bayley-III items often incorporate many recommended accommodations. Additionally, instructions are simplified, the language load is low for non-language concepts, some directions are unscripted, and response formats allow considerable flexibility (e.g., a child may indicate his or her choice on some items by touching, by pointing, by looking at, or by naming the object). In addition, some items allow the examiner to assist the child on part of the task (e.g., to stabilize the cup or pegboard or hand the disks to the child). The *Bayley-III Administration Manual* includes a special section that provides general suggestions to the clinician that may assist in providing accommodations and modifications specific to the needs of the child while still maintaining standardized administration methods.

Developmental Risk Indicators

Good clinicians remain alert to the display of atypical behaviors that may indicate developmental risk or impairment. Appendix B in the *Bayley-III Technical Manual* identifies behaviors that may be evident during the administration of certain items, and thus assists clinicians in expanding their focus beyond the Bayley-III items. Although the presence of these behaviors should not be used to diagnose a disorder, they may be clinically useful in determining the need for further evaluations.

Administrative Features

Efforts were made to facilitate the Bayley-III's administration. For example, reverse and discontinue criteria are consistent across subtests, clusters of items that comprise a series are clearly marked within the record form and administration manual, instructions are worded similarly across subtests to provide consistency and clarity, instructions are succinct and designed to facilitate comprehension, and sample responses are provided. Item titles closely reflect the assessment goal of the item (e.g., *Shifts Attention*). The spiral-bound Stimulus Book, with its low-angle easel back, allows the examiner to see over the book easily to observe the child's response.

The examiner has some flexibility in the choice of stimulus materials for items. For example, on some items the examiner is allowed to select materials that are deemed appealing to the child (e.g., Cognitive Item 28, *Pulls Cloth to Obtain Object*, requires the use of an "object of interest"), thus providing accommodation for individual differences, if needed, to enhance interest and motivation and to help ensure an accurate assessment.

The stimulus materials were selected to be sturdy, easily sanitized, latex-free, colorful, and thus appealing to children, easily manipulated, and meeting stringent safety criteria (e.g., no choking hazards for young children). In addition, efforts were made to limit the physical size of the kit and to provide a wheeled case for easy transportation. The administration and technical information is divided into two manuals to reduce the amount and weight of paper that must be transported to a testing site.

A computerized scoring assistant and PDA administration software are available to assist in administration, scoring, and calculation of scaled scores. Its use is ideal for multidisciplinary arena assessment, and to help the examiner plan interventions.

SCHOLARSHIP FOR THE BAYLEY SCALES

The domains and item content for the Bayley Scales represent a range of current scholarship on child development perspectives, grounded in infant and child research. The Bayley-III is derived from established developmental theory (e.g., Piaget, 1952; Vygotsky, 1962, 1978; Bruner, 1974–1975; Luria, 1976) and aligns with recent findings in child development research, including neuropsychological research and information processing (e.g., Aylward, 1988; Colombo & Cheatham, 2006; Colombo & Mitchell, 2009), functional social-emotional theory (Greenspan, DeGangi, & Wieder, 2001), and adaptive behavior (American Association on Intellectual and Developmental Disabilities, 1992, 2002) that support the employment of particular items within the domains. Item development and administration guidelines are consistent with basic underpinnings of child development, drawn from developmental research and theory that identify behaviors that typify important developmental milestones in young children.

The basis for the Cognitive Scale is informed by classic theory in child cognitive development (e.g., Piaget, 1952; Piaget & Inhelder, 1969; Vygotsky, 1978), as well as advances in the study of preverbal intelligence (e.g., Colombo & Frick, 1999; Colombo, McCardle, & Freund, 2009). Play facilitates cognitive and social-emotional development (Singer, Golnikoff, & Hirsch-Pasek, 2006). The use of tools (e.g., toys) as mediators of activity is linked to children's learning and intellectual development (Bruner, 1972; Bradley, 1985; *Toy Play*, 1994). Cognitive Scale items that reflect play include *Bangs in Play, Relational Play Series* items, and *Pushes Car*.

Children's understanding of numerosity has been used as an important marker of development. Research provides a greater understanding of the processes underlying numerosity (Baroody, Li, & Lai, 2008). For example, a study of toddlers' spontaneous attention to numbers found children's understanding and functional use of the concepts of *two* and *three* varies individually and by age, suggesting that the development of the concept of numerosity may require scaffolding by others as it may not occur spontaneously (Baroody *et al.*, 2008).

Cognitive development, language, and literacy development have been closely associated (e.g., Rose, Feldman, & Jankowski, 2009). Children's acquisition of generic concepts or kinds (e.g., "Apples are sweet" vs "I like this red apple") appear to develop spontaneously early in age (Gelman, Goetz, Sarnecka, & Flukes, 2008; Goldin-Meadow, Gelman, & Mylander, 2005).

Motor skills measured within the Bayley-III follow basic identifiable and generally universal milestones (Gesell, 1946; Thelen, 1995; Adolph & Berger, 2006). Although fine and gross motor skills are often thought to be affected by medical-biologic rather than environmental factors, some research suggests that these skills develop more slowly in young children from lower socio-economic families (Kelly, Sacker, Schoon, & Nazroo, 2006). Delays in fine motor skills also have been found in children with broader developmental delays, including those with autism (e.g., Provost, Heimerl, & Lopez, 2007; Provost, Lopez, & Heimerl, 2007). For example, stair-climbing ability, a gross motor skill, appears to develop universally within a predictable age range. Children with stairs in their homes were found to climb at an earlier age than those without stairs. However, the ability to descend stairs seemingly occurs at about age 13 months, and is independent of whether the home has stairs (Berger, Theuring, & Adolph, 2007). Delays in gross motor skills have been found in children with global developmental delays.

Adaptive functioning is often assessed when diagnosing, classifying, and providing intervention for individuals with various disabilities (Ditterline, Banner, Oakland, & Becton, 2008; Ditterline & Oakland, 2010), most notably mental retardation (American Association on Intellectual and Developmental Disabilities, 1992, 2002). Information on adaptive functioning together with cognitive, motor, and language development provides helpful information on the degree to which a child functions independently (Harrison & Oakland, 2003; Msall, 2005).

The five domains included in the Bayley-III, while measured independently, are not naturally independent of each other, and thus are somewhat interdependent. Greenspan (2004) described the reciprocal relationship between emotional, cognitive, and language development. The development of affective signaling (i.e., the ability to experience, comprehend, and communicate emotions) is posited to serve as a precursor to language and cognitive development (Greenspan and Shanker, 2007). Affect signaling includes six stages of development: self-regulation, shared attention, engagement, shared social problem-solving, emergence of symbols and language, and building bridges between ideas through complex affective interactions. Preliminary analyses using data gathered from the Bayley-III norming sample indicate a relationship between mastery of earlier, pre-symbolic stages of affect signaling, and language and cognitive skills.

OVERVIEW OF TEST STRUCTURE

The Bayley-III is based on a broad cross-section of infant and child research and other forms of scholarship. It follows a time-tested and long tradition of using standardized assessment procedures to provide toddlers and infants with tasks and situations that capture their interest and provide an observable set of behavioral responses.

The structure of the Bayley-III Scales allows clinicians to administer each of the five scales independent of others. This feature makes the instrument especially suitable for multidisciplinary and arena assessment. Each scale and subtest then may be administered and scored correctly and efficiently, consistent with the expertise that each member of the multidisciplinary team brings to the evaluation. In addition, such modes of assessment may facilitate qualitative observations of the child's behavior.

Performance measured by the Bayley-III is summarized through the use of various scores. These include scaled scores for each subtest, and composite scores for each scale, together with percentile ranks, developmental age equivalents, and growth scores. Discrepancy information is available to determine whether there are significant differences between a child's abilities in the domains measured, and how prevalent these differences are in the norming sample. A total score is not provided, because a total score that aggregates a child's performance on all five scales is not informative and is inconsistent with a central goal of the Bayley-III – namely, to promote an understanding of a child's strengths and weaknesses in reference to the five measured domains.

Assumes Typical Development

The Bayley-III utilizes an efficient administration design that relies on age-based start points, reverse, and discontinue criteria. When administering a subtest from the Cognitive, Language, or Motor Scales, the clinician begins by identifying the appropriate start point on the scale in accord with the child's age, or adjusted age. The reverse rule is followed if the child is unable successfully to complete any of the first three consecutive items from the start point, resulting in the clinician administering items from the start point for the previous age. After the child obtains a score of 1 on all of the first three items from the start point, additional items are administered in order until the child receives scores of 0 on five consecutive items, at which point the subtest is discontinued. This flexible administration format incorporated into a standardized procedure allows the Bayley-III to adapt to the individual child's temperament, age, and success rate. Items were ordered by difficulty within each subtest. Thus, early-appearing items generally are easier than later-appearing items. The order of items and administration structure (start point and discontinue rules) reflects typical early childhood development patterns.

This test format helps clinicians use standardized administrative procedures to identify development delays in most children. However, this format may not be suitable for some children who show atypical development or who evidence scattered strengths and weaknesses (e.g., due to traumatic brain injury) – qualities that may be referred to as splintered and uneven skill development. Information in Appendix C of the *Bayley-III Administration Manual* provides recommendations for adapting administrative strategies that possibly lead to needed qualitative information that supplements the test's quantitative information. In some instances, extending the assessment beyond the standardized format (e.g., testing the limits) may help provide a more accurate description of a child's strengths and weaknesses that informs intervention strategies.

A More Naturalistic Approach

A fully naturalistic approach would involve assessment of the child in his or her home environment. However, this approach has attendant issues when comparing children to a normative group, because the home testing environment cannot be standardized. The administration of the Bayley-III was designed to provide some flexibility in order to capitalize on the natural interests and attention of young children while maintaining standardized procedures. For example, Cognitive Scale Item 43, *Clear Box: Front*, requires the use of a small item of interest. The small duck is often used. However, other items can be used (e.g., the bracelet or car) when the child shows an interest in them. Such methods do not alter the test's validity, and instead may enhance it. The clinician should attempt – within the bounds of standardized administrative methods – to create conditions that optimize the child's performance by ensuring the child is motivated to perform at his or her highest level.

A number of items can be scored through incidental observation. A clinician familiar with these items (identified on the Observation Checklist) can score the behaviors during the course of the test session without the need to administer them. For example, a 9-month-old child who vocalizes during the test session, saying *ma-ma-ma-bad-ah*, would receive a score of 1 for Receptive subtest Item 8. However, if the child were silent during the preceding items, the clinician should attempt to induce vocalizations by modeling the desired sounds.

Parents have important roles in the evaluation and intervention process. For example, the administration of the Cognitive, Language, and Motor Scales may be facilitated by having the caregiver assist in presenting a stimulus item to the child. Thus, caregivers may gain further insights into the types of behaviors the child exhibits by participating more directly in its administration. Caregivers complete the Social-Emotional and Adaptive Behavior portions of the Bayley-III.

The Bayley-III's Caregiver Report presents the child's scores as a profile, thus highlighting the child's strengths and weaknesses. The report also provides an explanation of the qualities that were measured, as well as activities caregivers may use with their child to promote skill development.

Five Content Domains

Cognitive Scale

The Cognitive Scale assesses a uniform construct and thus does not have separate subtests. The scale emphasizes the assessment of mental development through methods that minimize language. Its 91 items assess children's sensorimotor development, exploration and manipulation of objects, object relations, concept formation, and memory. Infants complete tasks that measure their interest in novelty, attention to familiar and unfamiliar stimuli, and problem-solving. Preschool-aged children complete tasks that measure pretend play, and activities such as building with blocks, color matching, counting and solving more complex patterns.

For example, the progression of play development illustrates how items were developed for the Bayley-III. From birth to approximately age 2 years, exploration of play with objects is the predominant form (Pellegrini & Boyd, 1993). Mouthing and manipulation eventually become replaced by functional play (e.g., stacking blocks, pushing a car forward and backward) and pretense play (e.g., bringing a phone to one's ear and holding a pretend conversation) (Belsky & Most, 1981). From age 2 through approximately age 5 years, fantasy becomes the dominant form of play activity (Pellegrini & Perlmutter, 1989; Pellegrini & Boyd, 1993), with fantasy play shifting from self-referenced (e.g., pretending to brush their own hair) to other-referenced (e.g., pretending to brush a doll's hair). Older preschool-aged children become less dependent on realistic props and toys to enact their fantasy play (Trawick-Smith, 1990), and can continue to engage in play in the absence of such props (e.g., holding a pretend spoon to take a sip of pretend soup).

Language Scale

The Language Scale measures two major aspects of language: receptive and expressive communication skills. These skills are displayed differently, and may or may not develop independently. Receptive language typically precedes expressive language. Interventions for children diagnosed with either a receptive or expressive language disorder generally differ. The Bayley-III Language Scale items include some adapted from the *Preschool Language Scale – Fourth Edition* (Zimmerman *et al.*, 2002). The Bayley-III items provide broad content coverage in keeping with scholarship and clinical practices associated with language development.

The 49-item Receptive Communication subtest assesses preverbal behaviors, including a child's ability to recognize sounds, receptive vocabulary (e.g., ability to identify objects and pictures), and morphological development (e.g., pronouns and prepositions) and morphological markers (e.g. plurals, tense markings, and the possessives). Children's social referencing and verbal comprehension (e.g., how well they understand directions) skills are also assessed.

The 48-item Expressive Communication subtest assesses preverbal communication (e.g., babbling, gesturing, joint referencing, and turn-taking), vocabulary use (e.g., naming objects, pictures, and their attributes – color and size), and morpho-syntactic development (e.g., using two-word utterances, plurals, and verb tense).

Motor Scale

The Motor Scale assesses fine motor and gross motor skills separately. New items were added to expand the coverage across the age range, increase the focus on the quality of a child's movement and to provide greater content coverage in accord with scholarship and clinical practices associated with motor development.

The 66-item Fine Motor subtest assesses how well children use their eyes, fingers, and hands to engage their environment. Fine motor skills include muscle control of the eyes, prehension (e.g., grasping, stacking blocks), perceptual–motor integration (e.g., building simple structures), motor planning and speed (e.g., tracing an outline on paper), visual tracking (e.g., following an object), reaching (e.g., acquiring a block from across the table), functional hand skills (e.g., cutting paper with scissors), and response to tactile information (e.g., discriminating objects by touch).

The 72-item Gross Motor subtest assesses how well children control and move their body. Gross motor skills include head control in infants, and stepping, standing, walking, climbing, and running in toddlers and preschoolers. Items measure movement of the limbs and torso, static positioning (e.g., sitting, standing), dynamic movement (e.g., locomotion and coordination), balance, and motor planning.

Social-Emotional Scale

The 35-item Social-Emotional Scale identifies normal social and emotional developmental milestones of infants, toddlers, and preschoolers. This information is gathered through a questionnaire completed by the child's caregiver. The scale is derived from the *Greenspan Social-Emotional Growth Chart* (Greenspan, 2004). The Social-Emotional Scale measures children's functional emotional skills, including self-regulation and interest in the world; ability to communicate needs, engage others and establish relationships; use of emotions in a purposeful manner; and use of emotional signals to solve problems.

Adaptive Behavior Scale

The 241-item Adaptive Behavior Scale assesses the child's independent display of skills needed in normal daily living. Adaptive information is gathered through a questionnaire completed by the child's parent or primary caregiver. The scale is derived from the Parent/Primary Caregiver Form (for ages 0–5 years) of the Adaptive Behavior Assessment System – Second Edition (ABAS-II; Harrison & Oakland, 2003).

A General Adaptive Composite (GAC) provides an overall measure of adaptive development based on the following 10 skill areas: Communication (e.g., the child's speech, language, and non-verbal skills), Community Use (e.g., the child's interest in activities outside the home and ability to recognize various community locations), Health and Safety (e.g., how readily a child shows caution and an ability to avoid physical danger), Leisure (e.g., forms of play and the ability to follow rules), Self-care (e.g., the child's eating, toileting, and bathing behaviors), Self-direction (e.g., how readily the child shows self-control, follows directions, and makes choices), Functional Pre-academics (e.g., the child's skills at letter recognition, counting, and drawing simple shapes), Home Living (e.g., the degree to which a child helps adults with household tasks and cares for his or her personal possessions), Social (e.g., how well the child gets along with other people, uses manners, assists others, and recognizes emotions), and Motor (e.g., the child's locomotion skills and manipulation of the environment).

Limitations of Bayley-III and How Those are Addressed

Although the Bayley-III's structure provides considerable flexibility in administration and meets a broad range of applications, it may not be appropriate for every child. The norm sample included a large number of children who display normal behavior as well as differing clinical conditions. The norm sample did not include children with all disorders; however, the use of a scale with special needs children may be relevant even if its norms did not include children with similar special needs. Additionally, the full use of the Bayley-III with children with significant sensory impairments (e.g. blindness, deafness, or hard of hearing), severe spinal cord injuries (apart from cerebral palsy classification), and with other severe physical conditions may be precluded because the disorder may prevent a standardized administration. Children with suspected head trauma were included in the at risk category provided they were not currently affected by seizures or taking medication that would significantly impair functioning.

Appendix C of the *Bayley-III Administration Manual* describes the types of accommodations and modifications that can be made when administering the Bayley-III to children with special needs, as well as the types of modifications that may limit interpretation of standard scores. In addition, more investigation is needed to assess the application of the Bayley-III with children older than 42 months who evidence severe developmental delay.

Children included in the norm sample understood and spoke English, or their parents were able to communicate effectively in English. Norm data have not been obtained for children for whom English is not their first and primary language. Thus, test results should be interpreted with caution when assessing a child who does not speak or understand English. Researchers are urged to collect additional test data to determine if the performance of non-English-speaking children is comparable to that of the Bayley-III norm sample.

Atypical Development

The *Bayley-III Administration Manual* and *Technical Manual* include guidelines that help the clinician to gauge whether a child is exhibiting atypical behaviors indicative of developmental delay, and to frame the interpretation of those scores. Other information may help the clinician determine whether certain accommodations and modifications may invalidate the test results. Administration guidelines allow for clinicians to test the limits by administering item sets that occur beyond the bounds of the recommended administration start point and discontinue point.

SUMMARY OF FEATURES

The Bayley-III contains many features that make it a useful assessment tool for clinicians working with infants and toddlers. It complies with the latest federal, state, and professional guidelines for the assessment of children in schools, and covers a broad age range. Few other measures are available for use with children as young as 1 month to 42 months. The Bayley-III is normed on recent census data, and includes a significant number of children from diverse ethnic groups and parent education levels. It includes a number of children with a varied range of clinical conditions, including fetal alcohol exposure and pervasive developmental delay, thus helping guide professionals who work in early intervention. The

Bayley-III utilizes an engaging, play-based format, and permits a flexible approach to testing. It also encourages parent involvement in the assessment.

A number of different scores are available to help the examiner understand the child's information-processing capacity and weaknesses. Scaled scores, composite scores, growth scores, percentiles, and age-equivalents can all be derived.

Caregiver Reports are available to help parents better understand the range of skills demonstrated on the test, to determine the pattern of their strengths and weaknesses, and to mark progress. This information may inform intervention plans to help the child progress in areas of weakness and possibly promote a better outcome for young children.

References

Adolph, K., & Berger, S. (2006). Motor development. *Handbook of Child Psychology*, Vol. 2, *Cognition, Perception, and Language* (6th ed.), (pp. 161–213). Hoboken, NJ: John Wiley & Sons.

American Association on Intellectual and Developmental Disabilities. (1992). *Mental Retardation: Definition, Classification, and Systems of Support.* Washington, DC: Author.

American Association on Intellectual and Developmental Disabilities. (2002). *Mental Retardation: Definition, Classification, and Systems of Support.* Washington, DC: Author.

American Educational Research Association, American Psychological Association, & National Council on Measurement in Education. (1999). *Standards for Educational and Psychological Testing.* Washington, DC: Author.

American Psychiatric Association. (2000). *Diagnostic and Statistical Manual of Mental Disorders* (4th ed.) text revision. Washington, DC: Author.

Aylward, G. P. (1988). Infant and early childhood assessment. In M. G. Tramontana, & S. R. Hooper (Eds.), *Assessment Issues in Child Neuropsychology* (pp. 225–248). New York, NY: Plenum Press.

Baroody, A., Li, X., & Lai, M. (2008). Toddlers' spontaneous attention to number. *Mathematical Thinking and Learning, 10*(3), 240–270.

Bayley, N. (1993). *Bayley Scales of Infant Development* (2nd ed.). San Antonio, TX: The Psychological Corporation.

Bayley, N. (2006). *Bayley Scales of Infant and Toddler Development* (3rd ed.). San Antonio, TX: Pearson.

Belsky, J., & Most, R. K. (1981). From exploration to play: A cross-sectional study of infant free play behavior. *Developmental Psychology, 17*(5), 630–639.

Berger, S., Theuring, C., & Adolph, K. (2007, February). How and when infants learn to climb stairs. *Infant Behavior & Development, 30*(1), 36–49.

Bishop, D. V. (1997). Cognitive neuropsychology and developmental disorders: Uncomfortable bed fellows. *Quarterly Journal of Experimental Psychology: Human Experimental Psychology, 50*(4), 899–923.

Bradley, R. H. (1985). Social–cognitive development and toys. *Topics in Early Childhood Special Education, 5*(3), 11–30.

Bruner, J. S. (1972). Nature and uses of immaturity. *American Psychologist, 27*(8), 687–708.

Bruner, J. S. (1974–1975). From communication to language: A psychological perspective. *Cognition, 3*, 255–287.

Carr, J. (2005). Stability and change in cognitive ability over the life span: A comparison of populations with and without Down's syndrome. *Journal of Intellectual Disability Research, 49*(2), 915–928.

Colombo, J., & Cheatham, C. L. (2006). The emergency and basis of endogenous attention in infancy and early childhood. In R. Kail (Ed.), *Advances in Child Development and Behavior* (pp. 283–322). New York, NY: Academic Press.

Colombo, J., & Frick, J. (1999). Recent advances and issues in the study of preverbal intelligence. In M. Anderson (Ed.), *The Development of Intelligence* (pp. 43–71). Hove, UK: Psychology Press.

Colombo, J., & Mitchell, D. W. (2009). Infant visual habituation. *Neurobiology of Learning and Memory, 92*, 225–234.

Colombo, J., McCardle, P., & Freund, L. (2009). *Infant Pathways to Language: Methods, Models, and Research Disorders*. New York, NY: Psychology Press.

Cone-Wesson, B. (2005). Prenatal alcohol and cocaine exposure: Influences on cognition, speech, language, and hearing. *Journal of Communication Disorders, 38*, 279–302.

Davis, A. S. (2008). Children with Down syndrome: Implications for assessment and intervention in the school. *School Psychology Quarterly, 23*(2), 271–281.

Ditterline, J., & Oakland, T. (2010). Adaptive behavior. In E. Mpofu, & T. Oakland (Eds.), *Assessment in Rehabilitation and Health* (pp. 242–261). Boston, MA: Allyn & Bacon.

Ditterline, J., Banner, D., Oakland, T., & Becton, D. (2008). Adaptive behavior profiles of students with disabilities. *Journal of Applied School Psychology, 24* (2), 191–208.

Eisenhower, A. S., Baker, B. L., & Blacher, J. (2005). Preschool children with intellectual disability: Syndrome specificity, behaviour problems, and maternal well-being. *Journal of Intellectual Disability Research, 49*(9), 657–671.

Ernhart, C. B., Greene, T., Sokol, R. J., Martier, S., Boyd, T. A., & Ager, J. (1995). Neonatal diagnosis of fetal alcohol syndrome: Not necessarily a hopeless prognosis. *Alcoholism: Clinical and Experimental Research, 19*(6), 1550–1557.

Gelman, S., Goetz, P., Sarnecka, B., & Flukes, J. (2008). Generic language in parent–child conversations. *Language Learning and Development, 4*(1), 1–31.

Gesell, A. (1946). The ontogenesis of infant behavior. In L. Carmichael (Ed.), *Manual of Child Psychology* (pp. 295–331). New York, NY: John Wiley.

Goldin-Meadow, S., Gelman, S. A., & Mylander, C. (2005). Expressing generic concepts with and without a language model. *Cognition, 96*, 109–126.

Goorhuis-Brouwer, S. M., & Knijff, W. A. (2002). Efficacy of speech therapy in children with language disorders: Specific language impairment compared with language impairment in comorbidity with cognitive delay. *International Journal of Pediatric Otorhinolaryngology, 63*, 129–136.

Greenspan, S., & Shanker, S. (2007). The developmental pathways leading to pattern recognition, joint attention, language and cognition. *New Ideas in Psychology, 25*, 128–142.

Greenspan, S. I. (2004). *Greenspan Social–Emotional Growth Chart: A Screening Questionnaire for Infants and Young Children.* San Antonio, TX: Pearson.

Greenspan, S. I., DeGangi, G. A., & Wieder, S. (2001). *The Functional Emotional Assessment Scale (FEAS) for Infancy and Early Childhood: Clinical and Research Applications.* Bethesda, MD: Interdisciplinary Council on Developmental and Learning Disorders.

Hack, M., Klein, N. K., & Taylor, H. G. (1995). Long-term developmental outcomes of low birth weight infants. *The Future of Children, 5*(1), 176–196.

Halle, T., Forry, N., Hair, E., Perper, K., Wandner, L., Wessel, J., & Vick, J. (2009). *Disparities in Early Learning and Development: Lessons from the Early Childhood Longitudinal Study – Birth Cohort (ECLS-B).* Washington, DC: Child Trends.

Harrison, P. L., & Oakland, T. (2003). *Adaptive Behavior Assessment System* (2nd ed.). San Antonio, TX: Pearson.

Individuals With Disabilities Education Improvement Act of 2004, Pub. L. No 108–446, 118 stat. 2647 (2004). [Amending 20 U.S.C. §§ 1400 *et seq.*].

Kahn-D'Angelo, L. (1987). Is the small for gestional age, term infant at risk for developmental delay? *Physical & Occupational Therapy in Pediatrics, 7*(3), 69–73.

Kelly, Y., Sacker, A., Schoon, I., & Nazroo, J. (2006). Ethnic difference in achievement of developmental milestones by 9 months of age: The Millennium Cohort Study. *Developmental Medicine and Child Neurology, 48*, 825–830.

Koman, L. A., Smith, B. P., & Shilt, J. S. (2004). Cerebral palsy. *Lancet, 363*, 1619–1631.

Luria, A. R. (1976). *Cognitive Development: Its Cultural and Social Foundations.* Cambridge, MA: Harvard University Press.

Msall, M. (2005). Measuring functional skills in preschool children at risk for neurodevelopmental disabilities. *Mental Retardation and Developmental Disabilities Research Reviews, 11*(3), 263–273.

National Association of School Psychologists. (2009). *NASP Position Statement: Early Childhood Assessment.* Bethesda, MD: Author. Retrieved from http://www.nasponline.org/about_nasp/positionpapers/EarlyChildhoodAssessment.pdf.

National Research Council. (2008). Early Childhood Assessment: Why, What, and How. Committee on Developmental Outcomes and Assessments for Young Children. In C. E. Snow, & S. B. Van Hemel (Eds.), *Board on Children, Youth, and Families, Board on Testing and Assessment, Division of Behavioral and Social Sciences and Education.* Washington, DC: The National Academies Press. Retrieved from The National Academies Press website: http://www.nap.edu/openbook.php?record_id=12446&page=R2.

National Research Council and Institute of Medicine. (2000). From Neurons to Neighborhoods. The Science of Early Childhood Development. Committee on Integrating the Science of Early Childhood Development. In J. P. Shonkoff, & D. A. Phillips (Eds.), *Board on Children, Youth, and Families, Commission on Behavioral and Social Sciences and Education*. Washington, D.C: National Academy Press. Retrieved from The National Academies Press website: http://books.nap.edu/openbook.php?record_id=9824&page=R1.

No Child Left Behind Act, 20 U.S.C. § 6301 *et seq.* (2001).

Ounsted, M. K., Moar, V. A., & Scott, A. (1983). Small-for-dates babies at the age of four years: Health, handicap and developmental status. *Early Human Development, 8,* 243–258.

Patel, J., & Edwards, A. D. (1997). Prediction of outcome after perinatal asphyxia. *Current Opinion in Pediatrics, 9*(2), 128–132.

Pearson Education. (2008). *Factors Contributing to Differences Between Bayley-III and BSID-II Scores. (*Bayley-III Technical Report No. 2*).* San Antonio: Pearson Education. Retrieved from http://pearsonassess.com/NR/rdonlyres/85553691-1039-4964-8C1C-6F1E9506BE31/0/BayleyIII_TechRep2_postpubRX.pdf.

Pellegrini, A. D., & Boyd, B. (1993). The role of play in early childhood development and education: Issues in definition and function. In B. Spodek (Ed.), *Handbook of Research on the Education of Young Children* (pp. 105–121). New York, NY: Macmillan.

Pellegrini, A. D., & Perlmutter, J. C. (1989). Classroom contextual effects on children's play. *Developmental Psychology, 25*(2), 289–296.

Phelps, L. (2005). Fetal alcohol syndrome: Neuropsychological outcomes, psychoeducational implications, and prevention models. In R. C. D'Amato, E. Fletcher-Janzen, & C. R. Reynolds (Eds.), *Handbook of School Neuropsychology* (pp. 561–573). Hoboken, NJ: John Wiley & Sons.

Piaget, J. (1952). *The Origins of Intelligence in Children.* New York, NY: International University Press.

Piaget, J., & Inhelder, B. (1969). *The Psychology of the Child.* New York, NY: Basic Books.

Porter-Stevens, C., Raz, S., & Sander, C. J. (1999). Peripartum hypoxic risk and cognitive outcome: A study of term and preterm birth children at early school age. *Neuropsychology, 13*(4), 598–608.

Provost, B., Heimerl, S., & Lopez, B. (2007). Levels of gross and fine motor development in young children with autism spectrum disorder. *Physical & Occupational Therapy in Pediatrics, 27*(3), 21–36.

Provost, B., Lopez, B., & Heimerl, S. (2007). A comparison of motor delays in young children: autism spectrum disorder, developmental delay, and developmental concerns. *Journal of Autism & Developmental Disorders, 37*(2), 321–328.

Rose, S., Feldman, J., & Jankowski, J. (2009). A cognitive approach to the development of early language. *Child Development, 80*(1), 134–150.

Singer, D., Golinkoff, R., & Hirsh-Pasek, K. (Eds.). (2006). *Play = Learning: How Play Motivates and Enhances Children's Cognitive and Social–emotional Growth.* New York, NY: Oxford University Press.

Thelen, E. (1995). Motor development: A new synthesis. *American Psychologist, 50*, 79–95.

Toy Play in Infancy and Early Childhood: Normal Development and Special Considerations for Children with Disabilities (1994, June 6). (ERIC Document Reproduction Service No. ED386900) Retrieved July 25, 2009, from ERIC database.

Trawick-Smith, J. (1990). The effects of realistic versus non-realistic play materials on young children's symbolic transformations of objects. *Journal of Research in Childhood Education, 5*(1), 27–36.

Vargha-Khadem, F., Isaacs, E., van der Werf, S., Robb, S., & Wilson, J. (1992). Development of intelligence and memory in children with hemiplegic cerebral palsy. The deleterious consequences of early seizures. *Brain, 115*, 315–329.

Ventola, P., Kleinmam, J., Pandey, J., Wilson, L., Esser, E., Boorstein, H., & Fein, D. (2007). Differentiating between autism spectrum disorders and other developmental disabilities in children who failed a screening instrument for ASD. *Journal of Autism Developmental Disorders, 37*, 425–436.

Vygotsky, L. S. (1962). *Thought and Language.* Cambridge, MA: MIT Press.

Vygotsky, L. S. (1978). *Mind in Society: The Development of Higher Psychological Processes.* Cambridge, MA: Harvard University Press.

Wechsler, D. (2002). *Wechsler Preschool and Primary Scale of Intelligence* (3rd ed.). San Antonio, TX: Pearson.

Xu, Y., & Filler, J. W. (2005). Linking assessment and intervention for developmental/functional outcomes of premature, low-birth-weight children. *Early Childhood Education Journal, 32*(6), 383–389. doi: 10.1007/s10643-005-008-4.

Zimmerman, I. L., Steiner, V. G., & Pond, R. E. (2002). *Preschool Language Scale* (4th ed., English ed.). San Antonio, TX: Pearson.

2

The Bayley-III Cognitive Scale

Kathleen H. Armstrong and
Heather C. Agazzi

College of Medicine, University of South Florida, Tampa, FL

INTRODUCTION

The Bayley Scales of Infant and Toddler Development, Third Edition (Bayley-III; Bayley, 1993, 2006) is an individually administered instrument designed to assess the developmental functioning of infants, toddlers, and young children aged between 1 and 42 months. The Bayley-III provides coverage of the following five domains: cognitive, language, motor, adaptive, and social-emotional development. These domains are emphasized in the Individuals with Disabilities Educational Improvement Act of 2004 IDEA 2004, (United States Department of Education, 2004) as critical to the comprehensive assessment of young children, as they are key in documenting delays and are pertinent to informing response to intervention efforts.

Historically, the Bayley Scales have been viewed as the gold standard assessment tool for assessment and research with infants and toddlers. Thus, this revision can be expected to continue to provide valuable information about young children's developmental status (Bradley-Johnson & Johnson, 2007; Sattler, 2008). This chapter discusses the clinical administration and interpretation of the Bayley-III, outlines its strengths and weaknesses, and provides a case study that highlights its use with a toddler who displays developmental delays.

29

CONTENT

Among this scale's 91 items, 72 were retained from the prior scale, some are new, others were modified, and some were dropped. Nineteen items were added to extend the content to accommodate children through 42 months, and to align the test to be consistent with the latest developmental research regarding cognitive functioning. Research regarding information processing, processing speed, problem-solving, and play related to early cognitive development was utilized in this revision. The role of information processing in early cognitive development and its later relationship with intelligence was addressed by adding items that assessed novelty preference, attention, habituation, conceptual reasoning, and memory functioning (Colombo & Frick, 1999; Dougherty & Haith, 1997; Kail, 2000; Schatz, Kramer, Ablin, & Matthay, 2000). For example, Items 12 and 13 were included to address attention and habituation of very young infants. Items 84 and 90 were added to assess attention and memory skills in older children. Concepts thought to be critical to early learning (e.g., the ability to sort and group objects by color, size, and mass) are assessed by several items, beginning with Item 72.

Some items were modified to simplify their administration, such as Bayley-III Item 45, *Finds Hidden Object*, which replaced *Finds Toy under Reversed Cup*. Other items were revised to make the tasks more engaging for young children, such as Item 74, *Comparing Masses*, in which toy ducks replaced boxes. Scoring criteria also were revised to more accurately reflect the requirement of the task, such as in Item 49, *Pink Board Series*, in which the examinee receives credit for placing any piece in the puzzle. Forty-five items were dropped due to issues related to administration, scoring, low child interest, bias toward some groups, or their making little contribution to the scale.

Processing speed and problem-solving are thought to be critical to cognitive competence in young children; however, they remain understudied in psychological research on developmental testing (Rose, Feldman, & Jankowski, 2009). Processing speed refers to the rate at which one is able to complete a new task correctly. The Bayley-III attempts to assess processing speed with several items, beginning with those that assess a child's ability to focus and habituate, and extends tasks requiring the construction of puzzles and completion of a pegboard. Several of these items comprise a series that becomes increasingly difficult to perform. The items may be administered one after the other when the child is engaged and attentive. The successive administration of these and other related items helps to maintain the child's interest and motivation, and decreases the potential for challenging behaviors that may occur if an interesting toy is removed. Problem-solving requires reasoning, memory, and the synthesis of information. It is assessed by Item 43, the *Clear Box*, in which an attractive item is hidden behind a translucent screen.

The critical role of play in cognitive development has long been endorsed by early childhood researchers (Bruner, 1972; Piaget, 1952; Vygotsky, 1978). As such, many items that rely on play to assess cognitive development have been included. For example, early play skills (e.g., exploring objects, banging them together, dumping and filling) are assessed beginning at the 4-month-old entry level. Later functional play skills (e.g., placing a spoon in a cup, or putting a lid on a pot) are assessed through the *Relational Play Series*, beginning with Item 48. Symbolic and pretend play (e.g., feeding and bathing a doll) is observed beginning with Item 48, in which the child is provided with a baby doll and other objects of interest. First, the examiner places several objects in front of the child, including a cup, and provides a verbal prompt – "I'm thirsty. I need a drink." – and pretends to drink from the cup. Then, the examiner waits to see how the child will respond using these objects. Beginning stages of relational play include behaviors such as bringing the spoon to one's mouth, while more advanced relational play involves using objects with others, such as pretending to feed the baby doll. Simply modeling what the examiner does without expanding play (in this example, only drinking from a cup) does not receive credit.

Toys used to assess cognitive skills are bright, colorful, and interesting to infants, toddlers, and young children. Activities are designed to reflect a developmental approach long advocated by the National Association of Education for

Young Children (NAEYC) and the Division of Early Childhood (DEC) (Ostrosky & Horn, 2002). As an added advantage, these materials are economical, readily obtainable, and may provide caregivers with examples of materials and activities that can be used to stimulate their child's development in the home and school settings. For example, most young babies are immediately drawn to the glitter bracelet. Slightly older babies naturally enjoy placing items in and out of containers, and find searching for hidden objects entertaining, thus providing their caregivers with additional ideas for playing with them. Toddlers and preschoolers are often drawn to items that create an opportunity to develop their imagination through play. Older children enjoy the early learning games that involve concepts, numbers, and patterns. While administering the test, the examiner may point out these features to the observing parent or caregiver as examples of activities that they can use to develop skills important for success in preschool settings.

ADMINISTRATION

The Bayley-III has simplified administration procedures, making it easier for the examiner to focus more on engaging the child rather than on the administration of test items. Administration instructions are clear, having consistent basal and ceiling rules across all subtests for all items, and highlight a series of items that may be administered serially despite their item number within a subtest. Items on the cognitive domain do not require the child to respond verbally. This is important to consider when assessing the cognitive ability of children who display expressive language delays. Complying with IDEA 2004 requirements to include caregivers within the multidisciplinary assessment process (United States Department of Education, 2004), the optimum arrangement during testing is to have the primary caregiver and the examiner in the room with the child. In addition, the Bayley-III allows scoring credit in cases when the caregiver elicits a response from the child that the examiner was unable to elicit. However, credit is not awarded based on a caregiver's report of a skill alone.

Researchers and advocates in early childhood education and special education have questioned the appropriateness of testing young children, especially those with disabilities (Bagnato & Neisworth, 1994; Bracken & Walker, 1997; Nagle, 2007). As such, eight critical elements have been endorsed for early childhood assessment practice: useful, acceptable, authentic, collaborative, convergent, equitable, sensitive, and congruent (Neisworth & Bagnato, 2000). The Bayley-III takes these concerns into account, to the extent possible within a standardized assessment tool, by providing some flexibility when administering this test to children whose physical or sensory impairments may place them at some disadvantage. Furthermore, the examiner decides whether this tool is appropriate for answering the referral question. Any changes in administration that result in changes to standard administrative procedures should be noted on the protocol and reported with the interpretation of the results. Additionally, examiners who observe behavioral indicators of neurological impairment during testing should interpret the results with caution and refer the child as needed.

The *Bayley-III Adminstration Manual* explicitly addresses examiner qualifications rather than professional training/ certification of those who may administer and interpret this assessment tool. Examiners need to have training and experience in administering and interpreting comprehensive developmental assessments, and in the fundamentals of assessment procedures. They should also be competent in testing young children characterized by different cultural, clinical, and pre-academic experiences. Test interpretation should be consistent with those promulgated by the *Standards for Educational and Psychological Testing* (American Educational Research Association, 1999). Examiners who have not had formal training in assessment must be supervised by experienced and knowledgeable professionals. In addition, examiners must abide by state and federal laws and policies that may require certain professional or graduate training and the ability to function within a multidisciplinary team, as well as the skills to interpret results in a meaningful way.

SCORING

Each item on the Cognitive subtest has explicit administration and scoring criteria that are best practiced and learned before testing a child. The manual suggests examiners should become sufficiently familiar with the administration directions so as to not need to read from the manual during the assessment. Although the Bayley-III subtests may be administered in any order, examiners may choose to administer the Cognitive subtest first because the tasks are engaging and do not require a verbal response. Test entry point is determined based upon the child's age and this helps ensure the child's initial success.

In the case of infants born before the 37th week of gestation, the manual allows for age adjustment through 24 months of chronological age. The intention of age adjustment, also known as "corrected age" in the medical literature, is to take prematurity into account in assessing neurocognitive development, growth, and medical outcomes in preterm children (American Academy of Pediatrics (AAP), 2009). In order to make the adjustment, the prematurity is calculated in weeks and months, and is then subtracted from the chronological age. The resulting number of months and days are then recorded in the row labeled "Adjusted Age." Several calculators for determining age adjustments may be found online (March of Dimes, 2009), or may be downloaded as i-Phone applications. Best practices would include deriving summary scores for both adjusted and chronological ages.

The basal level is determined by obtaining a score of 1 on three consecutive items. Testing should continue until the ceiling is reached – namely, five consecutive scores of zero. Qualitative information (e.g., on the child's language and test behavior) ought to be recorded on the record form, as this information may help later when scoring and interpreting results.

Items that comprise a series are conveniently identified as such, and may be administered and scored at the same time. For example, the *Blue Board Series* begins with Item 51 (1 piece in 150 seconds), continues to Item 58 (4 pieces in 150 seconds) and finally to Item 66 (9 pieces in 75 seconds). Otherwise, items should be administered in order, as they are grouped by difficulty. Rules for scoring multiple responses are specified in the manual. As a rule of thumb, the best response is credited, but one should always consult with the manual. Timed items are cued by a clock symbol on the protocol, with the number of seconds specified – information that is helpful to the examiner.

Seating and positioning is not specified in the manual for the Cognitive subtest. We have found that supported sitting at a table across from one another works best for very young babies or for those children needing more stability. Toddlers may enjoy sitting on the floor with the examiner and parent, while older children may be most attentive when seated at a sturdy table and on a chair of a comfortable height. If evaluated in a playroom, the examiner should consider limiting distractions by removing other toys in order to engage the child in the testing. The examiner should be aware of signs of fatigue, and allow for breaks as needed.

As with the Bayley-III subtests, the total number of passes together with the number of unadministered items below the basal level are summed, resulting in a raw score. This raw score then is converted to a scaled score, using Table A.1 in the manual. The scaled score has a mean of 10 and a standard deviation of 3. A composite score that combines the cognitive and the social-emotional subtests is determined by using Table A.5. This composite score has a mean of 100 and standard deviation of 15.

All scores are recorded on the front page of the Bayley-III Record Form. The profile may be charted on page 2 of the Record Form. We have found the recording and profiling of scores to provide a useful visual aid when interpreting scores to caregivers. Discrepancies between scores also may be determined through using Table B.2 and then documenting them on page 2. Growth scores are a novel concept included in the Bayley-III, and may be used to document growth towards outcomes. Similar to height and weight charts used by pediatricians to document growth velocity, and educational assessment tools used for progress monitoring, Bayley-III cognitive growth scores provide an opportunity to chart and observe cognitive growth over time (Centers for Disease Control and Prevention (CDC), 2000; Ostrosky & Horn, 2002). Table B.6 is used to plot Bayley-III growth scores; this converts the raw score to the growth score equivalent. Then, the scores are plotted on a copy of the growth chart in Appendix H. There are growth charts available for ages

1–18 months, 18–36 months, and 24–42 months. Figure 2.1 provides an example of the Bayley-III Growth Chart utilized in the case study described below.

Finally, while developmental age equivalents may be obtained and are perhaps more understandable for caregivers

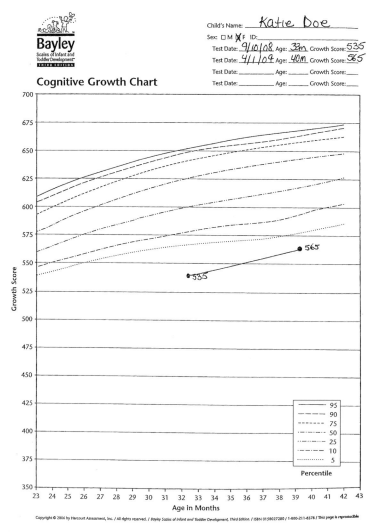

FIGURE 2.1   Case study: Cognitive Growth Chart for Katie Doe.

than standard scores, caution should be used in their application and interpretation. Developmental age scores are based upon the average age in months in which a given total raw score is obtained – for example, if the average raw score of 2-year-old children is 62, any child obtaining a score of 62 receives an age equivalent of 2 years. Thus, one cannot compare the child's performance to the peer group. Furthermore, the distribution of age scores does not represent equal units, and small raw-score changes may result in large changes in resulting developmental age equivalents. Percentile scores may offer a more straightforward explanation to parents of their child's position relative to the standardization sample; for example, a child who scores at the 50th percentile has performed better than 50 percent of similar age children in the norm sample (Sattler, 2008). We find age scores most useful in describing performance within the context of development for severely delayed children, who may exceed the age range for the Bayley-III.

INTERPRETATION

When interpreting results of young children, it is important to avoid equating their cognitive development with later intelligence. The Bayley-III was designed as a diagnostic tool to provide information that documents a child's current developmental status. This status may change rapidly as the child matures. Tests of intelligence assume a curvilinear function between the age of the child and the level of ability. Considerable variability in this developmental timing is normal for very young children.

Examiners are encouraged to follow a series of four steps when interpreting Bayley-III mean scores:

1. Describe the child's composite scores ($SD = 100$, $M = 15$) in light of the descriptive classifications in the manual, which range from Very Superior (130 and above) to Extremely Low (69 and below).
2. Compare scores on the Cognitive domain with others to determine possible discrepancies. For example, those on the Cognitive domain may be compared with those on Receptive

Communication, Expressive Communication, Fine and Gross Motor, and Social-Emotional domains.
3. Utilize the composite scores to describe overall development in the five domains.
4. Analyze scores from the adaptive behavior domain. The use of the Scoring Assistant to generate reports and plot scores greatly assists these efforts.

STRENGTHS AND CONCERNS

Strengths of the Bayley-III include current norms collected from a somewhat large ($n = 1,700$) and representative sample of US children aged from 16 days to 43 months, 15 days. Item development and selection reflect the latest research in child development. Administration is relatively easy, due to the design of the protocol and clarity of instructions. While the previous Bayley editions combined cognitive and language skills in the Mental Scale, the Bayley-III separates them into distinct domains; this, too, is a strength. Reliability and validity are adequate for clinical use. As noted previously, the completion of the cognitive domain does not require expressive language responses from the child, and thus expressive language delays do not affect a child's performance on this domain. An examiner is able to make corrections for prematurity up to 24 months according to the *Bayley-III Administration Manual*, which is consistent with guidelines from AAP, the March of Dimes, and others (AAP, 2009; March of Dimes, 2009). This adjustment is not endorsed in the manuals of similar infant and toddler assessment tools, and thus may present an ethical dilemma for the examiner.

Furthermore, the Bayley-III development is consistent with the IDEA 2004 requirements for a multidisciplinary team assessment of five domains, one of which is Cognitive. Parent or primary caregiver involvement is encouraged, thus facilitating testing, and providing parents and caregivers with insight regarding ways in which they may engage children in learning. The information yielded from the Bayley-III is helpful in diagnosing developmental delays and developing intervention plans. The growth scores may be utilized to document response to intervention. Finally, the design of the test enables examiners to easily transport the test to community settings, where assessments often occur.

The major weakness of the Bayley-III is a lack of research that supports its clinical utility. The Cognitive domain provides only general information that may be used for intervention and instructional purposes, as "the item sample is limited, 22% of the items are timed, and some of the items are of questionable educational relevance" (Bradley-Johnson & Johnson, 2007, pp. 339–340). These authors concluded that it remains unclear which aspects of cognition are being measured, since the Bayley-III was not designed to be used as a measure of intelligence or to predict academic achievement. The studies, which were completed by the test publisher and reported in the manual, are interesting, yet insufficient. Researchers, clinicians, and others are encouraged to conduct and report this form of research. Most published studies utilized the Bayley-II or even older editions, and differences between the older and current versions limit the relevance of findings from studies that used older versions. Researchers may elect to utilize the older edition when comparisons to longitudinal data sets are necessary.

The norms only extend to the age of 42 months. This, too, is a limitation, especially given the availability of other similar assessment tools that span a higher age range. Thus, if using the Bayley-III for toddlers, a different tool must be selected to assess the preschool population. As such, evaluators must utilize separate tools to identify children under the age of 3 (Part C) and over the age of 3 (Part B) for eligibility purposes under the IDEA 2004. Thus, certain states – for example, Florida – have mandated the use of assessment tools for eligibility that have a broader age range, for the purpose of achieving continuity across these programs, and for purposes of program evaluation. Given the historical efforts of the Bayley Scales towards understanding infant and toddler developmental functioning, it may be a strength that Bayley-III has continued to maintain its original purpose and focus on that population of very young children, rather than attempting to also assess older children's cognitive functioning and academic achievement.

USE IN CLINICAL POPULATIONS

A representative proportion of children with atypical development (10 percent) was included in the norm sample in an effort to enhance the representativeness of the sample. However, percentages of the children with various diagnoses were not provided. Special group studies have been completed on children with autism spectrum disorder, Down syndrome, language impairment, small gestational age, fetal alcohol exposure, cerebral palsy, and intrapartum asphyxia, and most received lower scores compared to a matched group from the norm sample (Bayley, 2006; Bradley-Johnson & Johnson, 2007). A study completed in Victoria, Australia, comparing cognitive outcomes of 201 very preterm (VP; < 28 weeks) or extremely low birth weight babies (ELBW; < 1,000 g) with 196 controls indicated that the mean values for all cohorts on the Cognitive Scales were higher than the normative mean, indicating that the Bayley-III Cognitive scores may be inflated (Anderson *et al.*, 2009). Comparison studies with other major early childhood assessment tools are reported in the manual, but again, data are limited (Bayley, 2006). Separate norms are not provided for clinical groups, given that the purpose of this tool is to assess developmental functioning and to help identify children with developmental delays. The Bayley-III has not been translated into Spanish, and there are no norms for non-English-speaking children. Thus, until more studies can be completed using the Bayley-III, its predictive ability must be considered with caution.

CASE STUDY: KATIE

Katie was referred to a child development clinic for a developmental evaluation subsequent to removal from her parents' custody and placement into the foster care system due to multiple concerns regarding her development. At age 2 years 5 months, Katie was unable to walk or feed herself, and showed little interest in her environment. She apparently had spent her days strapped in an infant seat, and she received her only nutrition, baby formula, by a bottle. Katie had not received any well baby check-ups or immunizations. Upon entry into foster care, her height and weight were below average (20th percentile) and her head circumference fell below the 5th percentile. She was described as having dysmorphic features, including close-set eyes, bushy eyebrows, and a left ear malformation. She had not received any form of early intervention.

When seen for the initial evaluation, Katie had been in foster care for 3 months. She walked stiff-legged, and held her arms upward. She was immediately affectionate toward the examiner and other adults. She showed interest in toys in the playroom, and tended to choose those that could be placed in and then tipped out from containers. She showed no interest in more imaginative toys, such as dolls, a toy kitchen, or a dollhouse. Katie was happy and agreeable when allowed to do what she wanted, but would fall to the floor when she disagreed. She did not point or use any words or gestures, and simply grunted. Simple commands were difficult for her to follow, and she did not respond when her name was called. Katie's results on the Bayley-III are presented in Table 2.1. As shown by the scores in this table, Katie's development was quite delayed compared with other toddlers, many of whom would soon be ready to begin the preschool experience.

Katie was determined to be eligible for early intervention services, based upon scores obtained on this evaluation with the Bayley-III together with other information. She began receiving weekly home visits from an early interventionist and a speech therapist, who worked with her foster mother to develop skills across development, with an emphasis on communication. She was enrolled in a medical program that included a pediatrician who managed her health needs and referrals for medical tests. Due to her significant delays along with mild dysmorphic features, Katie was referred for genetic testing to rule out Fragile X or other chromosome abnormalities, to an audiologist for an in-depth hearing evaluation, and to a neurologist for an MRI of her brain. All results were normal. Thus, her delays seemingly were due mainly to neglect. Termination of parental rights followed, and Katie was placed with a family who eventually adopted her.

We had the opportunity to evaluate Katie again 8 months later at 37 months of age, as part of the adoption process. Katie was now attending a special education preschool for children

TABLE 2.1   Results of Bayley-III Initial Evaluation

Domain/subtests	Scaled score	Standard score	Percentile rank	Age equivalent
Cognitive	–	65	1	–
Cognitive	3	–	–	16 months
Language	–	56	0.1	–
Receptive Communication	3	–	–	13 months
Expressive Communication	2	–	–	9 months
Motor	–	61	1	–
Fine Motor	4	–	–	17 months
Gross Motor	3	–	–	15 months
Social-Emotional	–	55	0.1	–
Adaptive Composite	–	47	0.1	–

Note. Katie's scores at 29 months of age.

with mild developmental delays. Her parents were fostering Katie's 6-month-old sister, who they also hoped to adopt. Katie presented as an active, happy, and engaging child who was quite interested in people and her surroundings. She would sometimes bring items to share with her mother, as well as going for an occasional hug. She had also developed a strong disposition since her last visit, and was more self-directed. She displayed mild temper tantrums, which, if ignored, went away. She could be redirected to tasks. She responded positively to praise and attention, and was proud of her work. Her communication skills were emerging; she now used words and jargon to express her wants and needs, and vocalized during her play. She had gained in height and weight since her last visit, though her head circumference was still below the 5th percentile. The results of the Bayley-III are summarized in Table 2.2, and Katie's growth scores may be seen in Figure 2.1.

While still delayed relative to her peers, we were delighted to observe the gains that Katie had made across all areas of development. Most improved were her social-emotional and

TABLE 2.2   Results of Bayley-III at Follow-up Evaluation

Domain/subtests	Scaled score	Standard score	Percentile rank	Age equivalent
Cognitive	–	70	2	–
Cognitive	4	–	–	21 months
Language	–	65	1	–
Receptive Communication	3	–	–	16 months
Expressive Communication	5	–	–	21 months
Motor	–	55	.1	–
Fine Motor	4	–	–	22 months
Gross Motor	1	–	–	16 months
Social-Emotional	–	80	9	–
Adaptive Composite	–	74	4	–

Note. Katie's scores at 37 months of age.

adaptive functioning, which we attributed to the positive impact of a stable and nurturing environment in which she had received proper nutrition and medical care, instruction in daily routines, and stimulation. She showed solid attachment to her adoptive mother, interest in the world around her, and enjoyed playing with toys much more appropriate for her age. Her mother reported steady improvement in communication skills. She will need continued special education services for some time, to address her overall development.

References

AAP Policy Statement. (January 1, 2009). *Age terminology during the perinatal period.* Retrieved October 20, 2009 from http://aappolicy.aappublications.org.

American Educational Research Association. (1999). *Standards for Educational and Psychological Testing.* Washington, DC: American Educational Research Association.

Anderson, P., Kelly, E., Charlton, M., Williamson, A., de Luca, C., Hutchinson, E., & Doyle, L. (2009). *Cognitive Outcome at 2 years in Very Preterm or Extremely Low Birthweight Infants born in Victoria in 2005.* Retrieved October 20, 2009 from http://www.abstracts2view.com/pas/view.php?nu=PASL1_2540.

Baby age calculator. Retrieved October 20, 2009 from www.appolicious. com/.../baby-age-calculator-big-blue-apps-::39380.

Bagnato, S. J., & Neisworth, J. T. (1994). A national study of the social and treatment "invalidity" of intelligence testing for early intervention. *School Psychology Quarterly, 9*, 81–102.

Bayley, N. (1993). *Bayley Scales of Infant Development* (2nd ed.). San Antonio, TX: Harcourt Assessment, Inc.

Bayley, N. (2006). *Bayley Scales of Infant and Toddler Development* (3rd ed.). San Antonio, TX: Harcourt Assessment, Inc.

Bracken, B. A., & Walker, I. K. C. (1997). The utility of intelligence tests for preschool children. In D. P. Flanagan, J. L. Genshaft, & P. C. Harrison (Eds.), *Contemporary Intellectual Assessment: Theories, Tests, and Issues* (pp. 484–502). New York, NY: Guilford Press.

Bradley-Johnson, S., & Johnson, M. (2007). Infant and toddler assessment. In B. Bracken, & R. Nagle (Eds.), *Psychoeducational Assessment of Preschool Children* (4th ed.) (pp. 325–357). Mahwah, NJ: Lawrence Erlbaum Associates.

Bruner, J. S. (1972). Nature and uses of immaturity. *American Psychologist, 27*(8), 687–708.

Centers for Disease Control and Prevention, National Center for Health Statistics. (2000). *CDC Growth Charts: United States.* Atlanta, GA: Author.

Colombo, J., & Frick, J. (1999). Recent advances and issues in the study of preverbal intelligence. In M. Anderson (Ed.), *The Development of Intelligence* (pp. 43–71). Hove, UK: Psychology Press.

Corrected Newborn Age Calculator. Retrieved October 20, 2009 from www. adhb.govt.nz/newborn/guidelines/admission/gacalc.htm.

Dougherty, T. M., & Haith, M. M. (1997). Infant expectations and reactions as predictors of childhood speed of processing and IQ. *Developmental Psychology, 33*(1), 146–155.

Kail, R. (2000). Speed of information processing: Developmental change and links to intelligence. *Journal of School Psychology, 38*(1), 51–61.

March of Dimes. (2009). Pregnancy and Newborn Health Education Center. Retrieved October 20, 2009 from http://www.marchofdimes.com.

Nagle, R. (2007). Issues in preschool assessment. In B. Bracken, & R. Nagle (Eds.), *Psychoeducational Assessment of Preschool Children* (4th ed.) (pp. 29–48). Mahwah, NJ: Lawrence Erlbaum Associates.

Neisworth, J. T., & Bagnato, S. J. (2000). Recommended practices in assessment. In S. S. Sandall, M. McLean, & B. Smith (Eds.), *DEC Recommended Practices* (pp. 17–27). Longmont, CO: Sopris West.

Ostrosky, M. M., & Horn, E. (2002). *Assessment: Gathering Meaningful Assessment Information.* Longmont, CO: Sopris West.

Piaget, J. (1952). *The Origins of Intelligence in Children.* New York, NY: International Universities Press.

Rose, S., Feldman, J., & Jankowski, J. (2009). Information processing in toddlers: Continuity from infancy and persistence of preterm deficits. *Intelligence, 37* (3), 311–320.

Sattler, J. M. (2008). *Assessment of Children: Cognitive Foundations* (5th ed.). San Diego, CA: Jerome M. Sattler, Publisher, Inc.

Schatz, J., Kramer, J. H., Ablin, A., & Matthay, K. K. (2000). Processing speed, working memory and IQ: A developmental model of cognitive deficits following cranial radiation therapy. *Neuropsychology, 14*(2), 189.

United States Department of Education. (2004). The Individuals with Disabilities Education Improvement Act of 2004. Retrieved August 12, 2009. from http://www.ed.gov/about/offices/list/osers/osep/index.html.

Vygotsky, L. S. (1978). *Mind in Society: The Development of Higher Psychological Processes*. Cambridge, MA: Harvard Press.

The Bayley-III Language Scale

Elizabeth R. Crais

Division of Speech & Hearing Sciences, The University of North Carolina at Chapel Hill, Chapel Hill, NC

INTRODUCTION

The Bayley-III (Bayley, 2006) aligns well with current federal legislation (IDEA, 2004), best practice guidelines, an array of early intervention fields (Sandall, Hemmeter, Smith, & McLean, 2005), and recent research findings. For example, the Bayley-III (Bayley, 2006) measures skills across the five domains (cognitive, language, motor, adaptive, and social-emotional) mandated by IDEA (2004) and partitions the domains into separate measurable sets of items so as to encourage interdisciplinary administration, diagnosis, and planning for the child and family. The Bayley-III (Bayley, 2006) was developed, in part, in response to heightened awareness of the need to understand children's skills across domains (Crais, Watson, & Baranek, 2009) and the requirements for multidisciplinary assessment across domains in IDEA (2004). The use of this scale enables various professionals on the assessment team (e.g., the psychologist, speech-language pathologist, occupational and physical therapist, special educator) to contribute their individual disciplinary knowledge, thus leading to an integrated description of the child. The Bayley-III can fit easily within most assessment models, including multi-, inter- and transdisciplinary, as well as arena-based, models.

The inclusion of parent information on the young child's social-emotional and adaptive skill development provides an avenue for the family–professional collaboration envisioned by many (Barrera & Corso, 2002; Summers, Hoffman, Marquis, Turnbull, & Poston, 2005; Crais, 2010). Further, the use of the Bayley-III encourages the inclusion of family members as active participants in the assessment process, by taking an active part in the direct assessment of their child through the use of parent report instruments. Thus, the Bayley-III's design utilizes evidence-based practices, ones that incorporate the best available research evidence, professional wisdom and experience, and consumer values and experience (Sackett, Straus, Richardson, Rosenberg, & Haynes, 2000).

The Bayley-III (Bayley, 2006) also provides results from assessment of both typically and atypically developing children (e.g., children who were premature, or those with Down syndrome) in order for professionals to have some idea of how these populations of children perform on this measure. In this way, professionals can compare their target child to the test norms to gain insight into the samples' representativeness to the target child.

Substantial changes have been made to the language items on the Bayley-III by expanding some content areas (e.g., prelinguistic, social, complex language components) and increasing the test's pragmatic and child-friendly features. An earlier edition of the Bayley, Bayley II (Bayley, 1993), incorporated the language items in the Mental Scales along with various other items (e.g., those assessing cognitive, perceptual, problem-solving, and personal/social skills).

The Bayley-III encapsulates language and related skills in one Language Scale with two subtests: Receptive Communication and Expressive Communication. The use of the term "communication" was selected consciously so as to reflect all aspects of related developmental behaviors, especially those involved in the prelinguistic stage of communication before more advanced stages of language emerge. In addition, in recognizing the importance of both receptive and expressive communication and the need to compare these two sets of skills, the Bayley-III divides them into separate subsets. The Bayley-III added a number of items that assess receptive and expressive skills, including paralinguistic skills and others for the higher ages.

The current chapter first provides a brief overview of the importance of measuring early communication and language skills in young children, and highlights their strong associations with later developmental and academic skills. The next section pinpoints specific behaviors that can be predictive of later development, and describes how the Bayley-III reflects the theoretical underpinnings, the best available research evidence, and professional consensus regarding these key areas. The subsequent section briefly touches on how the Bayley-III administration procedures enhance child and caregiver partic-ipation and ease administration. Sections on scoring and interpreting the test follow, with additional sections on the strengths and concerns of the Bayley-III, and the clinical pop-ulations best suited for its use are then provided. Finally, a case study illustrates the use of the Bayley-III Language Scale in assessing a young child who was referred because of delayed language skills.

CONTENT

Throughout this chapter, the term *language* will be used to represent any conventionalized symbol system (e.g., words, signs, picture symbols) the child may use to interact that is consistently recognized by others. On the other hand, the term *communication* refers to any means that the child uses to interact with others (e.g., eye gaze, gesture, facial expression, vocal-izations, words) or any combination of two or more means. Thus, language is only one form of communication, and communication can occur without language. The early means of communication often are thought of as developing during the prelinguistic (before the use of symbols) and early linguistic stages, and can also be used along with language to augment a message (e.g., pointing while saying "Look").

Language and communication skills play a major role in children's overall learning. The acquisition of language both allows and facilitates learning in many other domains, and is enhanced by advances in other domains (e.g., social-emotional, motor, cognitive, adaptive). Consider the constant interplay of language and communication skills with other domains in the life of children with varying disabilities (e.g., hearing loss, visual impairment, autism, severe physical disabilities). The mutual influences of development of language and other important domains become evident. In addition, theories of child development suggest that language acquisition, like other aspects of development, is a transactional process influenced by multiple ecological factors, including culture and home environment, along with caregiver and child characteristics (Bronfenbrenner & Morris, 1998; Chapman, 2000; Sameroff & MacKenzie, 2003).

The identification of children's early communication and language skills is essential to recognizing the child's strengths and weaknesses, and assists in predicting the child's later skills. The child's current communication performance is one of the best predictors of a child's future language (Brady, Marquis, Fleming, & McLean, 2004). In addition, children's early language abilities have positive relationships with later language and literacy skill development (NICHD Early Child Care Research Network, 2005). Finally, the level of symbolic play exhibited by young children predicts later language skills (Lyytinen, Laakso, Poikkeus, & Rita, 1999; Lyytinen, Poikkeus, Laakso, Eklund, & Lyytinen, 2001). For example, Lyytinen and colleagues (1999) observed that symbolic play skills at 14 months of age were predictive of receptive and expressive language at both 24 and 42 months. Thus, assessing various early communication and language skills in young children can be helpful in identifying children with disabilities who may need early intervention, and also can shed light on the ultimate prognosis of these children for advancing their communication and language skills.

Several content areas in the Bayley-III Language Scales are of particular interest because they reflect new clinical and research developments, notably across social-emotional skills, prelinguistic communication skills, and comprehension skills. In addition, items have been added to the upper reaches of the age range to help enhance the test's utility for older children. These areas are highlighted below with the clinical and theoretical rationale.

Social-Emotional Skills

Professionals engaged in early intervention work increasingly understand the importance of emotional and social development during early childhood (Guralnick, 2005). Children with significant attachment or emotion regulation difficulties may display secondary or concomitant communication delays. Important skills for early social and emotional development include attention and self-regulation; the ability to form relationships by means of mutual engagement and attachment; intentional two-way communication and reciprocity; prelinguistic means of communication, including gestures, gaze, and vocalization; and the use of symbols to express thoughts and feelings (Greenspan, DeGangi, & Weider, 2001; Zero to Three, 2005). Items from each of these categories ensure comprehensive assessment of social-emotional development.

In addition to the Social-Emotional Scale, the Language subscales also include a number of items reflective of social development. Several items investigate the child's attention to people, how the child responds to his or her name, reacts when interrupted in play, and understands inhibitory words. A child's failure to look up or orient to his or her own name or to respond to speech directed to him or her early in life marks an indicator associated with a later diagnosis of autism (Baranek, 1999; Filipek, Accardo, & Baranek, 1999; Zwaigenbaum, Bryson, & Rogers, 2005). Thus, for all children, and most particularly for those at risk for autism, identifying the child's ability to respond to speech is an important element within assessment.

Items documenting early mutual engagement and reciprocity are included in the Bayley-III. Their inclusion reflects increased recognition of the importance of social responsiveness and of the need to assess and intervene within natural environments (IDEA, 2004). Professionals are encouraged to work closely with caregivers to model and support children's learning and to provide services in natural environments (Bernheimer & Weismer, 2007; American Speech-Language-Hearing Association (ASHA), 2008). Thus, behaviors in these environments should be assessed to facilitate intervention planning. The added items provide an understanding of how the child responds to requests for, attends to, participates in, and initiates social routines; as well as imitates behaviors modeled by adults. These types of naturally occurring activities offer opportunities to promote children's learning throughout the day by using activities, materials, and people familiar to the child (Dunst, Hamby, Trivette, Raab, & Bruder, 2000; Bernheimer & Weismer, 2007). The professional's participation in the child's and family's natural environments enhances the assessment and intervention processes through the identification of the child's and family's preferred routines and interests, facilitates access to everyday materials and toys, and encourages effective arrangement of the environment to promote communication in familiar and functional activities (ASHA, 2008). Further, these types of activities are supported by transactional and social interaction theoretical positions that underscore the importance of transactional or interactive influences of the child and the environment, particularly with caregivers through their use of modeling, imitation, and other responsive communication strategies (Chapman, 2000; Sameroff & MacKenzie, 2003).

Prelinguistic Communication Skills

Prelinguistic communication has gained the attention of both researchers and clinicians for what it can offer in assessment and intervention planning. The relationship between the early use of communicative means (e.g., gaze, gestures, vocalizations, words) and later language skills in children with developmental delays is strong (McCathren, Yoder, & Warren, 2000; Wetherby, Goldstein, Cleary, Allen, & Kublin, 2003), as well as in those with autism spectrum disorders (ASD, Zwaigenbaum et al., 2005). In children who are identified as "late talkers," gesture use has been used to help predict which children will eventually "catch up" with their peers (Thal, Tobias, & Morrison, 1991). In addition, the production of early sounds, especially consonants, is closely associated with later language skills. The ability to use more than one consonant in an utterance is an important developmental milestone that many 24-month-old toddlers with delayed language do not achieve (Paul & Jennings, 1992). Further, 2-year-olds delayed in phonological development show a higher risk for speech delay at age 3 (Carson, Klee, Carson, & Hime, 2003). Therefore, phonological information can be useful in making decisions regarding "late talkers" and predicting their likelihood to exhibit typical language skills at age 3 or 4 years. The measurement of communication skills is an essential component when working with young children with or at risk for communication deficits – particularly those who are at the prelinguistic stage of development.

The ability to signal one's intentions also is critical at the prelinguistic level, and to the development of higher-level communication skills (Brady *et al.*, 2004). Twelve-month-olds often communicate intentionally about once per minute, 18-month-olds about twice per minute, and 24-month-olds about five times per minute (Wetherby, Cain, Yonclas, & Walker, 1988). Therefore, a limited rate of intentional communication may indicate deficits. The rate of intentional communication is predictive of language development in young children with developmental delay. Higher rates of non-verbal intentional communication are associated with improved language outcomes (Calandrella & Wilcox, 2000).

The functions of communication, or the reasons a child communicates, also influence both prelinguistic and future developmental levels. Common categories for indicating functions of communication include Bruner's (1981) classification of *behavior regulation* (e.g., requesting objects or actions, protesting), *social interaction* (e.g., greeting, showing off), and *joint attention* (e.g., showing, commenting). Use of specific types of communicative functions predicts later language skills, and can help differentiate children with different disability patterns. For example, joint attention skills predict comprehension and production skills in both typically developing children (Mundy & Gomes, 1998; Slaughter & McConnell, 2003) and those with autism spectrum disorders (Mundy, Kasari, Sigman, & Ruskin, 1995; Charman, Baron-Cohen, Swettenham, Baird, Drew, & Cox, 2003). Social interactions also predict expressive vocabulary in typically developing children (Mundy & Gomes, 1998) and those with ASD (Mundy, Sigman, Ungerer, & Sherman, 1986; McEvoy, Rogers, & Pennington, 1993). Furthermore, limited use of gestures in 9- to 12-month-old children has also been associated with later diagnosis of ASD (Colgan, Lanter, McComish, Watson, Crais, & Baranek, 2006). Thus, understanding and assessing the reasons a child communicates are vital when identifying current and potential future communication deficits.

Although there were some prelinguistic items on earlier versions of the Bayley, new items have been added to provide a richer picture of children at younger ages and of children who are developmentally within these very early stages. Several Bayley-III items enhance professionals' abilities to assess prelinguistic (and linguistic) communication skills, especially the child's intentionality or functions of communication. They include examining the child's ability to gain attention (social interaction), use consonants, use gestures (behavior regulation), direct other's attention (joint attention), and use words or words plus gestures in combination to meet personal needs.

Comprehension Skills

Comprehension skills also are key to children's current and future language skills. Comprehension deficits serve as barriers to language development, and are associated with future language deficits (Thal *et al.*, 1991). Comprehension skills in the second year of life predict later comprehension and production skills in children with typical and atypical development (Lyytinen *et al.*, 2001; Wetherby, Allen, Cleary, Kublin, & Goldstein, 2002; Wetherby *et al.*, 2003). In addition, good comprehension skills predict which children with early expressive language delays are most likely to display social and other behaviors similar to typically developing age-matched peers (Paul, Looney, & Dahm, 1991; Thal *et al.*, 1991; Whitehurst, Fischel, Arnold, & Lonigan, 1992; Paul, 2000).

More Complex Language Levels

Finally, additional and more complex items have been added to the receptive and expressive scales to assist in the evaluation of higher-level language skills. Receptive language items include understanding descriptive words, prepositions, terms such as "less than" or "least," past tense, and negatives.

Complex expressive language items include the use of future tense, four- to five-word sentences, descriptive phrases, and morphemes such as "ing" and prepositions. Many higher-level items came from the Preschool Language Scale-IV (PLS-4; Zimmerman, Steiner, & Pond, 2002), a widely used measure to identify children's language development, including those with language deficits.

ADMINISTRATION AND SCORING

The Bayley-III Language Scale is child- and family-friendly, and easy to administer. The instructions encourage test administrators to include a parent or familiar caregiver (e.g., early care and education teacher, babysitter) in the testing process to help the child feel more comfortable and to facilitate the administration of some items. Most Bayley-III items allow the examiner and/or caregivers to encourage the child to respond if he or she initially refuses to do so, as long as basic standardization procedures are followed. Some children, especially those with communication deficits, may be shy or hesitant. In these instances, professionals may elect first to play briefly with the child to encourage rapport, communication, and cooperation, and later to begin testing. Although preschool children without disabilities may perform equally well with familiar and unfamiliar examiners, children with communication difficulties may perform more poorly with unfamiliar examiners (Fuchs, Fuchs, Power, & Daly, 1985; Fuchs, Fuchs, Benowitz, & Barringer, 1987). Thus, examiners need to be particularly careful in how they first administer and then interpret test results with children unfamiliar to them. Examiners should confer with parents or other caregivers to determine whether the child's performance was typical or atypical compared with his or her behaviors in other settings or tasks.

Examiners are advised to begin the Language Scale administration by identifying the start point. As indicated on the record form, individual start points are identified for each of a series of age ranges, beginning in 1-month increments and gradually moving to 3- to 4-month increments. First, the examiner calculates the child's chronological age, and then uses the corresponding start point listed on the record form. The use of the correct start point is intended to help the examiner target items that are within the child's developmental language level, to avoid challenging the child with language items likely to be too difficult, and to enhance efficiency – a quality important to infant assessment – by avoiding those items that are likely to be too easy. The reversal rule also helps. An examiner who finds the items are too difficult invokes the reversal rule, thus drops back to the previous start point, and resumes with easier items. This is particularly important on the Language Scale, as beginning too high can frustrate the child and may make him or her less communicative. This backward progression continues until the child passes three items in a row, at which point the basal level is established and the examiner begins moving forward to complete the unadministered items. Similarly, the discontinue rule – stop when the child receives five errors in a row – ensures that the child has the opportunity to attempt as many items as possible within his or her developmental level. This feature is particularly useful on the Language Scales, as children sometimes have "spotty" performance, knowing some items but not others.

When working with children who were born prematurely (< 37 weeks gestation), the examiner identifies the child's adjusted age by taking into account the degree of prematurity. The conventional practice for infant/toddler assessments is to adjust for prematurity until 24 months of age (Wilson and Cradock, 2004), and the Bayley-III follows this practice. The examiner first subtracts the child's date of birth from the expected birth date, and then enters the number of months and days born prematurely to the record form under the Adjustment for Prematurity. The examiner then calculates the child's chronological age without adjustment by subtracting the date of birth from the date of test and calculating the child's age in months and days. The examiner then identifies the adjusted age by subtracting the number of days/months of prematurity from the age in months/days.

Although the Bayley-III Language Scale is fairly easy to administer, a few tips may help guide the examiner. The initial use of the Receptive Scale often provides an excellent introduction to testing, especially with children who may be shy or hesitant with strangers. In this way, the child initially is not required to talk until later, when the examiner has developed more rapport with the child.

The record form for the Language Scale enhances the ease of test administration, including the accurate recording of test-related data. The record form informs the test user of the overall start point, item description, materials, and the number of trials allowed, and gives brief descriptions of the scoring criteria. The record form also has a space to record additional information that could be useful in later testing, as well as interpreting the results and writing the report. Communication attempts (e.g., gestures, words, phrases) that the child uses during the testing can be documented in this area for later use in completing some test items.

When first learning how to administer the Language Scales, examiners may highlight key words or directions for some items in the *Bayley-III Administration Manual* to facilitate test administration. For example, on the Receptive Item 14 (*Responds to Social Routines*), highlighting the names of the social routines may help the examiner see them quickly. Recording a few notes on the record form also may be helpful. For example, on the record form by Receptive Item 14, an examiner may write *E11 & E17* to remember that R14 connects with Expressive Items 11 (participates in social routine) and 17 (initiates play interaction), thereby remembering that the child may receive credit for those items during Item 14. Additionally, Receptive Item 8 (sustains play with objects) also is linked to Item 10 (child interrupts activity). As a helpful reminder, the examiner may draw an arrow from Item 8 to 10 on the record form. Highlighting key materials on the record form also may be useful. For example on Receptive Item 18 (understands inhibitory words), the examiner may highlight *6 Blocks* – one of the possible activities to play with the child. A thorough exploration of both the Receptive and Expressive items may help the new examiner become aware of links both within a subtest and across the two language subtests, especially those on which a child's score on one item may influence scores on other items.

After completing the Language Scale, the calculation of the child's total raw scores is easy. On each of the Language Scales, the examiner counts the total number of items the child passed and adds that to the number of preceding items below the basal level. Scaled scores are found by locating the appropriate table in the manual for the child's age (or adjusted age), then the total raw score and the corresponding scaled score. The Receptive and Expressive scaled scores are then summed, the appropriate table and corresponding composite score are located, and the language composite score is obtained. Tables also provide percentile ranks and confidence intervals.

Both the scaled scores and composite scores can be recorded on the profile graphs on page two of the record form to help with interpretation. This graphical presentation facilitates a visual understanding of a child's strengths and weaknesses for professionals and parents. The examiner should determine whether the differences are statistically significant, and how common the differences are compared to similar data from the standardization sample. Comparisons can be made between all scaled scores except the Adaptive Behavior Scale. Using the Discrepancy Comparison Table, the examiner enters any two scaled scores, subtracts the difference, and locates the required difference to determine if the difference equals or exceeds the required difference, in which case it is significant. Examiners consult an additional table to determine the frequency of the difference seen in the standardization sample.

The scoring system also facilitates the calculation of a child's relative growth for each subtest by using that subtest's growth chart appropriate for the child's age. The growth scores range from 200 to 800, with a mean of 500 and a standard deviation of 100. For each subtest, the total raw score is plotted on the growth chart relative to the child's current age. As with most growth charts, lines indicate the growth of same-age peers at the 5th through 95th percentile bands. This feature is particularly helpful to chart the child's language status compared with peers, and to chart the rate of progress in language skills over time.

INTERPRETATION

Interpretation of the Language Scale (and overall) results is an ongoing process, beginning from the start of the testing through the scoring, validating the child's behaviors with parents or caregivers, and considering the aggregate of what is known about the child and his or her family. Experienced professionals know that the interpretation of a child's language scores is dependent on many qualities. These include the number of correct responses on the test, as well as how the child performed on the items, the parents' or caregivers' thoughts about the representativeness of the child's performance, other child qualities that may need to be considered (e.g., illness, fatigue, attention, amount of testing preceding this test, receptiveness to examiner), and the examiner's own perceptions of the child's communication and language skills during and surrounding the testing. The same scores obtained by two or more children may be interpreted somewhat differently depending on these factors.

The use of the Behavior Observation Inventory, found at the end of the Bayley-III record form, may facilitate this type of information. This Inventory includes a way to record examiner and parents' or caregiver ratings of the child's behavior, including behaviors that may have impacted the child's test performance (e.g., positive or negative affect, ease of engagement, alertness, anxiety). All professionals with testing experience can describe instances where any one or a combination of these factors impacted a child's language performance. Identifying these qualities and noting them on the child's report is important.

Behavioral observations of the child's language skills may be necessary to better describe and explain the scores obtained for the child. For example, those who read the report should understand the child's language scores in light of the highlighted behaviors. The language scores for many children will be viewed as representative of the child, and can lay the groundwork for ongoing intervention planning and progress monitoring. However, some children underperform on language measures, and their scores may not reflect their true potential. Professionals and parents are urged to identify additional strategies for gathering information on these children. For example, classroom observations, communication or language samples, or parent and teacher reports may need to supplement the language results. Consistent with federal legislation (e.g. IDEA, 2004), program eligibility should not be based only on data from a single test or measure. Therefore, the Bayley-III (or the Language Scale if used separately) can serve as the core assessment, with other measures to confirm and/or add information for making appropriate decisions about a child.

Comparisons of scores from the receptive and expressive subtests can be a vital part of interpreting the child's scores. For example, when the Receptive Composite is lower than the Expressive Composite, a discrepancy of 4 points occurred in 7.9 percent of the standardization sample. In contrast, when the Receptive Composite is higher than the Expressive Composite, a discrepancy of 4 points occurred in 10.2 percent of the standardization sample. Sattler (2001) indicates that differences that occur in less than 10 percent of the sample are unusual. Further, a statistically significant difference between subtests in favor of a child's expressive skills may indicate particular disorders (e.g., auditory processing, autism, William's syndrome) that are characterized by higher expressive than receptive skills in some children. In addition, the possible impact of the child's linguistic, cultural, medical, physical, and environmental background should be investigated, as they may help explain these differences.

An examination of commonalities across Receptive and Expressive subtests may also be helpful during the intervention planning process. For example, a child who shows weak interactive skills within social routines is often likely to have limited gestures and means of getting others' attention. Thus, interventions that focus on building stronger prelinguistic and social interactive skills (e.g., social reciprocity, use of gestures, vocalizations, and eye contact) may help facilitate attention-getting skills and, later, the use of words and word combinations. In addition, given that receptive skills typically are stronger than expressive skills, children whose receptive skills are poor need help to strengthen them along with a focus on facilitating their expressive skills.

Interpretation and intervention planning efforts focused on communication skills are also enhanced by examining developmental risk indicators of delayed or atypical behavior. The broad categories include atypical social behaviors (especially those that may characterize autism spectrum disorders), and attentional, motor and movement, hearing, and visual difficulties. Knowledge of these behaviors may help the examiner identify the need for further testing, and may be particularly useful during intervention planning focused on communication facilitation.

Additional information for interpreting language results may also be gained by using qualitative classifications of the child's composite scores. These range from very superior to extremely low. Tables in the *Technical Manual* enable examiners to identify the child's qualitative classification of the Language composite score and the percentage of scores from the standardization sample that fall within that classification. For example, the very superior and extremely low classifications represent the top 2.0 percent and the bottom 2.4 percent, respectively, of the 1,700 standardization scores. Children whose composite score falls below the 10 percent level would be classified as borderline, and are likely to need intervention. The use of these classifications can help examiners identify and compare the child's strengths and needs across the composite scores, as well as to communicate descriptively how the child performs.

STRENGTHS AND CONCERNS

The Bayley-III has many strengths that support its use across various testing situations and locations, and with children within the developmental age range covered by the test. The Bayley-III provides test scores and other information across the five domains specifically identified within IDEA (2004), thus adding to its overall utility. One of the primary purposes of the Bayley-III is to promote interdisciplinary administration, and therefore it should have strong appeal to early intervention teams. For speech-language pathologists who often use their own assessment tools, the opportunity to utilize an instrument that includes a valid and reliable way to measure language skills within the same testing framework as other professionals is a clear strength. Moreover, the ability to profile the child's skills across domains, utilize growth charts, and compare scores across testing times (e.g., pre- and post-intervention, annual reviews) also enhances the value of this test. Its flexibility of use across most assessment models (e.g., inter-, multi-, and trans-disciplinary) further increases its desirability. Being able to administer the Receptive and Expressive subtests in the order that makes the most sense with an individual child is a bonus. Further, the location of its administration is also flexible. Children can be seen in the setting that may be most comforting to them (e.g., home, childcare setting), and therefore their language may be more easily elicited.

The scoring process and the record form provide additional strengths of the Bayley-III. The use of information acquired on one item to complete other items without having to administer them is also an advantage. This is particularly useful on the Language Scale, as children will not always "produce" language when asked or prompted by an examiner, but may do so spontaneously at other points in the testing. Having all the information necessary to administer the Language Scale on the record form is also helpful when trying to engage the child, elicit communication skills, and follow the test protocol.

The only concern or caution is that the use of the Language Scale results alone to make critical decisions should be avoided. These results should be supplemented with information derived from additional sources, including interviews, observations, data from other measures, and medical and other records. Examiners can use informal interactions to gain added information about the child's communication or language skills, especially looking for possible behavioral differences displayed by the child across contexts. This information is necessary when forming a complete understanding of the child's communication and language skills.

USE IN CLINICAL POPULATIONS

The Language Scale may be used with children who exhibit various kinds of communication and language deficits. Additionally, the scale may be modified for use with children who display mild to moderate disabilities. The manual provides helpful guidelines about how to make modifications, and whether the modifications would substantially diverge from the standardized administration. The test is appropriate for most children referred due to language delays or disorders, whether language is the primary issue or one of several concerns. However, the use of the Language Scale with children who display severe physical or sensory disabilities should be avoided when their physical limitations preclude accurate assessment of their skills.

The Bayley-III data reported in the test's manual, which summarize the performance of children from several clinical populations, can guide professionals as to how children who display these differing diagnoses performed on the Bayley-III. These comparisons may be useful to professionals and parents when considering whether the child's language performance is representative of other children who share the same diagnosis. This information can facilitate intervention planning when identifying evidence-based practices that can be effective with this population of children.

One of the most popular measures to examine children's language skills is the Preschool Language Scale-4 (PLS-4; Zimmerman *et al.*, 2002). As expected, scores from the Bayley-III Language Scale and PLS-4 correlate highly, and both assess similar constructs. SLPs who practice in interdisciplinary settings should consider using the Bayley-III Language Scale in order to promote a more unified examination of the child when other professionals are using other subtests of the Bayley-III. In addition, the Bayley-III provides for easy comparison across subtests, and offers further (e.g., growth curves, atypical population scores, statistical comparison of differences across subtests) that other measures typically do not include. Therefore, the use of the Bayley III Language Scale when part of an interdisciplinary team that shares in the Bayley-III administration is highly recommended.

CASE STUDY: JACK

Jack, a 30-month-old boy, was referred by his parents because of their concerns about his delayed speech and inattentiveness. They also reported that Jack's preschool teachers were concerned about his limited ability to follow directions, play with other children, and interact with his teachers. Jack's parents also said they needed help deciding whether he was in the "right" preschool setting.

Pre-assessment Planning

A team member met with Jack's parents a week before the assessment. The purpose was to gather background information about Jack, identify his current skills and interests, discuss his parents' concerns, identify what his parents hoped to gain from the assessment, and plan for the upcoming assessment. His parents provided the following background information.

Background Information

Jack had a significant birth history of intrauterine growth retardation and jaundice. He also had a history of illness, with multiple sinus and ear infections, high fevers, and pneumonia. He had sinus surgery at 18 months, and tonsils/adenoids removed and ventilation tubes placed at 24 months. His responsivity to his parents was better after the tubes were inserted, and he began to say more words and sounds. His hearing currently, assessed through sound-field testing, is adequate for language learning; although he shows little response to speech, his responses to other sounds were appropriate.

By 12 months of age, Jack was using 20 to 30 words, although he has fewer words now. Getting his attention is difficult except during rough-housing or saying the alphabet. His parents said he understands most of what they say to him, but he also ignores them and does what he wants to do. He may imitate some sounds and words, but then does not use them on his own. When he wants something, he typically takes an adult's hand and leads them to the object. Jack sometimes just fusses, and his parents are not sure what he wants. He does not respond to his name or the names of common objects, but will pick up alphabet letters or numbers from 1 through 10 when they are mentioned by an adult.

Jack's parents reported that he is loving, tender, gentle, and playful, and his attachment to his parents seems secure. For example, he does not object to being left by them, even with strangers, but is happy when they return. Jack plays for a long time by himself, and his parents often intrude to get him to interact with them. He likes puzzles and watching videos; however, he does not watch when there is a lot of talking, and sometimes he just watches the credits. He does not exhibit any pretend play, and prefers to play rough-house and tickle games. He is a good problem-solver and is not tricked easily (e.g., he finds hidden things readily). Jack displays some obsessive tendencies; he does not like others to move or reorganize his toys, he often lines up his toys, and he does not like different foods to touch on his plate. He looks at books briefly, turning the pages quickly, and does not like his parents to read to him.

Assessment Plan

The Bayley Scales of Infant and Toddler Development, Third Edition (Bayley-III) and the MacArthur-Bates Communicative Development Inventory-Words and Gesture (CDI-WG, Fenson et al., 2006), a parent-report tool, were chosen for administration. A preschool observation also was arranged to gain information about Jack in another context.

Preschool Observation

After 1 hour of observation at his preschool and discussion with his teachers, it was clear that Jack's participation in the class was minimal. He spent most of the time moving around the room from area to area. His few interactions were initiated by teachers (e.g., diaper change, engagement in craft). Jack did not use any words, but jabbered unintelligibly. He picked up a few objects or toys and then quickly dropped them. He showed no interest in classroom activities, except to eat a bagel while roaming the room. His teachers said his behavior that day was typical, and they are concerned about his limited interactions, words, and following of routines.

Assessment Results and Observations (Primarily Language Components)

CDI-WG

The parent report on the CDI-WG confirmed that Jack has limited expressive and receptive language skills; his scores were well below the 10th percentile. Jack responds inconsistently to phrases (e.g.," no no," "give it to mommy") and to a few words (e.g., mom, dad, Sissy, ball, dog, no, eat, shoe, bath, bed, out). He inconsistently uses about 10 words to name objects, but not to request them. He says the numbers 1 to 10, and most of the alphabet letters. He uses a few gestures (e.g., reaches to be picked up, pushes things away) and plays peek-a-boo and chase. He demonstrates knowledge of simple actions on objects (e.g., uses a fork, comb) and sometimes imitates adults (e.g., puts on glasses, hat).

Bayley-III (Language Components)

Jack was able to sit and participate in most of the language assessment activities, with his parents next to him to help him attend. Knowing that Jack's language skills were below age level, the examiner considered the start point just below his age-matched one. This item (Item 19 on Receptive, *Identifying Three Objects*) appeared above Jack's competence, so the examiner began with Item 15. Jack immediately responded by looking at the book when named, did not respond to the cup and spoon, looked at the ball, but not the doll. Thus, Item 19 was not a pass, as expected. He did say "ball," and picked it up.

For Item 16 (*Identifies Object in Environment*), Jack has a Magnadoodle that he likes to draw on, so the examiner asked him where it was and if he wanted to "draw." He did not look for it, even though it was sticking out of his mother's bag. Other words his parents felt he may know were attempted (i.e., shoe, pants); however, he did not respond to them. Thus, the examiner dropped back to Item 13. The examiner tried a few social games (e.g., peek-a-boo, and itsy-bitsy spider), but he did not look or respond. When he was tickled, he laughed and smiled and even placed the examiner's hands on his tummy to request more. Later, when she asked "Tickle" while holding her fingers up (Item 14), however, he did not respond to this or other social requests ("peek-a-boo"). Therefore, the examiner moved to Item 10. Jack did not respond to his name when called while playing, and the examiner moved to Item 8. Jack is not easily engaged with toys, but did scribble with a pen for at least a minute (Item 8); however, he did not respond to his or any other names (Item 9).

Moving back to Item 6, Jack turned his head to locate the bell (Item 6), and responded to the rattle (Item 7). Thus, with these items and Item 8 (sustains play with object), Jack passed three consecutive items and the examiner moved forward to fill in the gaps. Jack did not respond to familiar words without objects or pictures present (Item 11), but did respond to "no–no" (Item 12). He had passed Items 13 (*Attends to Other's Play*) and 15 (*Identifies One Object*), but not Items 14 (*Responds to Request for Social Routine*) or 16 (*Identifies Object in Environment*). Thus, the examiner moved to Item 17, and Jack was able to respond correctly by looking at two pictures (dog and ball), but did not look clearly at the other named pictures (Item 21). Jack did not respond to the inhibitory words (i.e., wait, stop, my turn) for Item 18, had not passed Item 19 (identifies three objects) in the series, and nor did he follow one-part directions (Item 20) or identify clothing (Item 22). Therefore, he had five consecutive errors.

The Expressive Communication subtest was administered after taking a short break. Jack had used only a few words during the testing (i.e., dog, no, ball), but not the eight required on Item 23, so the examiner started with Item 20 (*Names One Object*). Jack had labeled the ball earlier, and demonstrated a pushing away gesture and said "no" to looking at a book. Thus, he received credit for Items 20 and 21 (*Combining a Gesture and Word*). He did not name any items in the picture book (Item 22), and was not easily engaged in the book. The examiner moved back to Item 17 (*Initiates Play*) and he received credit because he previously had taken the examiner's hands to tickle his tummy. Jack also had used two words (no, ball) during the testing, so passed Item 18. He did not receive credit for Item 23 (*Eight Different Words*), but used one word, "no," to clearly indicate his wants, and passed Item 19. He therefore had passed three consecutive items (Items 17–19). The examiner then moved to Items 24–26, which Jack did not pass. His parents indicated that he does not use *yes* or *no* when responding to questions (Item 24), and does not imitate (Item 25) or use two-word utterances (Item 26). Thus, Jack had five consecutive errors.

The examiner recognized the need for Jack and his parents to experience some success toward the end of the testing, and therefore brought out some test objects and played a hide and seek game with Jack. The use of games like this also can be instructive in modeling for parents how they might engage their child and label objects. Jack participated briefly by looking for the cup or spoon, while the examiner labeled each several times in a short time span. The examiner also brought out the Magnadoodle and watched Jack approximate the names of many alphabet letters drawn by his mother. After the testing, the examiner completed the Behavior Observation Inventory with Jack's parents. They noted his test behaviors were fairly typical, and said he was more cooperative than they had expected. This may be due to the fast-paced activities of the Bayley-III and the interesting objects used in the Language Scales.

Bayley-III Results

Jack passed 12 Receptive (scale score of 2) and 21 Expressive (scale score of 5) items for a total scale score of 7. His resultant language composite score of 62 placed him at the 1st percentile. His communication skills generally are well below what is expected for a child his age. The large and statistically significant difference between his receptive and expressive scores, favoring his expressive skills, is a pattern not seen in many children. Jack was able to respond to sounds in the environment, but did not respond consistently to his name or most other words used. This too is highly unusual when no hearing loss is present. He was most responsive to alphabet letters, which is not common for children at his developmental level. Jack was able to attend briefly to the examiner and his parents; however, he was not consistent in his attention, and was much less responsive than would be expected for a 30-month-old child. His attentional focus was much better in 1 : 1 structured situations than was observed in the classroom.

Jack's expressive communication was also limited, with use of few words (except naming the letters on the Magnadoodle), limited eye contact (except during tickle activities), limited gestures, infrequent vocalizations (except jabbering when unoccupied), and few communicative attempts toward adults (i.e., a few protests, one hand-over-hand request to get more tickling). His primary reasons for communicating were to regulate the behavior of others (e.g., get things he wanted, push things away) and for occasional social interaction to play tickle games. Jack showed very little functional play with any of the objects (except the ball and Magnadoodle), and no evidence of any symbolic play.

Case Conclusions

Information provided from the use of the Bayley-III indicated that Jack displayed a significant delay in language (composite 62, 1st percentile), cognitive (composite 75, 5 percent), social-emotional (composite 55, 0.1 percent), and adaptive (composite 45, < 0.1 percent) skills. Thus, his development is well below his age level in these areas. In contrast, his motor skills were within normal limits (Composite of 88, 16th percentile), and therefore a strength for him. All examiners noted that Jack's performance was affected by his limited attentional and interactive skills, and cautioned that the results are very likely underestimates of his overall abilities.

The language results indicate Jack has limited prelinguistic communication and play skills. He is unable to get his needs met consistently because of limited gesture use, inconsistent and unrecognizable vocalizations, and limited eye gaze. In addition, his engagement with others is inconsistent and highly dependent on the task/materials presented. His expressive language was also higher than his receptive language, thus demonstrating an atypical pattern. Further, Jack exhibited most of the developmental risk Indicators for Atypical Social Skills that characterize children with an ASD.

Further, Jack met criteria for a diagnosis of autism using the guidelines from the *Diagnostic and Statistical Manual-IV-TR* (American Psychiatric Association, 2000). Within the area of "qualitative impairment in social interactions," Jack had limited interactions with others, no instances of seeking other's attention for sharing enjoyment or interests, and showed very little social-emotional reciprocity except in tickle games and with letters and numbers. He had striking impairments in communication, particularly in both language reception and expression (i.e., few words, little response to spoken speech), and also had very limited play skills (i.e., limited functional play and no symbolic play). Jack showed a restricted range of interests, with his intense focus on alphabet letters and numbers, some obsessiveness over the placement of foods and toys, and some preoccupation with parts of objects. Therefore, Jack showed multiple behaviors that comprise each of the three areas necessary for a diagnosis of autism.

When discussing the findings with Jack's parents, the team pointed out Jack's strengths, including his motor and visual spatial skills, interest in numbers and letters, ability to attend in more structured settings, independent problem-solving skills, enjoyment of play with his parents, and his engagement for some activities (e.g., Magnadoodle, bubbles). When discussing a diagnosis of autism, his parents noted that two family members (father's uncle and cousin) display autism, and that other family members had worried that Jack also may have an autism spectrum disorder. The team supported the diagnosis with the test results across domains, their observations, and the parents' reports of his behaviors at home. Given the diagnosis, the team highlighted potential characteristics of an optimal learning environment for Jack, and suggested that intensive early intervention support be provided to the classroom teachers and his parents, along with a recommendation for speech-language services.

His parents also were given various ideas for building Jack's social and communication skills, including ways to use his strengths (i.e., tickle games, alphabet letters, and numbers) to build skills in other areas (i.e., social engagement). Jack's limited attention to books may be enhanced by initially using books with letters or numbers, and using common objects to pair with the pictures. His parents also were encouraged to focus on developing his functional and later symbolic play skills, recognizing that early play is highly predictive of later language skills. Additionally, gestures and other prelinguistic behaviors are early means to get one's needs met, and predict later language skills. Jack uses primarily contact gestures (e.g., pulling, pushing someone's hand), and primarily to regulate others' behavior. He needs to expand his repertoire and consistency of behavior regulation acts (e.g., giving something to get it fixed, reaching with vocalizations, and/or eye gaze). He also needs more social and joint attention gestures (e.g., showing, giving, and pointing). Early strategies to enhance these kinds of gestures are through both social interactions (e.g., grab bags with items to pull out) and behavior requests (e.g., trading turns with bubble jar, hats). His parents were also encouraged to continue to focus on his comprehension and productions skills by continuing to name common objects and play games with them (e.g., hiding, washing, pretending to eat them) and to play social games with Jack to enhance his vocabulary development (e.g., head, shoulders, knees, and toes; ring around the rosy) as well as his social awareness and responsiveness to others.

SUMMARY

The Bayley-III (Bayley, 2006) has many uses within the assessment process, and can help identify children with developmental disabilities in need of early intervention services. Specifically, the Bayley-III provides rich information on a child's strengths and weaknesses, and helps pinpoint areas in need of special interventions. The case study of Jack showed that the use of the Bayley-III's Language Scale provided a focus on prelinguistic behaviors, reasons for communicating, and social routines, as well as both expressive and receptive language skill – information that was key in identifying Jack's abilities and the gaps in his communication skills. Data from this scale added importantly to the overall picture of Jack's skills when combined with the other Bayley Scales. This information, along with clinical observations and parent report, helped guide professional judgments and decision-making in reference to Jack's diagnosis and intervention planning. The combination of professionally administered, parent reported, and clinically observed measures produced the best overall description of Jack, one seen by his parents as representative of his typical behaviors. The ultimate consensus gained between the professionals and Jack's family around his assessment will lay the foundation for collaborative work throughout the early intervention process. The use of the Bayley-III was instrumental in gaining this consensus.

References

American Psychiatric Association. (2000). *Diagnostic and Statistical Manual-IV-TR*. Arlington, VA: American Psychiatric Association.

American Speech-Language-Hearing Association. (2008). *Roles and Responsibilities of Speech-Language Pathologists in Early Intervention: Guidelines*. Available from www.asha.org/policy.

Baranek, G. T. (1999). Autism during infancy: A retrospective video analysis of sensory-motor and social behaviors at 9–12 months of age. *Journal of Autism and Developmental Disorders, 29*, 213–224.

Barrera, I., & Corso, R. (2002). Cultural competency as skilled dialogue. *Topics in Early Childhood Special Education, 22*(20), 103–113.

Bayley, N. (1993). *Bayley Scales of Infant Development* (2nd ed.) (*Bayley-II*). San Antonio, TX: The Psychological Corporation.

Bayley, N. (2006). *Bayley Scales of Infant and Toddler Development* (3rd ed.) (*Bayley-III*). San Bloomington, MN: Pearson.

Bernheimer, L., & Weismer, T. (2007). "Let me tell you what I do all day...": The family story at the center of intervention research and practice. *Infants and Young Children, 20*(3), 192–201.

Brady, N., Marquis, J., Fleming, K., & McLean, L. (2004). Prelinguistic predictors of language growth in children with developmental disabilities. *Journal of Speech, Language, and Hearing Research, 47*, 663–677.

Bronfenbrenner, U., & Morris, P. A. (1998). The ecology of developmental processes. In W. Damon, & R. M. Lerner (Eds.), *Handbook of Child Psychology* (5th ed.), *Theoretical Models of Human Development* (pp. 993–1028). New York, NY: Wiley.

Bruner, J. (1981). The social context of language acquisition. *Language and Communication, 1*, 155–178.

Calandrella, A., & Wilcox, J. (2000). Predicting language outcomes for young prelinguistic children with developmental delay. *Journal of Speech, Language, and Hearing Research, 43*, 1061–1071.

Carson, P. C., Klee, T., Carson, D. K., & Hime, L. K. (2003). Phonological profiles of 2-year-olds with delayed language development: Predicting clinical outcomes at 3. *American Journal of Speech-Language Pathology, 12*, 28–39.

Chapman, R. S. (2000). Children's language learning: An interactionist perspective. *Journal of Child Psychology and Psychiatry, 41*(1), 33–54.

Charman, T., Baron-Cohen, S., Swettenham, J., Baird, G., Drew, A., & Cox, A. (2003). Predicting language outcome in infants with autism and pervasive developmental disorder. *International Journal of Language and Communication Disorders, 38*, 265–285.

Colgan, S., Lanter, E., McComish, C., Watson, L., Crais, E., & Baranek, G. (2006). Analysis of social interaction gestures in infants with autism. *Child Neuropsychology, 12*(4), 307–319.

Crais, E. (2010). Testing and beyond: Strategies and tools for evaluation and assessment of infants and toddlers. *Language, Speech, Hearing Services in Schools*, in press.

Crais, E., Watson, L., & Baranek, G. (2009). Use of gesture development in profiling children's prelinguistic communication skills. *American Journal of Speech-Language Pathology, 18*, 95–108.

Dunst, C. J., Hamby, D., Trivette, C. M., Raab, M., & Bruder, M. B. (2000). Everyday family and community life and children's naturally occurring learning opportunities. *Journal of Early Intervention, 23*(3), 156–169.

Fenson, L., Marchman, V. A., Thal, D., Dale, P., Reznick, J. S., & Bates, E. (2006). *The MacArthur-Bates Communicative Development Inventories* (2nd ed.). Baltimore, MD: Paul H. Brookes Publishing Company.

Filipek, P. A., Accardo, P. J., & Baranek, G. T. (1999). The screening and diagnosis of autistic spectrum disorders. *Journal of Autism Developmental Disorders, 29*, 439–484.

Fuchs, D., Fuchs, L., Power, M., & Dailey, A. (1985). Bias in the assessment of handicapped children. *American Educational Research Journal, 22*, 185–197.

Fuchs, D., Fuchs, L., Benowitz, S., & Barringer, K. (1987). Norm-referenced tests: Are they valid for use with handicapped students? *Exceptional Children, 54*, 263–271.

Greenspan, S. I., DeGangi, G. A., & Weider, S. (2001). *The Functional Emotional Assessment Scale (FEAS) for Infancy and Early Childhood: Clinical and Research Applications*. Bethesda, MD: Interdisciplinary Council for Developmental and Learning Disorders.

Guralnick, M. J. (2005). *The Developmental Systems Approach to Early Intervention*. Baltimore, MD: Brookes.

Individuals With Disabilities Education Improvement Act of 2004, 34 C.F.R. § 300.7 (2004).

Lyytinen, P., Laakso, M., Poikkeus, A., & Rita, N. (1999). The development and predictive relations of play and language across the second year. *Scandinavian Journal of Psychology, 40*, 177–186.

Lyytinen, P., Poikkeus, A., Laakso, M., Eklund, K., & Lyytinen, H. (2001). Language development and symbolic play in children with and without familial risk of dyslexia. *Journal of Speech, Language, and Hearing Research, 44*, 873–885.

McCathren, R. B., Yoder, P. J., & Warren, S. F. (2000). Testing predictive validity of the communication composite of the Communication and Symbolic Behavior Scales. *Journal of Early Intervention, 23*(3), 36–46.

McEvoy, R., Rogers, S., & Pennington, R. (1993). Executive function and social communication deficits in young autistic children. *Journal of Child Psychology and Psychiatry, 34*, 563–578.

Mundy, P., & Gomes, A. (1998). Individual differences in joint attention skill development in the second year. *Infant Behavior and Development, 21*, 469–482.

Mundy, P., Sigman, M., Ungerer, J., & Sherman, T. (1986). Defining the social deficits of autism: The contribution of non-verbal communication measures. *Journal of Child Psychology and Psychiatry, 27*, 657–699.

Mundy, P., Kasari, C., Sigman, M., & Ruskin, E. (1995). Nonverbal communication and early language acquisition in children with Down syndrome and in normally developing children. *Journal of Speech and Hearing Research, 38*, 157–167.

NICHD Early Child Care Research Network. (2005). Pathways to reading: The role of oral language in the transition to reading. *Developmental Psychology, 41*(2), 428–442.

Paul, R. (2000). Understanding the "whole" of it: Comprehension assessment. *Seminars in Speech and Language, 21*(3), 10–17.

Paul, R., & Jennings, P. (1992). Phonological behavior in toddlers with slow expressive language development. *Journal of Speech and Hearing Research, 35,* 99–107.

Paul, R., Looney, S., & Dahm, P. (1991). Communication and socialization skills at ages 2 and 3 in "late-talking" young children. *Journal of Speech and Hearing Research, 34,* 858–865.

Sackett, D. L., Straus, S. E., Richardson, S. R., Rosenberg, W., & Haynes, R. B. (2000). *Evidence-based Medicine: How to Practice and Teach EBM* (2nd ed.). London: Churchill Livingstone.

Sameroff, A. J., & MacKenzie, M. J. (2003). Research strategies for capturing transactional models of development: The limits of the possible. *Development and Psychopathology, 15,* 613–640.

Sandall, S., Hemmeter, M. L., Smith, B. J., & McLean, M. E. (2005). *DEC Recommended Practices: A Comprehensive Guide for Practical Application in Early Intervention/Early Childhood Special Education.* Longmont, CA: Sopris West Education Services.

Sattler, J. (2001). *Assessment of Children: Cognitive Applications* (4th ed.). San Diego, CA: Author.

Slaughter, V., & McConnell, D. (2003). Emergence of joint attention: Relationships between gaze following, social referencing, imitation, and naming in infancy. *Journal of Genetic Psychology, 164*(1), 54–71.

Summers, J. A., Hoffman, L., Marquis, J., Turnbull, A., & Poston, D. (2005). Relationship between parent satisfaction regarding partnerships with professionals and age of the child. *Topics in Early Childhood Special Education, 25*(1), 48–58.

Thal, D., Tobias, S., & Morrison, D. (1991). Language and gesture in late talkers: A one year follow-up. *Journal of Speech and Hearing Research, 34,* 604–612.

Wetherby, A., Cain, D., Yonclas, D., & Walker, V. (1988). Analysis of intentional communication of normal children from the prelinguistic to the multiword stage. *Journal of Speech and Hearing Research, 31,* 240–252.

Wetherby, A., Allen, L., Cleary, J., Kublin, K., & Goldstein, H. (2002). Validity and reliability of the Communication and Symbolic Behavior Scales Developmental Profile with very young children. *Journal of Speech, Language, and Hearing Research, 45,* 1202–1218.

Wetherby, A., Goldstein, H., Cleary, J., Allen, L., & Kublin, K. (2003). Early identification of children with communication disorders: Concurrent and predictive validity of the CSBS Developmental Profile. *Infants & Young Children, 16,* 161–174.

Whitehurst, G., Fischel, J., Arnold, D., & Lonigan, C. (1992). Evaluating outcomes with children with expressive language delay. In S. F. Warren, & J. Reichle (Eds.), *Causes and Effects in Communication and Language Intervention, Vol. 1* (pp. 277–313). Baltimore, MD: Brookes.

Wilson, S., & Cradock, M. (2004). Review: Accounting for prematurity in developmental assessment and the use of age-adjusted scores. *Journal of Pediatric Psychology, 29*(8), 641–649.

Zero to Three. (2005). *Diagnostic Classification of Mental Health and Developmental Disorders of Infancy and Early Childhood* (Revised ed.) (DC: 0-3R). Washington, DC: Zero to Three Press (DC: 0-3R).

Zimmerman, I., Steiner, V., & Pond, R. (2002). *Preschool Language Scale* (4th ed.). Bloomington, MN: Pearson.

Zwaigenbaum, L., Bryson, S., & Rogers, T. (2005). Behavioral manifestations of autism in the first year of life. *International Journal of Developmental Neuroscience, 23*, 143–152.

The Bayley-III Motor Scale

Jane Case-Smith [1] and Helen Alexander [2]

[1] Division of Occupational Therapy, School of Allied Medical
Professions, The Ohio State University, Columbus, OH
[2] The Nisonger Center, The Ohio State University, Columbus, OH

INTRODUCTION

Gross and fine motor skills are essential aspects of a child's overall development. They allow a child to explore his or her environment, play with objects, demonstrate affection by reaching and holding, and demonstrate independence through mobility. Motor skills enable a child to master play skills, daily living skills (e.g., eating), and mobility. A child's ability to move and explore the environment influences his or her perceptual, cognitive, and social learning.

CONTENT

Neuromaturation

Our understanding of how motor skills develop in the child has evolved since the original work of Bayley (1969). The Bayley-III Scales reflect this expanded view of motor development. The original scales assumed that infant development reflects neuromaturation and genetic endowment. These assumptions led to a standardized set of procedures to elicit the sequence of skills that appear to be common to human development. Development was viewed to be lockstep, and individual variations in how children performed motor skills were not of great interest. Delays in infant development were attributed to genetic endowment or neurological deficit without considering the infant's environment and opportunities for learning. Since the original Bayley Scales, researchers (e.g., Gibson & Walker, 1984; Smith & Thelen, 2003; Spencer *et al.*, 2006) have demonstrated that, although most infants follow a typical developmental sequence, the ways in which typically developing infants perform specific skills is variable. For example, early reaching (Thelen, Corbetta, Kamm, Spencer, Schneider, & Zernicke, 1993) and crawling patterns (Adolph, Eppler, & Gibson, 1993) differ among infants. These researchers and others have demonstrated that infants organize motor actions around functional goals (see, for example, Thelen, 1995; Newell & McDonald, 1997; Lockman, 2000). Motor skill development is influenced by what the physical environment provides, including the objects available to the child. Children adapt locomotion patterns when they detect different possibilities for action. Learning new movement patterns and motor skills is a complex interaction of multiple factors. As infants and children develop strength and balance, their ability to detect possibilities for action improves. They frequently learn by attempting movements and learning through the consequences of their actions (Adolph *et al.*, 1993; Bushnell & Boudreau, 1993; Gottlieb, 1997; Lockman, 2000; Berger & Adolph, 2007).

The Bayley-III Motor Scales reflect four concepts that have emerged in recent motor development research:

1. Motor skills develop through the interaction of body systems – specifically, sensory, perceptual, and biomechanical systems
2. Learning and development are highly influenced by the child's social and physical context
3. How children perform motor skills varies across individual children
4. Functional outcomes motivate a child's development of motor skill.

Influence of Body System Interaction of Motor Development

In contrast to a hierarchical model of neural maturation (Halverson, 1937; Gesell & Amatruda, 1947), systems theory (also called *dynamic systems theory*) proposes a flexible model of neural organization in which the functions of control and coordination are distributed among many elements of the system rather than vested in a single hierarchical level (Van Sant, 1990). Infants' actions emerge from the interaction of many systems, both internal and external to the child (Thelen *et al.*, 1993; Spencer *et al.*, 2006). Factors that influence the development of gross motor skills include infant's size and weight, biomechanical attributes, neurological maturation, and the physical environment. Factors that influence fine motor skills include biomechanical characteristics, perceptual abilities, sensation, and cognition (Gordon & Forssberg, 1997; Newell & MacDonald, 1997).

For example, the pattern an infant uses to reach for an object is determined by biomechanic and kinematic factors such as weight of his or her arm, stiffness of joints, strength, and eye–hand coordination. The infant's reaching pattern also is influenced by how successful the child was in previous reach and grasp attempts (e.g., did the object move before he or she could attain it?), how motivated the child is to attain the object, and the child's general energy level, curiosity, and motivation. Within individual infants, these factors vary with time, activity demands, and environmental conditions. These systems (e.g., motor, sensory, perceptual, musculoskeletal, psychologic) are interdependent and work together such that strengths in one system (e.g., visual) can support limitations in another (e.g., kinesthetic).

The systems recruited to perform a task vary according to the novelty of the activity and the developmental stage. Early motor skills are guided by the visual system (e.g., first reach and head lifting), then motor, somatosensory, and visual systems become integrated (e.g., grasp and object exploration, and crawling, are influenced by multisensory input). Later in development, fine motor skills become increasingly influenced by cognitive skills (e.g., drawing, completing a puzzle). Dynamic systems theory represents an ecologic approach in that a child's functional performance depends on the interactions of the child's endowed and learned abilities, the characteristics of the desired task or activity, and the environment in which the activity is performed.

In dynamic systems theory, the body and environment are constantly changing and simultaneously influencing each other (Van Geert, 1998). In this approach, the therapist looks for periods of stability in learning and watches for signs that a child is ready to shift to a qualitatively higher level of behavior. By identifying the system variables that drive the transition from one level, the therapist can use those systems to facilitate learning. Variables that promote learning can relate to the child, the activity, or the environment. Physical growth and biomechanics may be more important for motor learning in infancy, while experience, practice, and motivation may be more influential in the learning motor skills in an older child (Thelen, 1995).

Influence of Social and Physical Context of Motor Development

Recent reviews of motor development research (see, for example, Gibson, 1988; Lockman, 2000; Humphry, 2009) discuss how physical, social, and cultural contexts influence development of motor skills. For example, physical possibilities for action, such as textured or inclined surfaces, strongly influence how the child moves (e.g., selects belly crawling, creeping, or bear crawling). When faced with the task of crawling on rough terrain, infants may alter motor behavior by extending their knees and "bear crawling." The physical characteristics of objects also can influence the skills that a child demonstrates. When a child reaches for a ball, the ball's size influences the shape of the child's hand and the approach taken (e.g., one hand versus two). These theories explain a child's development over time, and also are relevant in a specific testing context. The Bayley-III Motor Scale's items provide standard perceptual cues and possibilities for action across skill sets. The characteristics of the objects in the kit are designed to elicit specific skills (e.g., tightly fitting Legos elicit forceful grasp with both hands, coins elicit precision grasp, large crayons elicit various grasping patterns, stepping path elicits walking on a narrowed base of support). Social influences on the infant's performance also are considered (e.g., the Bayley-III Scales consider how the parent's presence may influence the child's performance). While the parent's presence is encouraged to promote the infant's feeling of safety and comfort during testing, specific cueing and prompting are discouraged. Because an infant's performance is context dependent, the Bayley-III Scales prescribe the environment so that the examiner evaluates the infant's response within a standardized context.

Variability in Motor Development

Research in dynamic systems theory has focused on explaining the ways new skills are learned (Thelen & Spencer, 1998; Thelen, Schoner, Scheier, & Smith, 2001). The learning of new movements or ways of completing an activity requires that previously stable movements be broken down or become unstable. New movements and skills emerge when a critical change occurs in any of the components that contribute to motor behavior. Motor change or skill transition in young children is envisioned as a series of events during which destabilization and stabilization of movement take place before the transitional phase in which movement becomes stable and functional (Piper & Darrah, 1994). Learning motor skills typically follows three stages. These stages are reflected in the Bayley-III Scale items that measure the steps of emerging skills.

First, the child experiments with different movement patterns, demonstrating high variability when performing an activity. Then, through these exploratory movements, the child determines which pattern is the most adaptive. Finally, the child selects the movement that is most adaptive (e.g., which pattern makes it easiest to rise from sit to stand, given the effects of gravity and available supports) and can be performed repeatedly and efficiently. These stages are reflected in Bayley-III Motor Scale item sequences and scoring criteria (e.g., items for young infants allow for more trials and more error, later items require more precision and skill).

Functional Outcomes Motivate Development

The motor system is self-organizing (Shumway-Cook & Woolacott, 2007), and is optimal in a functional task that has a goal and an outcome. Most functional tasks (e.g., walking, eating, and drinking) elicit a predictable pattern of movement.

Therefore, the task itself can organize the movements attempted. The infant becomes interested in mastering objects and physical play for functional purposes after a period of exploring objects and environment (e.g., perceptual learning). Infants realize that they have an effect on the environment, and their actions can produce functional outcomes through their exploration of objects and the environment. The outcomes that motivate an infant may be social (e.g., mother's smile) or physical (e.g., a toy moves, makes a sound). Functional tasks and outcomes begin to organize the infant's action (Gibson, 1988; Humphry, 2009) and actions are goal driven (Connolly & Dalgleish, 1989; Thelen *et al.*, 2001). By the end of the first year, infants handle and manipulate objects according to their purpose (e.g., use a spoon to eat, cup to drink) and move to obtain objects (McCarty, Clifton, & Collard, 2001). By 2 years, the toddler is holding a marker crudely but appropriately for drawing (Lockman, 2000). The Bayley Fine Motor Scales include functional items (e.g., drawing, eating with a utensil) that measure these goal-oriented functional skills that emerge during ages 2–4. These early motor skills demonstrate both self-organization and social learning.

The following sections illustrate how the Bayley Motor Scale items apply these interrelated concepts of motor development. How these concepts are used to interpret the child's performance on the Motor Scale items is also discussed.

Fine Motor Subtest

The Fine Motor subtest uses sets of related items to evaluate the fine motor skills that emerge from 1 month through 42 months. This scale's organization also helps the examiner appreciate the relationship within and among skills sets. Each skill set provides the examiner opportunities to observe and evaluate specific skills that contribute to a child's ability to effectively use his or her hands to play with toys, manipulate objects, and use tools. The following sections explain how a group of items measure the development of a skill set, what specific related skills are measured, and what underlying abilities can be analyzed by observing the child performing the items.

Ocular-motor Control

Ocular movements are foundational to a child's development of eye–hand coordination. Control of eye movement develops early, at 1–4 months, and is instrumental to an infant's desire to raise his head, to hold his head upright and steady in order to visualize his environment (Jouen, Lepecq, Gapenne, & Bertenthal, 2000). Eye gaze and tracking are among the first ways that an infant shows his interest in objects and people. The Bayley Scales' eye tracking items emphasize the infant's ability to cross the midline, which can discriminate between typical infants and those with a lesion in one brain hemisphere or immature integration of the two hemispheres. Eye tracking across the midline is a foundational skill for integrating the two sides of the body (e.g., transferring objects, banging two objects together, using two hands together to play). Therefore, tracking across the midline is an important indicator of potential developmental problems and of future fine motor skill performance. Table 4.1 lists the items that measure ocular motor skills, and the observations that can be made when administering these items.

Early Hand and Finger Movement

The infant's first hand and finger movements are reflexive. The neonate demonstrates a grasp reflex that

TABLE 4.1 Ocular Motor Skill

Item	Skill measured	Specific observations of systems involved
2. Eyes Follow Moving Person	Eye tracking.	Do eyes cross the midline?
3. Eyes Follow Ring (Horizontal)	Smooth eye tracking in horizontal plane.	Do eyes cross midline and follow the ring through an entire excursion right to left and back?
4. Eyes Follow Ring (Vertical)	Smooth eye tracking in a vertical plane at infant's midline.	Does the infant track with eyes together? In a partial arc? Is vertical tracking smooth?

(Continued)

TABLE 4.1   Ocular Motor Skill—cont'd

Item	Skill measured	Specific observations of systems involved
7. Eyes Follow Ring (Circular)	Coordinated eye tracking in a circle.	Do eyes demonstrate coordinated movement following the ring? Eye gaze may break away from the circle once or twice.
8. Head Follows Ring	With increased head control and coordination of eye and head movement, the infant turns his head to follow the ring.	Does infant move both head and eyes? It is typical for eye gaze to break away once or twice.
9. Eyes Follow Rolling Ball	Eyes track a rolling ball, which moves in a faster, more unpredictable path.	Do eyes track across midline without losing track of the ball's movement?

does not diminish until 2 or 3 months of age, and is not fully integrated into a voluntary grasp until 4 months (Charles, 2008). Although some authors characterize early finger movement as fisted (Gesell & Amatruda, 1947), the young infant (1–2 months) moves his fingers often, generally in full extension and full flexion. The Bayley Fine Motor subtest measures these early movements that appear to be non-purposeful but can be early indicators of muscle tone, activity levels, and asymmetries. Table 4.2 lists the items that measure early hand and finger movement.

Reach/Movement of Hands in Space

The connection between eyes and hands can be observed early in development. Infants as young as 5 days flail their arms more when they see an interesting object (Von Hofsten, 1984). At 1 month, infants reach for a mobile, although reaching is

TABLE 4.2   Early Hand and Finger Movement

Item	Skill measured	Specific observations
1. Hands are Fisted	Muscle tone and reflexive movements.	How much do hand and fingers move? What type of muscle tone characterizes the hand and arm?
6. Retains Ring	Grasp reflex. Ability to sustain grasp reflex for 2 seconds or more.	What type of muscle tone? What are predominant patterns of movement (flexion or extension) in holding and releasing the ring?
10. Keeps Hands Open	Inhibition of grasp reflex. Active extension of fingers such that hands appear open.	Is the grasp reflex integrated into a voluntary movement pattern? What type of muscle tone and how much movement does the infant have?
11. Rotates Wrist	Active supination of the forearm.	Is movement patterned in flexion and pronation? Active supination is a more mature movement pattern than active pronation and is a difficult motion for an infant with cerebral palsy. Observe if the child actively rotates rather than allowing hand to passively rotate using gravity.

inaccurate at this time. Gesell and Amatruda (1947) found that successful reaching was achieved by 4–5 months of age. When first reaching, the elbow is generally locked and the trunk moves with the arm (Berthier, Clifton, Gullapalli, McCall, & Robin, 1996). At 5–6 months infants tend to reach with two hands, and by 7–8 months they can reach with one hand; associated trunk movement is minimal (Rochat, 1992). Full postural support is needed for infants 4–7 months of age to reach accurately. As sitting balance improves in the 8- to 9-month-old, the infant reaches without postural support (Levin & Sveistrup, 2008). Postural stability is important to accurate reaching; Infants activate trunk muscles before making arm movements (Von Hofsten and Woollacott, 1989). The Bayley Fine Motor Scale (Table 4.3) measures the infant's refinement of accurate reach.

Grasping Patterns

The neonate's first reflexive grasp is elicited by touch. For example, the infant automatically closes his or her fingers around the parent's finger. The grasp reflex can be elicited

TABLE 4.3   Reach/Movement of Hands in Space

Item	Skill measured	Specific observations
5. Attempts to Bring Hand to Mouth	Hand to mouth, early midline orientation, arm flexion.	Is action purposeful? Generally the first hand to mouth is for self-comfort.
12. Grasps Suspended Ring	Combining of reach and grasp. Accuracy of reach.	How accurate is reach? Number of trials required to grasp. Over- or under-reaching. One- or two-hand approach.
13. Block Series: Reaches for Block	Accuracy of reach. One-hand reach.	What type of reach is used? Is there associated trunk movement? Does infant use a one- or two-hand approach?
14. Block Series: Touches Block	Accuracy of reach. One-hand reach.	What type of reach is used? Does the trunk move in association with arm movement?
16. Reaches Unilaterally	One-hand approach. Accuracy of reach.	Does child use one or two hands to obtain object? Does the child use isolated arm movement with minimal associated trunk movement?

through touch contact until 2 months of age. At 3–4 months infants begin to develop voluntary grasp, thus enabling them to sustain a grasp and hold onto objects of interest (Twitchell, 1970). A palmar grasp is used at this time (Castner, 1932) and continues through 24 weeks. The palmar grasp is characterized by a pronated hand and flexion of all fingers around the objects. By 28 weeks, the infant holds the object in a radial palmar grasp (Gesell & Amatruda, 1947) in which the radial fingers and thumb press the cube against the palm. This early pattern signifies the initial development of radial fingers as the skill side of the hand. Between 32 and 36 weeks the infant demonstrates grasp of the object in the fingers rather than the palm, and by 36 weeks of age the infant exhibits a radial digital grasp (Gesell & Amatruda, 1947) (see Figure 4.1). The infant prehends a small object between the radial fingers and the thumb. With the object held distally in the fingers, the infant can adjust the object within the hand, and can use it for various purposes while holding it.

When the infant first grasps a very small object (pellet size), a scissors grasp is used (Castner, 1932; Newell & McDonald, 1997). In a scissors grasp, typically observed at 8–9 months, a small object is prehended between the thumb and lateral

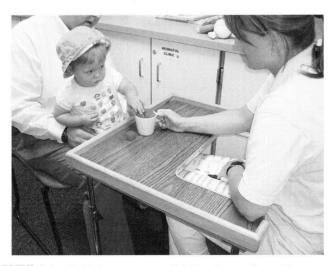

FIGURE 4.1 Child demonstrates radial digital grasp (Item 22).

border of the index finger after a raking movement of the fingers. By 10 months, the infant demonstrates an inferior pincer grasp (Gesell & Amatruda, 1947; Exner, 2005) in which the infant stabilizes the forearm on the table while grasping the cube and the object is held between the thumb and the distal lateral border of the index finger. By 1 year of age (52–56 weeks), the infant prehends and holds the object between the thumb and forefinger tip. Successful prehension using a superior pincer grasp (Halverson, 1937; Illingworth, 1991) is achieved without the forearm stabilizing on the surface.

A child's position and postural support can influence his or her grasping patterns. The *Bayley-III Administration Manual* specifies that the child should be well supported when seated – a condition particularly relevant for the grasping items. The size and shape of the object also highly influences the type of grasp observed. For this reason, standardized simple objects (the cube and pellet) are required. The progression of grasping patterns is measured in the block and pellet series (see Table 4.4; Figure 4.2).

Bimanual Coordination

The neonate exhibits both asymmetric and symmetric limb movements. The first bimanual reach is observed at 2 months, although swiping at objects such as a mobile can be unilateral. By 3 months, swiping increases and hand-to-hand interaction is observed with hands clasped on the chest. At 16 weeks, arm and hand symmetry predominates. Hands with or without an object are held together at midline (Case-Smith, 2006). The 5-month-old infant typically reaches with both hands, although may grasp the object with one (Fagard & Peze, 1997). At this age the infant transfers objects hand to hand, although release can be awkward. At 6 months, infants use a simultaneous bilateral approach to objects, often extending both arms together to the object or to be picked up by the parent. This strong symmetrical reaching pattern begins to change by 7 months. At this time, the infant uses a unilateral reach for small objects, and will continue to use a bilateral reach for large objects. The two hands interact frequently, with one hand holding a toy and the other hand manipulating it. At 7 months, infants actively transfer toys hand to hand while visually and tactilely exploring then. By this

TABLE 4.4 Grasping Patterns

Item	Skill measured	Specific observations
15. Block Series: Whole Hand Grasp	Use of palmar grasp. Voluntary and purposeful grasp (rather than reflexive).	Does the child show a voluntary grasp? Is he able to freely open and close fingers around block? Does he show interest in object?
17. Food Pellet Series: Raking Grasp	Whole hand, raking motion.	Is the child able to open and close hand around object? Is individual finger movement used in raking motion? Did the child secure pellet?
18. Block Series: Partial Thumb Opposition	Grasp using partial thumb opposition to the fingers.	Is the thumb active in grasp? Does the thumb adduct or partially rotate (oppose) to hold? Is block held in palm or is held in fingers?
20. Food Pellet Series: Whole Hand Grasp	Whole hand grasp is used to obtain the pellet. Pellet is held against the palm.	Do fingers extend and abduct in approach to pellet, then flex and adduct to grasp it? Does infant grasp pellet without raking and sliding it on the table?
22. Block Series: Thumb–Fingertip Grasp	Infant uses the thumb pads and fingertips to grasp the block.	Does the thumb oppose the fingers? Is the block held in the fingertips rather than proximal fingers?
24. Food Pellet Series: Partial Thumb Opposition	Infant grasps the pellet using partial thumb opposition against the lateral border of index finger.	Does the thumb actively oppose in grasp. Is the pellet held against the distal portion of the index finger?
26. Food Pellet Series: Thumb–Fingertip Grasp	Infant uses the pads of the thumb and index fingertip to grasp the pellet.	Does the thumb fully oppose the fingertips? Is the pellet held distally in the finger pads? Does the infant grasp it without forearm support?

FIGURE 4.2   Pellet is used to elicit a superior pincer grasp (Item 26).

age, active supination and isolated wrist movements enable the infant to rotate and turn objects for visual inspection. At 8 months, the infant waves toys in the air and bangs them on the table, and can combine objects by banging them together. The early development of bimanual coordination is measured in three items (Table 4.5).

Functional Use of Objects and Tools/Prewriting Skills

The ability to use tools is important to many human occupations. The Bayley Fine Motor Scale examines the young child's development of pencil grasp and drawing skills as the foundational skills needed for writing. This series of items, which spans $3^1/2$ years, provides thorough and specific

TABLE 4.5 Bimanual Coordination

Item	Skill measured	Specific observations
19. Transfers Ring	Object is transferred hand to hand.	Does the child release the ring with one hand and grasp with other hand?
21. Transfers Block	Small object transfer hand to hand.	Does the child smoothly release the block with one hand and grasp with other hand?
23. Brings Spoons or Blocks to Midline	Brings objects together at midline.	Can the child hold two objects and bang together at midline without dropping?

information about the child's development of pre-writing skills.

A 2-year-old typically grasps a pencil or marker using a palmar grasp. Initially the forearm is pronated, although most toddlers prefer to use a supinated grasp. With the forearm supinated, the toddler holds the pencil between the thumb and proximal fingers with fingers extended. This transitional grasp is the child's first effort to move the pencil more distally in the fingers and use the thumb to control it (see Figure 4.3). By 3 years, the child typically uses a static tripod grasp in which the pencil is held in the distal phalanges of the thumb, index, and middle fingers, with the wrist slightly extended and the forearm somewhat supinated. The tripod grasp becomes dynamic when the child learns to move the pencil with the fingers rather than the wrist. The dynamic tripod grasp emerges between ages 4 and 5, and appears to be important to forming small letters in writing tasks.

Both sensory and motor functions are important to the development of these skillful patterns of movement. The use of a dynamic tripod grip is associated with kinesthetic perception (Schneck, 1991). Proficiency using a dynamic tripod grip also relates to joint laxity (Summers, 2001). These researchers and

FIGURE 4.3   Various transitional grasps can be observed as children first learn to use a pencil or crayon (Item 34).

others (e.g., Manoel & Connolly, 1998) suggest that young children demonstrate a wide variety of pencil or crayon grips, with many of the grips functional for drawing and later writing.

Young children begin to scribble between 12 and 24 months of age. Typically, these first efforts at drawing are scribbling marks that have no representational intent. By age $3^1/_2$ the child can name what he or she has drawn, although it may not resemble the name given to it. Beery, Buktenica, and Beery (2006) cited the original research of Gesell to document the age ranges for the development of drawing skills. This sequence has been documented across many studies using the Beery Test of

Visual Motor Integration and the Bayley Scales (see, for example, Marr & Cermak, 2002; Daly, Kelly, & Krauss, 2003). Children learn to first draw a vertical line at midline (18–24 months). A horizontal line is more difficult because it requires the ability to cross the midline or integrate the two hemispheres. Children ages $2-2^1/_2$ can draw horizontal lines (Beery *et al.*, 2006); 2-year-old children also draw circular overlapping strokes. The Bayley Fine Motor item for circular strokes requires the child only to make a circular shape, imitating the examiner's model of a circle.

Drawing circles and crosses is foundational to writing letters. A cross is similar to several letters and is perceptually difficult because the child must cross the midpoint of a vertical line going from left to right. This skill requires crossing the midline and having some sense of crossing a line at right angles (Kephart, 1960). Therefore, this skill is more advanced than drawing horizontal lines, and does not emerge until age 4. The Bayley Fine Motor Scale measures two levels of making a cross: imitation and copying. The angles of the intersecting lines are assessed when scoring this item.

The square is the most difficult drawing task. This drawing task is difficult because the child must form corners by stopping the pencil and changing directions. By age 4, children learn to draw a four-cornered square, making it is the last item on the Fine Motor Scale (see Table 4.6).

CONTROL OF FINGER MOVEMENTS, REFINED GRASP AND PLACEMENT, KINESTHETIC PERCEPTION

By 10 months of age, infants demonstrate a wide variety of hand and finger movements. They mouth, wave, bang, rotate, and transfer objects. Finger skills develop that enable infants to manipulate objects within the hand. At 9–10 months of age, isolated finger movement emerges – a key skill to learning to manipulate objects. The infant now can poke with the index finger and pick up a small object in a precision grip (Pehoski, 2006). These isolated finger movements often are motivated by the object's texture and form as the infant runs his fingers over and around the object to explore its surfaces. From 10 to 18 months, the infant further refines this ability to differentiate individual finger movement and manipulate objects, and also

TABLE 4.6   Functional Use of Objects and Tools/Prewriting skills

Item	Skill measured	Specific observations
28. Grasp Series: Palmar Grasp	Whole hand grasp of the crayon to mark on the paper.	Does the child orient the crayon to the paper? Does he hold the crayon with forearm supinated or pronated? Is grasp firm and child is able to make a mark?
34. Grasp Series: Transitional Grasp	Holds crayon with partial thumb opposition. The thumb is close to the writing end.	Are the fingers partially extended and is the crayon held in the proximal fingers?
37. Grasp Series: Intermediate (Tripod) Grasp	Grasps the crayon using a static tripod or quadruped and makes a mark.	Is the crayon held more distally in the finger pads? Are the thumb and index finger near to the writing end of the crayon? Are the fingers flexed?
48. Grasp Series: Dynamic Grasp	Grasps the crayon or pencil with a dynamic grasp that enables control of the crayon to make precise marks.	Do the finger and thumb move while drawing with the crayon or pencil? Is the crayon mobile within the grasp so the child can draw precise controlled lines?
30. Scribbles Spontaneously	Child purposely scribbles.	Does the child mark the paper purposely, rather than accidentally?
32. Imitates Stroke Series: Random	Child draws stroke in any direction.	Does the child make a purposeful stroke?
39. Uses Hand to Hold Paper in Place	Child uses one hand to stabilize the paper while using the other hand to draw.	Does the child use cooperative actions of the two hands, with one assisting the action of the other? Does he or she use two hands together in an activity?
40. Imitates Stroke Series: Horizontal	Child makes a horizontal stroke within 30° of the horizontal.	Does the child cross the midline? Can he or she draw a line parallel to the table's edge?

TABLE 4.6 Functional Use of Objects and Tools/Prewriting skills—cont'd

Item	Skill measured	Specific observations
43. Imitates Stroke Series: Circular	Draws a mostly curved shape. Can be a spiral.	Does the child draw smooth circles? Does he or she rotate at shoulder or wrist when drawing a circular stroke?
53. Imitates Plus Sign	Child draws two intersecting lines that are within 30° of the other.	Does the child draw in segments, breaking the line at the cross? Does the child draw a continuous line? Draws lines at angles other than 90°?
59. Traces Designs	Child traces circle, square, diamond (at least two). He does not leave the inner or outer boundaries of the tracing patterns.	Does the child use continuous strokes rather than segments?
60. Imitates Square	Child draws a four-sided figure with four distinct corners and gaps no larger than $1/4$ inch at the corners.	Does the child change directions at corners? Does he or she draw using a continuous stroke rather than segments?
61. Copies Plus Sign	Child draws two intersecting lines, each within 30° of the horizon and vertical lines. The lines should extend beyond the point of intersection.	Does the child draw straight versus wavy lines? Does the child understand how to cross the vertical line with a horizontal line?
66. Copies Square	Child draws a four-sided figure with four distinct corners and gaps no larger than $1/4$ inch (same criteria as for Imitates a Square).	Do the lines intersect about midway? Are the lines about the same length? Are they straight versus wavy?

shows increasing control of object release. During age 2, the infant learns to precisely release an object in a specific space. Precision release requires well developed control of intrinsic muscles (Exner, 2005). Efficient object release requires regulation of grip force and timing of the placement of the object so that it is not dropped (Pehoski, 2006). Refinement of finger movement relates to improvements in the infant's haptic perception (i.e., perception of objects' form, shape, consistency, and texture through active touch) (Bushnell & Boudreau, 1993). As infants and toddlers (9–18 months of age) demonstrate increasing skill in manipulating objects within their hands, they learn to discriminate the texture, consistency (i.e., hardness), and shape of objects.

Buttoning and other tasks in which an object is inserted in a slot or hole require that the object be adjusted in the hand. Children as young as 2 years move objects within one hand (Exner, 1990). They move small objects in and out of their palms (termed translation) by age 3 (see Figure 4.4). In-hand

FIGURE 4.4   Precision grasp and release and arm control are required to accurately place a coin in a slot (Item 35).

manipulation is not frequently observed in 3-year-olds, because they tend to grasp too tightly and cannot easily move the object from one part of the hand to another. Various in-hand manipulation patterns are observed in children by age 4 (see Table 4.7).

TABLE 4.7 Controlled Finger and Hand Movement

Item	Skill measured	Specific observation
25. Lifts Cup by Handle	Combines grasp with arm movement. Beginning skills for cup drinking.	Does child hold cup in fingertips? Is forearm partially supinated?
27. Turns Pages of Book	Prehends single page in fingers, adducts arm which is holding page to turn it.	Does the child separate pages with his fingers? Does he move fingers when turning the pages? Are movements smooth?
29. Isolates Extended Index Finger	Isolated finger movement, able to combine flexion and extension.	Does child demonstrate full index finger extension with other fingers flexed?
33. Places 10 Pellets in Bottle (60 seconds)	Precision grasp with precision placement.	Does the child hold the pellet distally? Are precise grasp and release used?
35. Coins in Slot	Precision grasp with placement that requires correct orientation of object.	Does the child hold the coin in fingertips? Does he demonstrate a precise release? Does he orient the coin to the slot using wrist and forearms movements?
49. Tactilely Discriminates Shapes	Manipulation and fine movements, tactile and kinesthetic perception.	Do isolated finger movements follow the texture and shape of objects?
57. Buttons 1 Button	Manipulation, precision placement, correct orientation of object.	Does child use in-hand manipulation (shift) to move the button through the button hole? Do hands work together cooperatively?

(Continued)

TABLE 4.7   Controlled Finger and Hand Movement—cont'd

Item	Skill measured	Specific observation
62. Taps Finger	Isolated, rhythmic, controlled finger movement.	Does child tap his finger on the table quickly, rhythmically, and without apparent effort?
63. Places 20 Pellets in Bottle	Precision grasp with precision placement.	Does the child exhibit fingertip pincer grasp on the pellet? Does the child exhibit precise release? Can the child move quickly and smoothly?

STACKING BLOCKS AND BLOCK DESIGN: COMBINING GRASP, RELEASE, AND CONTROLLED MOVEMENT OF ARM IN SPACE

When children stack blocks, they use a precision grasp to prehend the cube, precision release to place the cube on top of another, and stability of arm in space. Controlled release along with control of force when placing the object are important aspects of object manipulation. A release at a specific location and time requires the fingers to open gently and gradually, using intrinsic muscle to guide the action. In addition to precision release, stacking blocks requires that the child hold his or her arm in space. This control requires cocontraction at the shoulder, elbow, and wrist (e.g., coordinating a stabilizing action at three joints). Holding the arm in space also involves kinesthetic and proprioceptive feedback from the joints so that the child can monitor and maintain the arm's position (Exner, 2010). These skills develop between 1 and 3 years – a period when the child is able to stack a tower of 10 cubes (see Figure 4.5).

The 3-year-old also develops the ability to copy block designs based on a model. This visual motor integration skill involves a perceptual understanding of the design and an ability to plan how to copy that design. Visual motor integration at ages 3 and 4 also is seen in the child's drawing skills. The ability to visualize a block design requires understanding of space and three dimensions, and demonstrates the child's

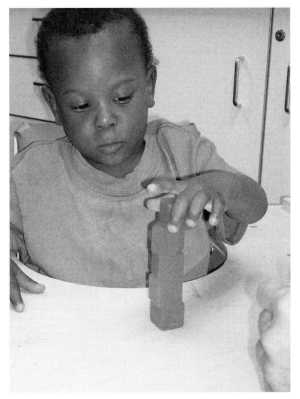

FIGURE 4.5   *Stacking Blocks* (Item 54) requires stability at the shoulder and proximal arm, precision grasp and release, and visual perceptual skills to align the blocks.

integration of proprioception, vision, and movement. Table 4.8 lists the block stacking items, while Figures 4.6 and 4.7 show the stacking items that use Legos™.

Tool Use and Motor Planning

Skillful tool use involves holding a tool within the hand and moving it dynamically (i.e., the hand must provide stability and mobility). The use of scissors to cut requires a child to adjust the scissors within the hand and then move the blades while holding with fingers through the scissors' loops. Virtually all tools, including eating utensils, scissors, and writing tools,

TABLE 4.8   Stacking Blocks and Block Design

Item	Skill measured	Specific observations
31. Block Stacking Series: 2 Blocks	Child places one block on another.	How is object released? Does the child demonstrate control of arm in space? Ability to correctly align the blocks?
38. Block Stacking Series: 6 Blocks	Child stacks at least six blocks.	Does the child release each block so that it stays balanced on top of the others? Does the child perceive where to place the block to center it on the others?
44. Builds Train of Blocks	Child places at least four blocks in a row, touching each other.	Does the child perceive that the blocks are aligned? Does the child place the blocks so that sides align and edges meet?
50. Builds Wall	Child replicates a wall of four blocks, two stacked blocks next to two stacked blocks.	Does the child perceive the design and motor plans how to replicate it? Does he place the blocks centered on each other with edges aligned?
52. Builds Bridge	Child replicates the bridge with one block stacked on two blocks with gap in between.	Is the top block balanced and centered on the bottom blocks? The two bottom blocks must have gap between.
54. Block Stacking Series: 8 Blocks	Child stacks at least eight blocks.	Are the blocks centered and aligned? Does the child use a precision release and manipulate the blocks to align them? Does the child control his arm in space to center his hand when stacking?
56. Builds T	Child replicates the T. Blocks are aligned although there may be small gaps between blocks.	Does the child perceive the design and motor plan how to replicate it? Does the child manipulate the blocks precisely so that they are aligned correctly?
58. Builds Steps	Child replicates three steps.	Does the child perceive the design and motor plan how to replicate it? Observe child's method for building the design.

TABLE 4.8   Stacking Blocks and Block Design—cont'd

Item	Skill measured	Specific observations
36. Connecting Blocks: Apart	Child pulls all blocks apart.	Does the child demonstrate adequate strength to easily pull apart the blocks? Does the child apply resistive force to pull blocks apart?
42. Connecting Blocks: Together	Child puts all Legos together. Connector knobs on each block must be correctly aligned and secured to another block.	Does the child demonstrate strength to connect legos? Does child apply sufficient resistive force to fit Legos together?

require manipulation within the hand or manipulation while holding them. Adjusting and efficiently using tools means that they are held with a gentle force that is graded to the weight, size, and shape of the tool, and the force needed to use it

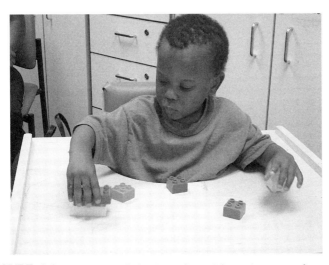

FIGURE 4.6   *Connecting Blocks: Apart* (Item 36) requires strength, as the Lego™ blocks provide resistance. The child must take all of the blocks apart to receive credit.

FIGURE 4.7 *Connecting Blocks: Together* (Item 42) requires strength and precision to fit blocks together. The child must put all of the blocks together to receive credit.

effectively (e.g., the force needed to paint compared to the force needed to cut cardboard).

The effective use a tool such as scissors in the hand requires integration of sensory (i.e., haptic, proprioceptive, kinesthetic) and motor (i.e., fine, isolated finger movement) systems. This integration of sensory and motor systems skills requires several years to develop. Skillful use of scissors to cut does not develop until $3^1/_2$–4 years of age. When developing scissors skills, children first hold the scissors in pronation and move the blades by extending and flexing their fingers. At 2–3 years of age, the entire hand opens and closes with the scissors' actions. Activating the scissors by using this motion limits control of the scissors, resulting in a child unable to cut on a line. By age 4, the scissor blades are moved using the radial digits and the ulnar fingers are kept in a flexed (closed) position, thus offering stability to the fingers moving the scissor blades. By age 4, the child can cut on a line or cut out a circle with fair accuracy.

In addition, cutting with scissors is a two-handed skill that requires one hand to hold the paper while the other manipulates the scissors. Both hands move dynamically, one repositioning the paper and the other holding and moving the scissors with a controlled movement that opens the blades only partially so that the paper stays within the blades (i.e., the child cuts on a line rather than snips the paper). Motor planning is required to move the paper in the correct direction and to guide the scissors along a line. Scissors skills require integration of sensory and motor systems; thus, they do not mature fully until ages 5–6. They are among the last items on the Fine Motor Scale (Table 4.9).

Gross Motor Subtest

The Bayley-III Gross Motor subtest is designed to test a child's ability to perform specific gross motor tasks essential for movement and play between birth and 42 months of age. These items measure head control, trunk control and locomotion, and motor planning (Bayley, 2006). The assessment of these skills provides the examiner with an opportunity to observe how early acquired foundational skills lead to more complex and challenging patterns of movement. Children's ability to move within and explore their environment can have a substantial impact on their overall development. The Gross Motor subtest comprehensively measures a child's accomplishment of a motor skill. Clinicians can use these items to observe how the child performs a broad range of gross motor and locomotion skills (see the qualitative indicators in the tables below). In addition, the quality of a child's movement can be specifically rated using the Behavior Observation Inventory and the Developmental Risk Indicators in the Bayley-III. The use of these combined tools provides a comprehensive profile of a child's gross motor and locomotion skill development (Bayley, 2006).

TABLE 4.9   Tool Use and Motor Planning

Item	Skill measured	Specific observations
46. Imitates Hand Movements	Motor planning. Ability to imitate a movement from a model. Integration of the two body sides	Does child automatically imitate movement versus observe and hesitate when imitating? How does child attend to and assimilate the movement patterns?
47. Snips Paper	Use of a dynamic tool in a primitive way.	How does child grasp scissors? Does he use two hands cooperatively during cutting activity?
51. Cuts Paper	Correctly uses a dynamic tool in a simple eye–hand task.	How does the child hold and position the scissors? Does the child use two hands together cooperatively?
55. Cuts on Line	Dynamic tool use. Eye–hand coordination. Bimanual coordination.	How does child grasp scissors? Position arm and hand? Use two hands together?
64. Cuts Circle	Dynamic tool use. Eye–hand coordination. Bimanual coordination. Motor planning.	How does child grasp scissors? Position arms and hands? Cooperatively use two hands together?
65. Cuts Square	Dynamic tool use. Eye–hand coordination. Bimanual coordination. Motor planning.	How does child grasp scissors? Position arms and hands? Control hand and arm action? Does child demonstrate cooperative use of two hands together?

Early Movement

In typical motor development, neonates respond reflexively to environmental stimuli. Their movements initially often are random and not necessarily purposeful, except for hand-to-mouth behavior for self-calming. Primitive reflexes become less prominent as postural reactions and more purposeful movements appear. Infants begin to turn their heads, track visually, reach toward toys, and roll over in response to visual, auditory, and tactile stimuli in their environment. These early movement experiences create the foundation for higher-level motor skill performance (Effgen, 2005; see also Table 4.10). Continued development of motor control, balance, and postural control and stability leads to the acquisition of more complex gross motor skills.

Postural Stability and Control

Postural stability is defined as the ability to maintain or control the center of mass in relation to the base of support for functional movements and balance. The terms *postural stability* and *postural control* are often used interchangeably. Static (i.e., stationary) and dynamic (i.e., control during movement) balance and postural control are believed to be necessary for functional motor performance. As infants acquire gross motor skills, they must develop adequate levels of postural control and balance to support movement and function. Feedback

TABLE 4.10 Early Movement

Item	Skill measured	Specific observations
1. Thrusts Legs in Play	Random anti-gravity movement in supine.	Do movements appear to be random, variable, and of different frequencies and amplitudes?
2. Thrusts Arms in Play	Random anti-gravity movement in supine.	Do movements appear to be random, variable, and of different frequencies and amplitudes?
6. Makes Crawling Movements	Reciprocal, alternating random movements in prone.	Are movements becoming more coordinated? Does the child alternate arm and leg movement?
14. Rolls from Side to Back	Limb movements that begin to produce mobility.	Do limb movements lead to whole body movement? Rolling generally is the infant's first experience of mobility and gives the infant an early sense of movement through space.

postural activity is movement that a child makes in response to sensory input from the environment. In contrast, anticipatory (or feedforward) postural control implies postural adjustments that are made in anticipation of voluntary movement. Feedback postural control develops earlier than feedforward postural control (Shumway-Cook & Woollacott, 2007; Westcott, Lowes, & Richardson, 1997).

In typically developing children, postural control develops in a cephalocaudal manner. Infants achieve head control, trunk control, and then standing stability. Adequate feedback and feedforward responses are necessary for functional movement (Shumway-Cook & Woollacott, 2007; Westcott *et al.*, 1997). Head control develops closely in conjunction with ocular-motor and vestibular control (Shumway-Cook & Woollacott, 2007). Infants experience feedback head control when learning to stabilize and move their heads upright as they are held and moved by caregivers. They learn feedforward head control when they move their heads in a purposeful effort to visualize their environment. Other examples of feedback and feedforward postural control can be found in Gross Motor subtest items. After infants produce somewhat random movements, they begin to develop sufficient motor control to produce more purposeful movements that allow them to stabilize in various postures and also begin to move between different postures or positions. Many of these purposeful whole-body movements emerge concurrently with and provide the proximal stability for reaching and grasping skills (see Tables 4.11–4.13).

Balance and Locomotion

Several authors (Dietz, Richardson, Atwater, & Crowe, 1992; Richardson, Atwater, Crowe, & Dietz, 1992) have studied the impact of sensory systems on balance. Infants and young children aged 4–24 months rely primarily on their visual systems to control their balance during gross motor skill performance. Children begin to use somatosensory information between ages 3 and 6, and exhibit mature use of their vestibular system later, between ages 7 and 10, at which time they are able to resolve sensory conflict and use all

TABLE 4.11 Head Control

Item	Skill measured	Specific observations
3, 4, 9. Controls Head While Upright Series: Lifts Head, 3 seconds, 15 seconds (Supported at Shoulder)	Initial purposeful upright head control against gravity.	Is child able to grade movements and control head when supported upright?
5. Turns Head to Side (Prone)	Anti-gravity head lifting or neck extension.	Does the child lift head from the surface to turn to each side?
7. Controls Head in Dorsal Suspension (Elevated Supine)	Anti-gravity neck flexor control.	Can the child maintain head in midline and avoid falling posteriorly into gravity?
8. Controls Head in Ventral Suspension (Lifted from Prone)	Anti-gravity head control when suspended in prone.	Can the child maintain midline and avoid falling anteriorly into gravity?
10. Holds Head in Midline (Level Supine)	Initial midline visual and motor orientation.	Can child sustain visual focus and head control in midline?
11. Holds Head Upright While Carried	Upright head control during movement.	Can child sustain midline head control while being moved in different planes and at varying speeds?
13. Rights Head (suspended upright)	Righting reactions of the head in both frontal and sagittal planes.	Does child respond to movements by righting head back to midline in various planes?

sensory systems to control balance. Therefore, children do not reach more adult-like balance abilities until ages 7–10 years, and can be expected to have more inconsistent balance abilities with visual dominance when younger than age 7. Berger and Adolph (2007) studied the role of experience in the development of balance and locomotion. Infants often engage in various mobility activities on varying textures and surfaces throughout the day. These activities provide experiences for

TABLE 4.12   Movement in Prone

Item	Skill measured	Specific observations
12, 17. Controls Head While Prone Series: 45, 90°	Anti-gravity head control with progression to more upright position.	Does child exhibit coordinated control of neck flexor and extensor muscles for movement; does visual gaze approach horizontal plane? Does child raise head to 90°?
15, 18, 21. Elevates Trunk While Prone Series: Elbows and Forearms, Shifts Weight, Extended Arms	Head control in conjunction with upper trunk extension and upper limb weight bearing; ability to shift weight and reach with upper limbs; prone position becomes more functional for play and movement.	Does child exhibit coordinated use of neck and trunk flexor and extensor muscles; demonstrate increased activation of abdominal and shoulder muscles for weight shifts; increased use of low trunk and pelvic muscles in extended arms position?

"BAYLEY-III" is a trademark, in the US and/or other countries, of Pearson Education, Inc. or its affiliate(s).
From: Bayley Scales of Infant & Toddler Development, Third Edition (Bayley-III). Copyright © 2006 NCS Pearson, Inc. Reproduced with permission. All rights reserved.

them to learn to adapt balance and locomotor strategies for more efficient mobility.

Infants and children with delayed gross motor skills lack the repetition and practice that accompanies experience with movement. The progression to upright standing and walking skills requires maturity and stability of an infant's postural system. Although the walking pattern continues to mature through age 7, the most significant changes in an infant's walking pattern occur during the first 4 months of independent walking (Shumway-Cook & Woollacott, 2007). An understanding of the development of balance and postural control is important when assessing gross motor abilities in infants and children. Clinically, therapists often will observe the timing of righting and equilibrium responses in children during both static and dynamic movements in order to assess strategies for balance. Information about a child's postural control and balance is valuable (see Figure 4.8). Poor postural control and inappropriate timing of balance responses often lead to motor

TABLE 4.13 Early Movement/Rolling

Item	Skill measured	Specific observations
20. Rolls from Back to Sides	Purposeful movement leads to mobility on the floor.	Often occurs accidentally initially with lower limb flexion (Item 24)
24. Grasps Foot with Hands	Anti-gravity flexor movement of lower limbs; upper limb reaching and body exploration.	Does the child elevate pelvis from the surface using abdominal muscle control? This movement pattern stretches the hamstring muscles and provides tactile and proprioceptive exploration of feet and legs for body awareness
25. Rolls from Back to Stomach	Purposeful movement leads to mobility on the floor for exploration.	Rolling typically is initiated with trunk and limb flexion and then completed with trunk and limb extension. Does the child incorporate righting responses of neck and trunk?

"BAYLEY-III" is a trademark, in the US and/or other countries, of Pearson Education, Inc. or its affiliate(s).
From: Bayley Scales of Infant & Toddler Development, Third Edition (Bayley-III). Copyright © 2006 NCS Pearson, Inc. Reproduced with permission. All rights reserved.

delays and inadequate motor performance during functional motor tasks. Tables 4.14–4.16 define specific observations for the balance.

BI-PEDAL AND UNI-PEDAL BALANCE AND MOTOR SKILLS

Infants develop stability and control on two limbs following the emergence of standing and walking skills without assistance. Table 4.16 describes the pattern of events that leads to the ability to stand and walk independently. Infants practice these skills hundreds of times a day (Berger & Adolph, 2007) to improve their balance, coordination, and muscle strength. Infants begin to practice skills on one limb as they become more proficient on two limbs. Changes occur as infants progress from double-support gait to single limb stance and higher-level gross motor skill performance. The demands of strength, stability, and balance increase

FIGURE 4.8 *Squats Without Support* (Item 45) combines balance, postural control, strength, and motor planning.

TABLE 4.14 Sitting

Item	Skill measured	Specific observations
16, 19. Sits with Support Series: Briefly, 30 seconds	Emergence of upright postural control and balance.	Does child demonstrate evidence of trunk extension through thoracic and lumbar regions?
22, 26. Sits Without Support Series: 5 seconds, 30 seconds	Progressive independence with sitting balance.	Does child demonstrate midline stability and static balance, neutral pelvic position, and wide base of support with lower limbs?
23. Pulls Up to Sit	Neck, trunk, and upper limb flexor control.	Does child tuck chin and pull with arms flexed to obtain upright position?
27. Sits Without Support and Holds Object	Progressive independence with sitting balance; feedback postural control emerging for righting responses.	Static balance improves to allow movement around midline without loss of balance. Does child exhibit emerging weight shifts and reaching?

TABLE 4.14 Sitting—cont'd

Item	Skill measured	Specific observations
28. Rotates Trunk While Seated	Dynamic sitting balance and anticipatory or feedforward motor control; mature righting and equilibrium responses.	Does child demonstrate dynamic movement of pelvis and weight shifts with reaching? Does child rotate trunk when sitting and freely moving legs into various positions?

TABLE 4.15 Precursors to Walking

Item	Skill measured	Specific observations
29. Makes Stepping Movements	Reciprocal lower limb movements with upright posture.	Does child exhibit sufficient postural control and hip stability to maintain upright posture and move legs?
30. Crawls Series: On Stomach	Forward movement in prone.	Does child exhibit reciprocal limb movements? Not all infants crawl in prone.
31. Crawls Series: Crawl Position	Ability to assume quadruped position from prone.	Can child push up on extended arms and activate abdominal muscles to elevate trunk and flex lower limbs? This posture requires balanced activation of flexor and extensor muscles.
32. Moves from Sitting to Hands and Knees	Transitional movement between positions.	How does child use weight shifts and trunk rotation to assume the quadruped position? Skillful transitional movements are key to developing higher-level mobility skills.
33. Supports Weight	Upright postural control and lower limb weight bearing.	Does child exhibit pelvic stability and lower limb extensor control?

(*Continued*)

TABLE 4.15   Precursors to Walking—cont'd

Item	Skill measured	Specific observations
34. Crawls Series: Crawl Movement	Locomotion in quadruped.	Initial crawling movements often are uncoordinated. Can child progress toward reciprocal limb movements?
35. Raises Self to Standing Position	Transitional movement to standing.	Does child exhibit a mature transition pattern of half-kneeling to stand? This transitional movement is key for proficient standing and walking.
36. Bounces While Standing	Ability to perform controlled lower limb movements in standing.	Bouncing indicates the emergence of eccentric muscle strength in lower limbs which is necessary for transitions and walking. How much control does child exhibit at hips and knees when bouncing?
37. Walks Series: With Support	Purposeful forward stepping movements with support.	Is postural control and pelvic stability sufficient for upright posture? Early walking is characterized by variable lower limb coordination although forward stepping is achieved.
38. Walks Sideways With Support	"Cruising" or walking along support surfaces while holding on.	Does child demonstrate controlled side-stepping? Cruising is a key skill for development of pelvic muscle strength (especially laterally) which is essential for standing and walking.
39. Sits Down With Control	Ability to lower to the floor with control while holding on to support surface (without falling to floor).	Does child exhibit eccentric muscle control in lower limbs through entire range of lowering movement (controlled lowering)?

TABLE 4.15   Precursors to Walking—cont'd

Item	Skill measured	Specific observations
40. Stands Alone	Ability to stand without assist or support surface; feedback postural control.	How long can child stand alone? How stable is child in standing? Emergence of righting and equilibrium responses in standing position is uncoordinated initially and then progresses to subtle movements.
41, 46. Stands Up Series: Alone, Mature	Ability to achieve standing position without support.	Skill combines balance, postural control, strength, and motor planning.

"BAYLEY-III" *is a trademark, in the US and/or other countries, of Pearson Education, Inc. or its affiliate(s).*
From: Bayley Scales of Infant & Toddler Development, Third Edition (Bayley-III). *Copyright © 2006 NCS Pearson, Inc. Reproduced with permission. All rights reserved.*

TABLE 4.16   Walking

Item	Skill measured	Specific observations
42. Walks Series: Alone	Ability to walk at least 3 steps without support.	How stable does child appear in stepping? Pattern of movement often begins uncoordinated with stiff limb movements and decreased balance.
43. Walks Series: Alone With Coordination	Ability to walk at least 5 steps with coordination and balance.	Do arm and leg movements appear coordinated? Pattern is more coordinated with better balance; months of practice are required for walking pattern to mature.
44. Throws Ball	Ability to throw a ball forward without support or loss of balance in standing. Evidence of feedforward postural control to stabilize proximally at the trunk to allow for distal movements of the upper limbs.	Do arms move freely and with coordination without associated trunk movement? Can child release ball efficiently without falling backward?

(Continued)

TABLE 4.16 Walking—cont'd

Item	Skill measured	Specific observations
45. Squats Without Support	Ability to transition between standing and squatting positions.	Can child lower slowly and then briefly maintain a squatting position before returning to standing? Skill combines balance, postural control, strength, and motor planning.
48. Walks Backward 2 Steps	Ability to maintain upright balance while walking at least 2 steps backwards without assist.	Does child exhibit pelvic stability? Is hip extension sufficient for stepping backwards? This skill signifies the emergence of body awareness (position in space).
53. Walks Sideways Without Support	Ability to maintain upright balance while walking at least 2 steps sideways without assist.	Does child step sideways with coordination, demonstrating minimal sway and good balance? Requires pelvic stability, specifically hip abduction; emergence of body awareness (position in space). This skill also requires motor planning.

significantly when moving from two limbs to one limb, as well as to higher-level skills such as running, jumping, and hopping (Shumway-Cook & Woollacott, 2007; see also Figure 4.9). Muscle force and power are required to propel the body forward and lift the body off the ground while running, jumping, and hopping. See Figure 4.10. Stair negotiation (Figure 4.11) requires the combination of specific muscle strength, reciprocal limb movement, and single limb stability. Tables 4.17–4.19 list the observations that can be made when administering the higher-level gross motor skill items.

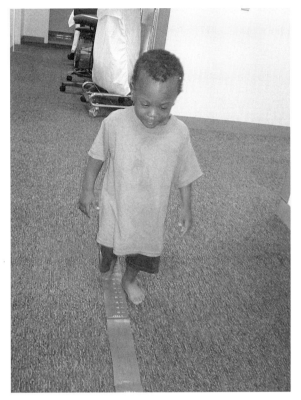

FIGURE 4.9   *Walks Forward on Path* (Item 56) requires balance and postural control on a narrowed base of support.

ADMINISTRATION AND SCORING

Directions for administering and scoring of the Bayley Scales are described well in the manual. The sections below elaborate on the manual's instructions, and define situation-specific considerations for administering and scoring the Motor Scales.

Preparing the Testing Environment

As with other of the Bayley-III Scales, the environment should be playful yet highly structured. The examiner establishes specific rules and expectations for performance that allow

FIGURE 4.10 *Jumping From Bottom Step* (Item 54) requires motor planning for pre-jumping position and then muscle power for take-off.

the child to make some decisions about testing sequence or where to sit. The manual provides explicit instructions regarding the testing environment, stating that it should be free of distractions, quiet, well lit, and comfortable. The examiner should make efforts to establish rapport with the child in order to elicit his or her best performance. When working with very young children, examiners should talk gently and positively with both the parent and the infant. Infants who perceive their parent is comfortable with the examiner are likely to trust the examiner and to engage with him or her. The display of positive affect, relaxed appearance, and administrative structure is important when working with all young children.

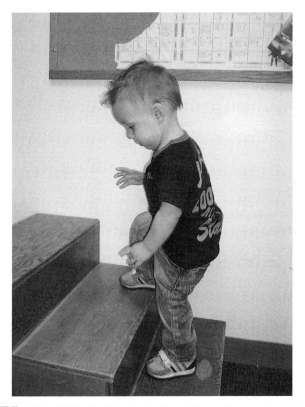

FIGURE 4.11 *Walks Up Stairs Series* (Item 47) combines postural stability, single limb balance, and concentric muscle control.

As much as possible, the examiner should attempt to establish a routine of turn-taking, with items quickly presented and the child responding automatically. The transition from one set of test materials and items to another can occur quickly during testing. At times, unexpected change can become confusing to the child because he or she may not understand why the examiner takes the toys away. One strategy to avoid this confusion is to present the next toy before removing the present toy. This allows the child to become engaged in the new toy and ignore the old toy being removed. Testing can flow smoothly when this rhythm is established.

TABLE 4.17   Single Limb/Base of Support Challenges/Motor Planning

Item	Skill measured	Specific observations
Runs With Coordination	Ability to progress from walking to faster movement pattern of running.	Does child exhibit rapid, even, and coordinated limb movements? A lower limb flight phase and upper limb coordination are not necessary with emergence of running.
51. Balances on Right Foot Series: With Support 52. Balances on Left Foot Series: With Support	Ability to balance and stabilize on one limb with support.	Emergence of balance and stability on one limb; righting responses are immature and pelvic stability is still developing.
55. Kicks Ball	Ability to maintain balance on one limb while kicking a ball forward with the other limb without support.	Single limb stability and balance responses are more proficient. Does child demonstrate true single limb stance versus walking into the ball when kicking?
56. Walks Forward on Path	Ability to walk forward while maintaining at least one foot on stepping path.	Is child stable on a narrow base of support? Does he attempt to put one foot in front of the other?
60, 69. Balances on Right Foot Series: 2 seconds, Alone; 8 seconds, Alone 61, 70. Balances on Left Foot Series: 2 seconds, Alone; 8 seconds, Alone	Ability to balance and stabilize on one limb without support.	Observe increased proficiency in pelvic stability with decreased sway of movement. Does child use mature balance strategies that allow for longer periods of single limb stance?
62. Walks on Tiptoes 4 Steps	Ability to take at least 4 steps unassisted without heels touching the floor.	Does child use more skillful balance strategies when on tiptoes? Demand for postural stability increases on an altered/smaller base of support.

TABLE 4.17   Single Limb/Base of Support Challenges/Motor Planning—cont'd

Item	Skill measured	Specific observations
63. Walks Backward Close to Path	Ability to walk at least 5 feet backward unassisted while staying close to stepping path.	Increased demand for body awareness (position in space) and motor planning. Does child exhibit balance and postural stability in backward walking?
65. Imitates Postures	Ability to imitate specific body positions and movements in standing.	Observe postural stability and motor planning. Item requires attention to and interaction with examiner.
66. Stops From a Full Run	Ability to stop running with control within 2 steps of the end of the stepping path.	High demand of postural stability and control; requires increased muscle power for push off. Does child exhibit eccentric muscle control and balance to stop movement quickly?
71. Walks Heel To Toe	Ability to walk along the entire stepping path with heel near toes of other foot.	Does child exhibit mature balance and stability on a narrowed base of support?

"BAYLEY-III" *is a trademark, in the US and/or other countries, of Pearson Education, Inc. or its affiliate(s).*
From: Bayley Scales of Infant & Toddler Development, Third Edition (Bayley-III). *Copyright © 2006 NCS Pearson, Inc. Reproduced with permission. All rights reserved.*

TABLE 4.18   Stair Negotiation

Item	Skill measured	Specific observations
47. Walks Up Stairs Series: Both Feet on Each Step, With Support	Ability to walk up at least 3 steps using wall or handrail (unassisted by examiner).	Observe how the child combines postural stability, single limb balance, and concentric muscle control.
49. Walks Down Stairs Series: Both Feet on Each Step, With Support	Ability to walk down at least 3 steps using wall or handrail (unassisted by examiner).	Observe how the child combines postural stability, single limb balance, and eccentric muscle control.

(Continued)

TABLE 4.18   Stair Negotiation—cont'd

Item	Skill measured	Specific observations
57. Walks Up Stairs Series: Both Feet on Each Step, Alone	Ability to walk up at least 3 steps *without* using wall or handrail (unassisted by examiner).	Does the child demonstrate stability and controlled stepping when not holding handrail? Demands on postural stability and single limb balance increase due to lack of upper limb assist.
58. Walks Down Stairs Series: Both Feet on Each Step, Alone	Ability to walk down at least 3 steps *without* using wall or handrail (unassisted by examiner).	Does child demonstrate balance and controlled eccentric muscle movement when descending stairs? Demands on postural stability and single limb balance increase due to lack of upper limb assist.
64. Walks Up Stairs Series: Alternating Feet, Alone	Ability to walk up at least 2 steps using wall or handrail (unassisted by examiner) demonstrating an alternating foot pattern.	Does child demonstrate controlled and alternating leg movements? Skill significantly increases the demand on concentric strength and single limb stability.
67. Walks Down Stairs Series: Alternating Feet, Alone	Ability to walk down at least 2 steps using wall or handrail (unassisted by examiner) demonstrating an alternating foot pattern.	Does child demonstrate controlled and alternating leg movements? Skill significantly increases the demand on eccentric strength and single limb stability.

"BAYLEY-III" is a trademark, in the US and/or other countries, of Pearson Education, Inc. or its affiliate(s).
From: Bayley Scales of Infant & Toddler Development, Third Edition (Bayley-III). Copyright © 2006 NCS Pearson, Inc. Reproduced with permission. All rights reserved.

At very young ages, most children perceive immediately that they are expected to perform. They generally engage easily when the bright and colorful Bayley-III items are presented. Most Fine Motor Scale items are adaptable (i.e., they can be used in various play actions – for example, the cubes can be used to build, stack, place in, or knock over. Other items (e.g. crayon and scissors) also can be used in various ways. In

TABLE 4.19 Jumping/Hopping

Item	Skill measured	Specific observations
54. Jumps From Bottom Step	Ability to jump to the ground with feet together or leading with one foot.	Does child exhibit strength and control to jump with feet together? Requires pre-jump/flexed hip and leg position and then significant muscle power to leave the surface of the step; landings are controlled by eccentric leg muscles.
59, 72. Jumps Forward Series: 4 inches, 24 inches	Ability to jump progressively farther forward on the ground.	Does child demonstrate strength to jump forward? Muscle power increases with distance jumped; take off and landing with feet together displays more mature pattern.
68. Hops 5 Feet	Ability to balance on one limb and hop consecutively forward at least 5 feet.	Skill requires the highest demand for postural stability, balance, and lower limb muscle strength and power.

addition, children intuitively know or have experienced playing with these objects; thus, minimal instruction may be needed. Therefore, some items can be scored based on the child's play before specific instructions are given. Children enjoy drawing and stacking activities because there are no right or wrong answers, and children can play with them in various ways. A certain amount of free play should be allowed before structuring the child's actions. Many Gross Motor subtest items can be observed during free play. Setting up the testing environment to encourage movement and exploration will facilitate administration of many gross motor items.

Examiners often begin Bayley-III Scales testing with the Fine Motor subtest. Compared to items on the Cognitive Scale, those measuring fine motor skills may be seen as being easier, more fun for some, and an extension of a child's prior experiences (e.g., blocks and crayons). Most items can be modeled by the examiner, thus reducing verbal commands. We recommend that Bayley Scales motor testing begins with the Fine Motor items.

The Gross Motor subtest can be administered with flexibility. Children may benefit from an opportunity to move when their attention strays during testing of other scales. Some examiners administer the gross motor items at the end of the testing session to avoid the child's possible reluctance to return to tabletop testing activities. Regardless of the sequence, flexibility and creativity during administration of gross motor items will lead to better testing success.

Postural Support

The examiner prioritizes safety and comfort when administering the Bayley Fine Motor and Gross Motor items. Infants' needs for external postural support change within the first year. Young infants can be positioned supine on the floor or supported in the parent's lap or an infant seat. These positions provide the head support that is important for the eye tracking and reaching items (i.e., the first 12 Fine Motor items). Beginning with Item 13, the infant is seated. However, full support of trunk remains important, particularly if the infant demonstrates poor postural stability. For infants aged 5–6 months, sitting in the parent's lap may provide optimal support and comfort. Once the infant is 7–8 months old, if sitting stability is good, the items can be administered on the floor, in a cube chair at a small table, or in the parent's lap.

For all Fine Motor items, the child should display good postural stability; if such stability is limited, external support of his or her trunk is needed. Inadequate postural support negatively affects the quality of fine motor skills (Exner, 2005). When children feel unstable, they use their hands for postural support and have less control of fine hand and finger movements. Postural instability also affects the child's ability to use his or her eyes to guide hand movements.

Item Sequence and Flow of Test Administration

The Fine Motor and Gross Motor subtests include item series that assess related skills and use the same materials; these items can be easily administered in a sequence without switching objects. Administering item series in a sequence promotes flow and test organization. Administering the series also allows the therapist to better engage the child, and the child to show increasingly higher-level skills with minimal cueing, thus facilitating a quicker and more organized test administration.

The examiner may begin with the block series because the child can play with the blocks in various ways. The blocks have a universal design that makes them easy to handle. The child's familiarity and experience with blocks can be helpful at the beginning of testing as the child settles into the testing environment, becomes comfortable with the examiner, and begins to understand the expectations. As the child handles the cube, crayon, and pellet, the examiner scores the grasping pattern items in addition to the items that rate how these objects are used in functional activities (e.g., stacking and drawing).

Knowledge of all of the items in a series will allow the examiner to score the series more accurately and efficiently. Efficiency also is achieved by grouping items that use similar materials or props. Stopping and starting test administration frequently to score items in the record book may lead to a distracted and less engaged child. For example, an examiner can administer all appropriate items using the stepping path at one time while the child is engaged. Also, a child can be encouraged to jump off the lowest step after completing the stair negotiation items. As a child crawls across the mat, the toy of interest can be moved up onto a low surface to encourage pulling up to stand and then cruising. These strategies may facilitate more continued movement and play for more efficient test administration.

The Bayley-III Fine Motor items may be embedded with the Cognition and Language items. When testing with an interdisciplinary team, examiners may alternate administering Fine Motor, Cognition and Language items. This administration format enables examiners to maintain a flow of test items without any down time for set up, thus working to maintain the child's attention. The Fine Motor and Cognitive Scales use some of the same items, and thus can be used in a sequence for both scales. A number of the tasks for both scales are similar, thus enabling the child to understand performance expectations (e.g., when presented with puzzles, pegboard, blocks, Lego blocks, and pellets in a bottle). The Bayley Gross Motor items can be administered intermittently as a break from the table-top activity or at the end as a play activity to reward the child for test completion.

Influence of the Environment on the Child's Performance

As noted above, both the physical and social environments influence motor performance. The examiner should think carefully about the influence of the testing environment on the child's performance. The manual recommends that examiners use a quiet, non-cluttered environment for testing. As the testing progresses, the examiners should maintain a well organized environment where distractions are minimal. When testing in a large room with toys, in order to maintain attention the child can be seated facing a wall or corner so that he or she is unable to see the play spaces and toys. The test items can be placed on the floor beside the examiner and out of the child's view.

Both positive and negative environmental conditions are likely to impact a child's success with motor performance and testing. Positive conditions include the examiner's or parent's encouragement to attempt an item or engage in a motor activity. Negative conditions include sound and visual distractions that limit the child's ability to perform an item. The examiner should monitor the effect of these factors to evaluate whether or not a child's test performance reflects his or her true ability.

The testing environment is set up to encourage movement and exploration, as this will allow for spontaneous observation of many gross motor items, especially pre-walking and early walking skills. For many of the early motor items, objects of interest are used to engage an infant. Using bright and enter-taining toys can be an effective method to facilitate gross motor performance. When working with infants, a mat on the floor is useful to provide a firm, flat surface for rolling, sitting, and crawling skills. In anticipation of transitions to standing, the testing space should have a sturdy bench, chair, or other low surface. Stairs can be very enticing for many children, which may lead to easy administration of the stair negotiation items. However, some children have difficulty leaving the stairs to engage in other testing items. More efficient testing is facilitated by isolating the stairs from a larger space used to test other gross motor skills whenever possible. Examiners should be cautious to guard children on the stairs to ensure safety.

The caregiver's presence can influence the child's performance. Generally, the caregiver can promote cooperation and compliance with the testing instructions; however, the caregiver is not always a positive influence and sometimes can divert the child's attention away from the testing items. When assessing infants and toddlers, the caregiver must be present in the room and preferably holding the infant. Toddlers often are more independent and may separate from the caregiver to interact with the examiner, although they generally prefer the caregiver to stay nearby and may seek support and assurance on occasion. When testing 3-year-olds, the caregiver's presence may or may not facilitate the child's best performance. The examiner should quickly assess whether or not the caregiver's presence facilitates optimal performance and, if not, suggest testing the child without the caregiver present. An ideal evaluation room has windows that allow caregivers to observe the testing without the child knowing that they are watching.

Children who are reluctant to separate from their caregiver may be difficult to engage in gross motor testing. Having a parent demonstrate the items may be helpful in increasing a child's participation. However, careful attention must be made to the administration of the items to ensure testing conforms to the standardized guidelines. Another strategy may be to engage the child in free play, using various toys before beginning testing. Building rapport with the child during this pre-administration time may increase his or her later willingness to participate. Finally, many infants cry in unfamiliar situations and settings; however, they may continue to participate in testing through bouts of crying and fussing. Unless the parent specifically requests testing be halted, an infant's crying does not necessarily mean testing must be discontinued. For example, a crying child placed a short distance from the caregiver may crawl or walk in his or her direction, thus allowing the examiner to observe a particular test item.

Interpretation

Interpretation Based on Skill Sets

The skill sets of related items help to interpret the child's performance by identifying a pattern of performance. Analyzing the child's pattern within item groups is helpful in informing diagnosis and developing intervention goals and plans. These plans and goals are facilitated by acquiring rich information on a child's fine and gross motor skill development, including their movement and manipulation, grasping patterns, bimanual coordination, strength, visual motor skills, motor planning, and tool use, together with early movement and locomotor skills. The identification of a child's strengths and limitations within and across the skill sets enables intervention planning.

Interpreting Variability in Performance

Children learn by first experimenting with movement. When learning a skill, movement may be varied and performance inconsistent. These steps in skill development can easily be observed when administering the Bayley-III Motor Scales. Items on which a child performs inconsistently or with variability represent skills under development. A child may have high interest in these items and make repeated attempts, yet does not meet the criteria. These emerging skills may become the goals and plans for intervention. They also should become the focus for evaluation reports, as they define the child's level and stability of performance.

Variability in performance may occur for various reasons, including limited experience. Thus, attempts are made to determine which activities a child has and has not previously experienced. Observations of the child's approach to tasks may enable the examiner to hypothesize the environment's influence on the child's skills. Performance on the Fine Motor subtest is particularly influenced by the amount of practice that the child has had with tools and toys. A child who never has used a crayon or scissors is unlikely to know what to do with these in the test items. He may display looks of curiosity, explore the items or attempt to use them in awkward ways (e.g., poking through the paper with the scissors). Some children may show a lack of interest because they have no idea how to use certain objects. The examiner should verify with the parent how much opportunity the child has had to play with objects and tools, particularly when performance with the crayon or scissors is inconsistent with performance on other fine motor items.

Variability or delay in gross motor performance also may be due to various conditions, and should be analyzed carefully. For example, specific impairments (e.g., deficits in muscle strength, postural control, or selective motor control) may affect a child's gross motor performance.

Relying on the dynamic systems theory, the evaluator should consider how environmental factors and past experience may have influenced skill development. For example, an infant with limited exposure to prone play activities may perform poorly on the prone items during administration of the Bayley Scales. The "Back to Sleep" campaign recommended by the American Academy of Pediatrics (AAP Task Force, 1992) has negatively affected the acquisition of gross motor skills for many infants. Results from multiple studies (Davis, Moon, Sachs, & Ottolini, 1998; Liao, Zawacki, & Campbell, 2005; Majnemer & Barr, 2005; Pin, Eldridge, & Galea, 2007) report delayed and/or altered early gross motor achievement in infants who are placed in a supine position for sleeping and play and experience limited exposure to prone positioning during awake play time. The performance of children with limited exposure to stair negotiation (no or restricted access) may be below age-level expectations. Parents may restrict a child's use of stairs at home and elsewhere due to safety concerns, thereby limiting the child's opportunities to acquire and practice stair negotiation skills.

A child's ethnic background also may influence the development of gross motor skills. Literature exploring motor development among children of Asian and European ethnic backgrounds suggests that differences exist in the rate and sequence of motor development in these populations of infants and children (Mayson, Harris, and Bachman, 2007). For example, children of Chinese descent tend to have lower muscle tone, with greater flexibility of joints, but also somewhat lower postural stability in the early months. Although the normed sample of the Bayley-III includes children of various ethnic backgrounds represented in the United States population, a child's ethnic background should be considered when interpreting performance and gross motor subscale scores.

These examples of environmental and ethnic influence on motor performance support the validity of dynamic systems theory. These should be considered when interpreting a child's scores on the Bayley-III Scales to determine whether motor delay is due to a neurological impairment or to other factors. These considerations require clinical judgment and a clear understanding of fine and gross motor development. They also are important for diagnostic and treatment recommendations.

Interrelationship of Scales

Behaviors are due to an interaction of interrelated systems – e.g., fine motor performance is influenced by visual and tactile systems; gross motor by visual, proprioceptive and vestibular systems. Because performance in one domain often relates to performance in other domains, the Motor Scale scores should be interpreted in the context of other Bayley Scale scores. Fine motor skills are strongly related to cognitive skills. For example, earlier editions of the Bayley Scales (1969, 1993) embedded the fine motor items within the Mental Scale. A separate Fine Motor subtest was created first for the third edition (Bayley, 2006). An examination of skill sets may help with understanding the possible influence of cognition on fine motor performance. Cognition may have a minimal impact on some skill sets (grasping patterns, ocular motor skills) and a greater impact on others, especially those that require an integration of systems (e.g., visual motor coordination and motor planning). Many items for age 3 years require visual motor integration, motor planning, and perceptual skills. These skills are considered to be part of a cognitive set, and to reflect early intellectual development.

The influence of cognition on fine motor skills is determined by examining the child's cognitive score. If it is below normal, the evaluator examines the child's performance on specific items that are more complex (e.g., have multiple steps) or are language-based (the child must follow a specific instruction). Low Fine Motor scores are likely to be influenced by cognitive delays when children also performed below age expectations on these items. The examiner should document this reasoning in the report as a possible interpretation of the child's performance.

Performance across all subscales may not be congruent for all populations of children. A child may display average performance on particular subscales, and below average performance on others. For example, children with autism or intellectual disability may display normal gross motor performance, and low language, cognition, and fine motor performance. Children with cerebral palsy may displayed low motor performance but average cognitive and communication abilities. Understanding that performance may vary in different subscales, examiners should attempt to elicit an accurate level of performance across all skill domains to appropriately define a child's developmental profile.

STRENGTHS AND CONCERNS

The Bayley-III Motor Scale can provide a valid assessment of a young child's fine and gross motor skills. It can be used for various purposes. This revision serves a number of purposes.

Standard scores contribute to determining a child's level of function for an appropriate diagnosis (e.g., cerebral palsy, developmental coordination disorder).

- Standard scores can help determine a child's eligibility for professional services
- The comprehensive set of items provides complete information for intervention planning
- The items provide repeated opportunities to evaluate the quality of movement and emergence of new skills
- Because the scale appears to be sensitive to change in motor skills, it is an assessment of choice to measure a child's progress in an intervention program or to track developmental progress.

Other strengths of the Motor Scale include the following:

- The items are presented in a logical sequence for testing

- The scale can be administered and scored in a reasonable time period
- The test covers key developmental fine and gross motor milestones
- Criteria for mastery (credit) are defined clearly for most items.

The Bayley-III Motor Scale has a few limitations. The scoring criteria do not allow for partial credit for emerging skills. Some important fine motor items are part of the Cognition Scale rather than the Fine Motor Scale. Puzzle completion and peg placement measure fine motor skills as well as cognitive skill. The examiner should note the child's visual motor integration, motor planning, precision grasp and release when completing the puzzle and peg Cognitive Scale items. Additional Fine Motor Scale items that assess bimanual coordination and in-hand manipulation (i.e., removing a small lid from a bottle, buttoning) would increase the scale's comprehensiveness. Additional Gross Motor Scale items would be helpful to test overall skill mastery, including rolling prone to supine, standing without support for longer time periods while performing functional tasks (e.g., playing with a toy or reaching), and jumping up off the floor before testing jumping from a low step. Jumping up and clearing the feet from the floor is a significant motor milestone due to the demands of postural control, balance, and muscle force/power required. Clinicians should record their observation of these skills on the protocol.

USE IN CLINICAL POPULATIONS

Children with Autism Spectrum Disorder

When testing a child with a known diagnosis, the examiner can make accommodations that help ensure a successful testing session. For example, the use of standardized tests with children who display autism spectrum disorder (ASD) can be challenging (National Research Council, 2001). However, many children with ASD can successfully complete a standard assessment, producing valid results when the examiner accommodates to the child's restricted interests and preferred communication methods. For example, children with ASDs, such as Asperger's syndrome, often prefer highly structured, repetitive activities. The child may engage in a structured activity such as stacking or lining up blocks, but have no interest in an unstructured activity such as drawing. Young children who display ASD symptoms are most likely to engage if first presented with a puzzle, the pegs, the cube blocks, or coins in a slot items. These items are repetitive and structured, are likely to be of interest, and should be among the first items administered.

The test behaviors of some children with specific diagnoses also can demonstrate variability. For example, children with ASD often have scattered scores, with some skills above age level (e.g., coins in the bank or puzzles) and others below age level (e.g., drawing). A pattern of scattered item performance is typical of children with ASD and others who have narrowly focused interests and rigid activity preferences.

A retrospective review of clinical records found 9 percent of a clinic population of children with ASD had diagnosed muscle hypotonia and gross motor delay. Delayed acquisition of independent standing and walking skills was the primary gross motor finding (Ming, Brimacombe, & Wagner, 2007). Identification of gross motor delays in children with ASD is important to provide diagnostic information and appropriate treatment recommendations.

Children with ASD often do not follow verbal instructions. Thus, when allowed by the item's standardization, modeling and verbal cueing are likely to be more effective ways to communicate instructions. At times, exaggerated cueing and gesturing may be needed to maintain their interest and focus on the items. Pre-walking and walking motor items are less difficult to administer with this population, since the children are more willing to engage with toys and objects than with people. Once the child identifies an object of interest, the examiner can use this object to engage the child in testing activities without relying on verbal cueing. The administration of higher-level fine and gross motor items may be more difficult when a child with ASD does not attend to directions.

An examiner also may improve participation in testing by altering the testing environment and using increased physical cues. For example, the examiner can instruct the child to step over low obstacles in his or her path to assess single leg balance, initially jump holding the child's hands to encourage spontaneous jumping, "chase" the child to encourage running, place visual cues on the stepping path to attract attention, and utilize stairs without a rail or wall to test this skill without support while guarding closely for their safety. Imitation typically is a core deficit in this population. Thus, Item 65 on the Gross Motor Subscale, *Imitates Postures*, may be one of the most challenging to administer. Children with ASD are likely to fail this item if they refuse to attend to the examiner. Motor planning and body awareness should therefore be assessed during spontaneous motor play (e.g., climbing on playground equipment).

Children with ASD often perform on their own terms, and examiners may need to wait for them to respond or to try an item a number of times in different ways. These children may have difficulty sustaining attention, and may need frequent breaks. Examiners often can succeed in administering the Bayley Scales and obtaining valid scores for children with ASD if they persevere, are patient and wait for the child's response, adapt the sequence of items, are flexible about where the items are administered, minimize verbal cueing, give visual cues, and set up a reward system (e.g., give juice when child stays attentive and seated). The Bayley-III Adaptive Behavior Scale provides the parent's report on children's daily functional performance, giving context to how children use motor skills in daily living skills. Although parents report on the child's functional skills in self-care, home and school living gives important insights into the child's daily use of functional motor skills, observation of motor performance remains important for identifying the interventions that may be useful for improving motor skill.

Children with Cerebral Palsy

Deficits in postural control and balance have been identified in children with developmental disabilities. Children with cerebral palsy (CP) demonstrate deficits in anticipatory postural adjustments (feedforward postural control) as measured by electromyography and a force plate (Liu, Zaino, & McCoy, 2007). Deficits in postural control and balance during walking were studied in two groups of children with CP using three-dimensional motion analysis and force plates. Children with CP displayed distinct differences in their control of center of mass and center of pressure (Hsue, Miller, & Su, 2009). Children with CP also display underdeveloped postural control mechanisms and specific reliance on visual feedback for balance (Shimatani, Sekiya, Tanaka, Hasegawa, & Sadaaki, 2009).

Children with CP and poor postural stability need external support to perform testing items. For infants, external support can be provided by sitting on the parent's lap or in an infant's seat with support to both head and trunk. For older children, a chair with high back and arm rests (e.g., a Rifton⊗ chair) should be used. The table height should allow the child to comfortably rest his or her arms on the table with elbows flexed to 90°. Children with very low postural stability can remain in their own wheelchair with the fine motor items placed on a wheelchair tray.

Children with CP often exhibit slow or delayed responses, and should be given plenty of time to complete fine and gross motor items (i.e., for items that are not timed as part of the scoring criteria). Often children with CP attempt the fine motor tasks but are unable to meet the criteria (e.g., inaccurate tracing, drawing figures that do not meet criteria). Narrative descriptions of movement difficulties can complement the scaled scores to provide a comprehensive picture of the child's abilities.

The reach and grasping pattern items should be administered to both hands and scored separately when a child with CP has asymmetrical involvement. This method provides information on the different levels of function for the right and left sides. Items that require coordination of two hands together often are challenging for such children and the examiner may, for example, decide to steady the paper for them so that they are more successful in drawing. The *Bayley-III Administration Manual* allows for these adaptations in administration.

The fine and gross motor growth curve often falls in the 5 to 10 percentile range for children with CP. As the scale's motor skill demand increases (e.g., items for 30–42 months), children with CP may plateau, falling further below the typical growth curve.

Children with Visual Impairment

Accommodations also are likely to be needed to obtain optimal performance from children with visual impairments. The *Bayley-III Administration Manual* provides guidance on testing children with visual impairment (see pages 224–225). The lighting in the room should be natural sunlight if possible. The examiner should consult the parent on the effect of glare and whether low light or bright light is best. A child can have loss of peripheral or central vision, and thus the examiner should position the test items where the child's vision is best. Some of the Fine Motor items do not require vision, and can be used to determine grasping patterns, some tool use, and use of two hands together. However, a number of the fine motor items cannot be adapted for children with low vision, and thus the scale cannot be administered and scored using the standard instructions in most cases.

The Fine Motor items and their tools are simple, and their use somewhat intuitive. Thus, their use can provide an estimate of the child's fine motor development, and an indication whether fine motor skills are age appropriate. The child with visual impairment should exhibit age appropriate performance on items that allow the child to use haptic perception (e.g. grasping patterns, object transfer, and connecting blocks) and show delays on others (e.g. stringing beads, stacking blocks, drawing or cutting with scissors).

Facilitating movement and gross motor performance in children with visual impairments can be accomplished using toys, bright lights, and musical or sound features. Examiners should use their ability to localize sound as a means to encourage movement. For example, children may raise their head upright to listen to a sound, demonstrate a weight shift in sitting when reaching toward a sound made by a rattle or bell, crawl or walk toward a musical toy, or squat to retrieve a musical toy. Examiners should reduce all peripheral sounds in a child's environment during testing to minimize confusion and increase attention and participation. Additionally, sounds from a toy coming from one direction and the examiner's voice from another direction may cause confusion. The examiner should provide simple and direct instructions to the child and repeat them as needed to encourage participation in testing. Finally, rapport with the child, established initially through free play activities, may be especially beneficial with children with visual impairments and contribute to establishing trust in the examiner and the testing environment.

Children with Intellectual Disability

Children with intellectual disability (ID) may need multisensory cueing to understand the test's instruction. Demonstrating or modeling the item to supplement verbal instructions should be considered. The administration instructions for most fine motor items provide for modeling them. The examiner can repeat the demonstration and instructions for some items.

Children with ID may have a short attention span, and the examiner may need to use a verbal cue, pointing or tapping to help the child refocus on the task. The examiner may move to an easier item if the child becomes resistant to more difficult items, and later return to the more difficult items. Children with Down syndrome often do not comply with item administration. When testing, the examiner can insert play opportunities to maintain their cooperation. When performance is charted on the Fine Motor Growth Chart, the progress of a child with ID may plateau at 30–36 months when the fine motor items require integration of visual and tactile perception (e.g., Item 49, *Tactilely Discriminates Shapes*; Item 53, *Imitates Plus Sign*) and cognitive skill (e.g., Item 46, *Imitates Hand Movements*; Item 52, *Builds Bridge*).

Using the Gross Motor Growth Chart, children with ID may show a plateau in gross motor skills when the items require them to follow specific instructions (e.g., hop on one foot, walk heel-to-toe). By age 3, the Gross Motor testing can be challenging for children who attend poorly or have cognitive and/or receptive communication difficulties that decrease their ability to follow directions. Testing higher-level gross motor skills requires children to attend to the examiner and follow simple directions. In these cases, every attempt should be made to accommodate to the child's level of understanding by keeping commands as simple as possible, using more physical demonstrations, and engaging the child with interesting toys. Provision of both verbal cues and physical demonstration whenever possible will maximize the child's ability to understand expectations. Examiners should adapt test administration within the limits of standardized testing to elicit as many skills as possible. The use of careful adaptation, creativity, and problem-solving in item administration is likely to enhance accuracy of motor skill assessment when working with children with ID.

CASE STUDY: MATTHEW

The following evaluation report for a child with suspected ASD illustrates how the Bayley Motor Scales can provide a comprehensive picture of developmental motor skills and at the same time provide qualitative information on the child's performance, including characteristics that reflect his ASD. Informal observation of his play and social interaction preceded formal testing using the Bayley Motor Scale. Playful interaction prior to and during testing was important because it provided a context for his performance on standardized testing, allowed the therapists to understand how to interact with him, and built rapport that promoted his compliance with the test items. Adapted behaviors also were assessed using the Adaptive Behavior Scale, and were documented in this report because they strongly relate to motor skills and were important in developing goals for an intervention plan. This report on motor skills contributed to Matthew's initial diagnosis of ASD.

Matthew's evaluation presented various challenges to his team. His decreased levels of attention, participation, and social interaction, in addition to his restricted interests, required the

CHILD'S NAME: MATTHEW P

Age at time of assessment: 2 years, 14 days

Evaluators: Physical and Occupational Therapy

Introduction

Matthew was referred by Dr Smith for a comprehensive evaluation due to concerns about speech and language and social skills. Matthew attended the evaluation with his parents, who also expressed these concerns and their interest in obtaining a diagnosis. Please refer to the Developmental Pediatrician's report for details of Matthew's medical history, which is significant for twin gestation and prematurity. Matthew's developmental history includes crawling by 8–10 months and walking by 12–13 months of age.

Past motor assessments include the Infant-Preschool Play Assessment Scale through the local early childhood program. Areas of concern were communication, cognitive/problem-solving, self-care, and fine motor. No gross motor concerns were reported by Matthew's parents today. They recently learned he is eligible to attend a center-based program at Easter Seals this Fall.

This developmental evaluation for Matthew was conducted through parent interview, observation of motor skills during play activities, and standardized Motor Scale of the Bayley Scales of Infant and Toddler Development-III (Bayley-III).

Clinical Observations and Test Results

Behavioral Observations

Matthew actively explored the testing room and engaged in various motor and play activities. He demonstrated intermittent eye contact and social interaction when approached by the examiners, but did not consistently initiate interaction during play. Matthew had difficulty transitioning between toys, and was very resistant to the examiners' attempt to engage him in play (especially when they altered the play routine). He performed some imitation of simple motor movements during motor play (kicking a ball, throwing a ball in a basketball goal, jumping from a step), but displayed difficulty imitating more novel movements and tasks. He did not demonstrate reciprocal and interactive gross motor play with the examiners (i.e., passing a ball or pushing a truck back and forth).

Matthew self-initiated play. He was interested in the slide, balls, and cars. He investigated a number of the toys in the room, and played with the dollhouse for several minutes. Most of his play was at a functional level. Some pretend play was developing. However, it mostly was one-step pretend play on self. His play demonstrated understanding of cause and effect, and object permanence. However, he did not pretend that objects represented different things. He played in proximity to the therapists, and did not interact consistently. He rarely followed their instructions, or did so only when he was interested in the activity. His interactions with the therapists were brief, and he often broke interactions to pursue his own interests. He was upset easily when instructed to perform an activity in a specific way, or one that did not interest him. He was active, yet would only stay with an activity of interest to him (e.g., climbing the steps and playing with the dollhouse).

Results of the Bayley Scales of Infant and Toddler Development

The **Bayley Scales of Infant and Toddler Development, Third Edition (Bayley-III)** is a standardized norm-referenced assessment used to examine gross and fine motor, cognitive, language, social-emotional, and adaptive skills in children ages 1 to 42 months. Standard scores between 8 and 12 are considered to be in the average range, scores of 6 or 7 are considered to be below average, and scores of 5 or below are considered to be in the poor range. His performance was compared with others his age.

On the **Gross Motor subtest**, Matthew's raw score of 54 was converted to a scaled score of 9. The scaled score mean is 10, with scores below 8 falling greater than 1 standard deviation below the mean (below average). His score indicates gross motor skill performance within the average range for his age. See table below.

On the **Fine Motor subtest**, Matthew's raw score of 33 was converted to a scaled score of 6. See table below.

When Fine and Gross Motor subtests were averaged, Matthew received a standard score of 9; his composite score is 85 (with 100 the mean). These scores indicate his fine motor performance is delayed. However, when his entire motor performance is compared to his age peers, his motor skills are only slightly below average. His motor composite percentile rank is 16, with the 50th percentile representing the middle score.

BAYLEY MOTOR SCALE SCORES

Scale subtest	Raw	Standard
Gross Motor	54	9
Fine Motor	33	6

Motor Observations

Matthew's movement patterns were observed to be symmetrical and coordinated during basic mobility and play, and mildly decreased during higher-level or more challenging gross motor tasks. Matthew demonstrated mild muscle hypotonicity (muscle tone), but exhibited functional levels of strength, range of motion, postural control, and balance during mobility and gross motor skills. One exception was mild decreased muscle power for push off during attempts to jump off the floor.

Matthew was observed to ascend and descend stairs using a step-to-foot pattern and a rail; he demonstrated an emerging ability to alternate feet when ascending with a rail, and to ascend and descend several steps without a rail (step-to-foot pattern), balance on a single leg for 1–2 seconds, walk across a line with one foot on/one off, and ride a push toy. He used an immature pattern to come to standing through four-point versus half-kneeling. He attempted to jump, but was unable to clear his feet from the floor or jump from a low step. He was able to run at a functional speed. He demonstrated appropriate balance when walking on level and unlevel surfaces. He was very hesitant to climb on a small slide initially, but later mastered the equipment. Galloping was not observed.

Matthew demonstrated consistent use of two hands together in cooperative activity. He appeared to be right-hand dominant, using the left hand as an assist. He used isolated finger movement to manipulate, but did not use his finger tips as much as expected. His grasping patterns with the marker were immature, although at 2 years a tripod grasp is not expected.

Given paper and a marker, Matthew scribbled using a fisted grasp. Matthew preferred structured activities; he completed the blue and pink puzzles on the Cognitive Scale and lined up the cubes. He did not stack the cubes, and his parents reported that he does not like to stack. He placed 10 pellets in the bottle, demonstrating a proficient pincer grasp. He seemed to like activities with repeated actions. He placed 10 coins in the slot. Although he did not take Lego bricks apart, his parents reported that he plays with Lego at home. His propensity for activities with repeated or stereotypic movements was noted, and was worrisome to both his parents and the examiners.

Adaptive Behavior

Matthew's adaptive behavior ranged from a standard score of 5 to 8. His percentile rank was 71, indicating moderate delays in adaptive behavior. His strengths were pre-academics and motor skills, and his lowest scores were health and safety, communication, and social. He scored well in pre-academics because he knows his letters and he knows the sounds of letters.

In areas of some delay, Matthew's parents report that he is not always aware of safety issues and sometimes acts impulsively. He does not always stop when his parents tell him to stop. He is not careful around dangerous items. He wanders off in a public place, thus creating a safety issue. He is delayed in social interaction, and often prefers to play on his own.

Matthew's parents call him a picky eater. His eating skills were delayed, with limited use of utensils and primarily finger feeds. He has a strong preference for a limited number of foods.

Social interaction is a primary parental concern. His skills in playing with others are limited, yet seem to be emerging. He is learning to share his toys and to greet others. He imitates the actions of others at times.

Impressions

Results of the Bayley-III Gross Motor subtest indicate that Matthew's gross motor performance is within the average range for his age. He demonstrated emerging jumping and stair negotiation skills. His mobility and gross motor performance were functional, although he demonstrated mild difficulty with coordination of movements during more challenging tasks. He demonstrated limited ability to imitate movements, which is important for learning higher-level motor skills and engaging in reciprocal play activities with peers and adults.

Results of the Bayley-III Fine Motor Subtest and Adaptive Behavior Scales indicate that Matthew's overall performance is moderately delayed, with strengths in structured activities and delays in unstructured activities (e.g., drawing). He has strengths in pre-academics and gross motor skills, and limitations in communication and social skills. He has functional hand skills; however, he has limited interest in pretend play or drawing.

Matthew's adaptive behavior is slightly to moderately delayed, with strengths in self-directed play and pre-academics. His self-directedness was viewed as a potential issue for learning to interact with his peers and participate in social play. Skills in social interaction should be a focus of intervention.

Recommendations

1. Direct physical therapy services are not recommended for Matthew due to his age appropriate level of gross motor skill development. His intervention team should monitor his independence on stairs and his development of jumping skills in the next few months. A re-evaluation by a physical therapist would be appropriate in 6–12 months if concerns arise.

2. As part of a comprehensive and intensive behavioral intervention, Matthew should receive both direct and consultative occupational therapy services. The focus of these services should be intervention to enhance pretend play, promote social play and social interactions, and improve fine motor skills with emphasis on drawing and visual motor integration skills.

3. The team also recommends a comprehensive feeding evaluation. This evaluation should consider possible sensory processing issues as part of his picky eating.

4. Matthew should be encouraged to imitate movements during play (e.g., hand/body movements with songs, pretending to be a specific animal) and to engage in more reciprocal motor play (e.g., passing a ball, rolling a car/truck back and forth). These

types of activities should help improve his motor imitation skills
for continued motor learning.

5. Matthew would benefit from involvement in community
   activities to further develop his muscle strength and motor
   coordination (gymnastics, swimming, playground activities,
   etc.). These activities also allow for social interaction and
   development of motor play skills with peers.

therapists to adapt the testing environment. He refused to sit at
a table for extended testing periods. Thus, many items were
administered in various locations within the testing room. The
therapists also administered items by alternating with each
other to capture Matthew's interests and adapt to his activity
level. Gross motor play in a large motor room allowed for
observation of motor activity, social interaction, motor planning, and safety awareness. An accurate profile of Matthew's
development was obtained during testing with the Bayley-III,
utilizing flexibility, creativity, patience, and a team approach.
Following administration of the Bayley-III, the physician-led
team discussed their observations and scored the Childhood
Autism Rating Scale (Schopler, Reichler, & Renner, 1988). His
score indicated autism of moderate severity.

Based on the Bayley-III results and the diagnosis of autism,
therapy services were recommended as part of a comprehensive program. Additional recommendations for follow-up were
given to the family. As is typical of many children with ASD,
gross motor skills were a strength area and fine motor performance showed deficits in visual motor integration, motor
planning, and cognitive related skills. The Bayley-III Motor
Scale findings demonstrated Matthew's strengths, and
contributed to understanding his impairments.

References

Adolf, K. E., Eppler, M. A., & Gibson, E. J. (1993). Development of perception of
  affordance. In C. Rovee-Collier, & L. P. Lipsitt (Eds.), *Advances in Infancy
  Research, Vol. 8* (pp. 51–98). Norwood, NJ: Ablex.
American Academy of Pediatrics Task Force on Infant Positioning and SIDS.
  (1992). Positioning and SIDS. *Pediatrics, 89*, 1120–1126.

Bayley, N. (1969). *Bayley Scales of Infant Development*. San Antonio, TX: Psychological Corporation.

Bayley, N. (1993). *Bayley Scales of Infant Development* (2nd ed.). San Antonio, TX: Psychological Corporation.

Bayley, N. (2006). *Technical Manual of Bayley Scales of Infant and Toddler Development* (3rd ed.). San Antonio, TX: Harcourt Assessment, Inc.

Beery, K. E., Buktenica, N. A., & Beery, N. A. (2006). *Beery–Buktenica Developmental Test of Visual Motor Integration* (5th ed.). Los Angeles, CA: Western Psychological Services.

Berger, S. E., & Adolph, K. E. (2007). Learning and development in infant locomotion. *Progress in Brain Research, 164*, 237–255.

Berthier, N. E., Clifton, R. K., Gullapalli, V., McCall, D., & Robin, D. (1996). Visual information and objects size in the control of reaching. *Journal of Motor Behavior, 28*, 187–197.

Bushnell, E. W., & Boudreau, J. P. (1993). Motor development and the mind: The potential role of motor abilities as a determinant of aspects of perceptual development. *Child Development, 64*, 1005–1021.

Case-Smith, J. (2006). Hand skill development in the context of infants' play: Birth to 2 years. In A. Henderson, & C. Pehoski (Eds.), *Hand Function in the Child: Foundations for Remediation* (2nd ed.) (pp. 128–141). St Louis, MO: Mosby.

Castner, B. M. (1932). The development of fine prehension in infancy. *Genetic Psychology Monographs, 12*, 105–193.

Charles, J. R. (2008). Typical and atypical development of the upper limb in children. In A.-C. Eliasson, & P. A. Burtner (Eds.), *Improving Hand Function in Cerebral Palsy: Theory, Evidence and Intervention*. London, UK: MacKeith Press.

Connolly, D., & Dalgleish, M. (1989). The emergence of a tool-using skill in infancy. *Developmental Psychology, 25*, 894–912.

Daly, C. M., Kelly, G. T., & Krauss, A. (2003). Relationship between visual motor integration and handwriting skills of children in kindergarten: A modified replication study. *American Journal of Occupational Therapy, 57*, 459–462.

Davis, B. E., Moon, R. Y., Sachs, H. C., & Ottolini, M. C. (1998). Effects of sleep position on infant motor development. *Pediatrics, 102*, 1135–1140.

Dietz, J. C., Richardson, P. K., Atwater, S. W., & Crowe, T. K. (1992). Performance of normal children on the Pediatric Clinical Test of Sensory Interaction for Balance. *Occupational Therapy Journal of Research, 11*, 336–356.

Effgen, S. K. (2005). Child development and appraisal. In S. Effgen (Ed.), *Meeting the Physical Therapy Needs of Children* (pp. 41–107). Philadelphia, PA: F.A. Davis Company.

Exner, C. (1990). The zone of proximal development in in-hand manipulation skills of non-dysfunctional 3- to 4-year-old children. *American Journal of Occupational Therapy, 44*, 884–891.

Exner, C. (2005). The development of hand skills. In J. Case-Smith (Ed.), *Occupational Therapy for Children* (5th ed.) (pp. 304–355). St Louis, MO: Mosby.

Exner, C. (2010). Evaluation and interventions to develop hand skills. In J. Case-Smith, & J. O'Brien (Eds.), *Occupational Therapy for Children* (6th ed.). St Louis: Mosby/Elsevier.

Fagard, J., & Peze, A. (1997). Age changes in interlimb coupling and the development of bimanual coordination. *Journal of Motor Behavior, 29*, 199–208.

Gesell, A., & Amatruda, C. S. (1947). *Developmental Diagnosis*. New York, NY: Harper & Row.

Gibson, E. (1988). Exploratory behavior in the development of perceiving, acting and the acquiring of knowledge. *Annual Review of Psychology, 39*, 1–41.

Gibson, E., & Walker, A. S. (1984). Development of knowledge of visual tactual affordance of substance. *Child Development, 55*, 453–460.

Gordon, A. M., & Forssberg, H. (1997). Development of neural mechanisms underlying grasping in children. In K. J. Connolly, & H. Forssber (Eds.), *Neurophysiology and Neuropsychology of Motor Development* (pp. 214–231). London, UK: MacKeith Press.

Gottlieb, G. (1997). *Synthesizing Nature–Nurture: Prenatal Roots of Instinctive Behavior*. Hillsdale, NJ: Erlbaum.

Halverson, H. M. (1937). Studies of the grasping responses of early infancy. *Journal of Genetic Psychology, 51*, 371–449.

Hsue, B. J., Miller, F., & Su, F. C. (2009). The dynamic balance of the children with cerebral palsy and typical developing during gait. Part I: spatial relationship between COM and COP trajectories. *Gait & Posture, 29*, 465–470.

Humphry, R. (2009). Occupation and development: A contextual perspective. In E. B. Crepeau, E. S. Cohn, & B. A. B. Schell (Eds.), *Willard & Spackman's Occupational Therapy* (pp. 22–32). Philadelphia, PA: Lippincott Williams & Wilkins.

Illingworth, R. S. (1991). *The Normal Child: Some Problems of the Early Years and Their Treatment* (10th ed.). Edinburgh: Churchill Livingstone.

Jouen, F., Lepecq, J.–C., Gapenne, O., & Bertenthal, B. I. (2000). Optic flow sensitivity in neonates. *Infant Behavior and Development, 23*, 271–284.

Kephart, N. C. (1960). *The Slow Learner in the Classroom*. Columbus, OH: Merrill.

Levin, M. F., & Sveistrup, H. (2008). Postural control for reaching and hand skills. In A.-C. Eliasson, & P. A. Burtner (Eds.), *Improving Hand Function in Cerebral Palsy: Theory, Evidence and Intervention*. London, UK: MacKeith Press.

Liao, P. M., Zawacki, L., & Campbell, S. K. (2005). Annotated bibliography: effects of sleep position and play position on motor development in early infancy. *Physical & Occupational Therapy in Pediatrics, 25*(1/2), 149–160.

Liu, W. Y., Zaino, C. A., & McCoy, S. W. (2007). Anticipatory postural adjustments in children with cerebral palsy and children with typical development. *Pediatric Physical Therapy, 19*, 188–195.

Lockman, J. J. (2000). A perception–action perspective on tool use development. *Child Development, 71*, 137–144.

Majnemer, A., & Barr, R. G. (2005). Influence of supine sleep positions on early motor milestone acquisition. *Developmental Medicine & Child Neurology, 47*, 370–376.

Manoel, E. J., & Connolly, K. J. (1998). The development of manual dexterity in young children. In K. J. Connolly (Ed.), *The Psychobiology of the Hand* (pp. 177–198). Cambridge, UK: Cambridge University Press.

Marr, D., & Cermak, S. (2002). Predicting handwriting performance of early elementary students with the Developmental Test of Visual Motor Integration. *Perceptual and Motor Skills, 95*, 661–669.

Mayson, T. A., Harris, S. R., & Bachman, C. L. (2007). Gross motor development of Asian and European children on four motor assessments: a literature review. *Pediatric Physical Therapy, 19*, 148–153.

McCarty, M. E., Clifton, R. K., & Collard, R. R. (2001). The beginnings of tool use by infants and toddlers. *Infancy, 2*, 233–256.

Ming, X., Brimacombe, M., & Wagner, G. C. (2007). Prevalence of motor impairment in autism spectrum disorders. *Brain & Development, 29*, 565–570.

National Research Council. (2001). *Educating Children with Autism*. Washington, DC: National Academy Press.

Newell, K. M., & MacDonald, P. V. (1997). The development of grip patterns in infancy. In K. J. Connolly, & H. Forssberg (Eds.), *Neurophysiology and Neuropsychology of Motor Development* (pp. 232–245). Cambridge, UK: Cambridge University Press.

Pehoski, C. (2006). Object manipulation in infants and children. In A. Henderson, & C. Pehoski (Eds.), *Hand Function in the Child: Foundations for Remediation* (pp. 143–160). St Louis, MO: Mosby.

Pin, T., Eldridge, B., & Galea, M. P. (2007). A review of the effects of sleep position, play position, and equipment use on motor development in infants. *Developmental Medicine & Child Neurology, 49*, 858–867.

Piper, M., & Darrah, J. (1994). *Motor Assessment of the Developing Infant*. Philadelphia, PA: W.B. Saunders.

Richardson, P. K., Atwater, S. W., Crowe, T. K., & Dietz, J. C. (1992). Performance of preschoolers on the Pediatric Clinical Test of Sensory Interaction for Balance. *American Journal of Occupational Therapy, 46*, 793–800.

Rochat, P. (1992). Self-sitting and reaching in 5- to 8-month-old infants: The impact of posture and its development on eye–hand coordination. *Journal of Motor Behavior, 24*, 210–220.

Schneck, C. M. (1991). Comparison of pencil grip patterns in first graders with good and poor writing skills. *American Journal of Occupational Therapy, 45*, 701–706.

Schopler, E., Reichler, R. J., & Renner, B. R. (1980). *The Childhood Autism Rating Scale*. Los Angeles, CA: Western Psychological Services.

Shimatani, K., Sekiya, H., Tanaka, Y., Hasegawa, M., & Sadaaki, O. (2009). Postural control of children with developmental disorders. *Journal of Physical Therapy Science, 21*, 7–11.

Shumway-Cook, A., & Woolacott, M. (2007). *Motor control: Theory and Practical applications* (3rd ed.). Philadelphia, PA: Lippincott Williams & Wilkins.

Smith, L. B., & Thelen, E. (2003). Development as a dynamic system. *Trends in Cognitive Science, 7*, 343–348.

Spencer, J. P., Corbetta, D., Buchanan, P., Clearfield, M., Ulrich, B., & Schoner, G. (2006). Moving toward a grand theory of development: In memory of Esther Thelen. *Child Development, 77*, 1521–1538.

Summers, J. (2001). Joint laxity in the index finger and thumb and its relationship to pencil grasps used by children. *Australian Occupational Therapy Journal, 28*, 132–141.

Thelen, E. (1995). Motor development: A new synthesis. *American Psychologist,* *50,* 79–95.

Thelen, E., & Spencer, J. P. (1998). Postural control during reaching in young infants: A dynamic systems approach. *Neuroscience and Behavioral Reviews,* *22,* 507–514.

Thelen, E., Corbetta, D., Kamm, K., Spencer, J. P., Schneider, K., & Zernicke, R. F. (1993). The transition to reaching: mapping intention and intrinsic dynamics. *Child Development, 64,* 1058–1098.

Thelen, E., Schoner, G., Scheier, C., & Smith, L. B. (2001). The dynamics of embodiment: A field theory of infant perseverative reaching. *Behavioral and Brain Science, 24,* 1–86.

Twitchell, T. E. (1970). Reflex mechanisms and the development of prehension. In K. Connolly (Ed.), *Mechanisms of Motor Skill Development.* London, UK: Academic Press.

Van Geert, P. (1998). A dynamic systems model of basic developmental mechanisms: Piaget, Vygotsky, and beyond. *Psychological Review, 105,* 634–677.

Van Sant, A. (1990). Life-span development in functional tasks. *Physical Therapy, 70,* 788–798.

Von Hofsten, C. (1984). Developmental changes in the organization of pre-reaching movements. *Development Psychology, 20,* 278–288.

Von Hofsten, C., & Woollacott, H. M. (1989). Postural preparations for reaching in 9-month-old infants. *Neuroscience Abstracts, 15,* 1199.

Westcott, S. L., Lowes, L. P., & Richardson, P. K. (1997). Evaluation of postural stability in children: current theories and assessment tools. *Physical Therapy, 77,* 629–645.

5

The Bayley-III Social-Emotional Scale

Cecilia Breinbauer[1], Twyla L. Mancil[2],
Stanley Greenspan[1]

[1] *Interdisciplinary Council on Developmental and Learning Disorders*
(ICDL), Bethesda, MD
[2] *University of Florida, Gainesville, FL*

INTRODUCTION

Early efforts to address the social-emotional needs of young children often were limited to diagnostic services. However, recent models focused increased attention on early identification, prevention, and intervention services, including attention to the emotional and social development of infants and young children (National Research Council and Institute of Medicine, 2000; Bagdi & Vacca, 2005; Briggs-Gowan, Carter, Bosson-Heenan, Guyer, & Horwitz, 2006). This attention has spawned increased interest among clinicians and researchers as to the importance of accurately assessing emotional and social development in young children, especially given the unique challenges of assessing children at such young ages (Lavigne *et al.*, 1993; Salvia, Ysseldyke, & Bolt, 2007; Briggs-Gowan & Carter, 2008). This attention, in turn, has led to the need for standardized norm-referenced measures to assess social and emotional qualities in young children.

The Bayley-III Social-Emotional Scale is an outgrowth of this interest. The scale, designed for children from birth to 42 months of age, focuses on the acquisition of functional social-emotional milestones that broadly represent social-emotional patterns and significant accomplishments, not just specific or isolated emotions or social skills (Bayley, 2006a). Thus, the scale assesses the attainment of important age-related milestones, including the capacity to engage and use a range of emotions, experiences, and expressions, as well as to comprehend various emotional signals and to elaborate upon a range of feelings through the use of words and other symbols.

The assessment of social-emotional functioning of infants and young children should focus on behaviors that occur in naturalistic settings. Thus, the Bayley-III Social-Emotional Scale relies on information provided by primary caregivers, including parents. Examples include whether the caregiver has observed the child looking at interesting sights, enjoying being danced with in their arms, and using words with peers. Caregivers are best able to know the functional behaviors of their children, and thus serve as reliable respondents (Bayley, 2006a).

CONTENT

The items on the Bayley-III Social-Emotional Scale are derived from the *Greenspan Social-Emotional Growth Chart: A Screening Questionnaire for Infants and Young Children* (Greenspan, 2004). This instrument has been recommended as an early screening tool for young children (including those who may display autism spectrum disorders) by many organizations, including *First Signs*, a national non-profit organization with the mission of educating parents and professionals about the early signs of autism and related disorders (NECTAC, 2008; First Signs, 2009). The chart identifies six areas of social-emotional growth for children from birth to 42 months of age. The six stages incorporate the following eight functional emotional milestones (Bayley, 2006a):

Stage 1, 0–3 months: growth in self-regulation and interest in the world
Stage 2, 4–5 months: engagement in relationships
Stage 3, 6–9 months: use of emotions in an interactive purposeful manner

Stage 4a, 10–14 months: use of interactive emotional signals or gestures to communicate

Stage 4b, 15–18 months: use of interactive emotional signals or gestures to solve problems

Stage 5a, 19–24 months: use of symbols or ideas to convey intentions or feelings

Stage 5b, 25–30 months: use of symbols or ideas to express more than basic needs

Stage 6, 31–42 months: creation of logical bridges between emotions and ideas.

Thus, during Stage 1, ages birth to 3 months, the scale assesses the development of self-regulated behaviors and interest in the world – qualities commonly observed in normally developing infants. During this period, the sensory and emotional responses of infants become organized and regulated. Thus, they are able to focus on sensations and to interact with others in pleasurable ways, including responding to touch and the approach of others, and taking enjoyment from objects in their environment (Bayley, 2006a). For example, infants in this stage will likely exhibit interest in most sounds, focus their attention on the caregiver without overly dramatic affects or sensory stimulation, and enjoy being quickly lifted into the air.

By Stage 2, 4–5 months, infants typically engage in relationships with others and exhibit positive emotions with caregivers, including physical signs of satisfaction, such as smiling, cooing, glances, blowing bubbles, and moving arms in a joyful way (Bayley, 2006a). Thus, at this stage, an infant may coo or smile at seeing a favorite person or make a curious or annoyed face in response to play.

Toward the end of Stage 3, 6–9 months, infants use emotions in an interactive and often purposeful manner. Thus, they use emotional expressions and motor actions with their caregivers (e.g., reaching for or crawling/toddling toward a caregiver, or exchanging two or more expressions) (Bayley, 2006a). Typical behaviors at this stage may include smiling and reaching out to be picked up, or pointing at a toy and making a distinct sound. Interactive communication continues through Stages 4a and 4b.

At Stage 4a, ages 10–14 months, infants and toddlers use emotional signals and gestures to communicate and to organize their emotions and behavior to form interactions and chains of socially meaningful communication. Thus, during this stage young children generally demonstrate warmth, joy, or exploration by responding to caregiver actions, and are able to respond in a back-and-forth manner to indicate wants and needs (Bayley, 2006a). Typical behaviors during this stage may include returning funny faces to caregivers, reaching out for a hug, stopping an action when the caregiver shakes his or her head, and looking at something to which the caregiver points.

At Stage 4b, ages 15–18 months, children use interactive emotional signals or gestures to solve problems. Thus, toward the end of this stage toddlers commonly exhibit socially meaningful problem-solving interactions that involve a range of emotions along with a continuous exchange of emotional signals (e.g., facial expressions, motor gestures, and possibly words) (Bayley, 2006a). Children who master this stage are able to search for an object of interest by looking, and to copy or imitate sounds while playing with a caregiver. Other stage-related examples include leading a caregiver to a door, banging on the door to indicate a want or need, and engaging a caregiver to search for a wanted toy.

Stage 5a, ages 19–24 months, is characterized by a child's ability to use symbols or ideas to convey intentions or feelings, facilitated in part by their expanding receptive and expressive language skills. The emergence of pretend play patterns, both with others and alone, constitutes a major milestone of Stage 5a. Children now use words or other symbolic means of communication to understand simple questions and express intentions or feelings (Bayley, 2006a). Thus, typical behaviors at this stage may include feeding or hugging a doll, conveying wants with one word (e.g., "Hug" or "Eat"), and responding to simple verbal commands.

Stage 5b, 25–30 months, is characterized by children's use of symbols or ideas to express more than basic intentions or feelings. Thus, they now are able to communicate two or more ideas when expressing intentions or feelings, and to comprehend and express more complex emotional themes (Bayley,

2006a). Their ability to comprehend and express more complex ideas and emotions enables children to begin to establish logical relationships between emotions and ideas. Typical behaviors at this stage may include pretending to be a cartoon or movie character, stating "Want that" or "No want" when communicating wants or needs, and using words with peers.

Stage 6, 31–42 months, is characterized by children's ability to connect symbolic elaboration of complex intentions and feelings in pretend play and verbal expressions, and to form connections between emotions expressed by self and others (Bayley, 2006a). Thus, a child now is able to understand the difference between fantasy and reality (Bayley, 2006a). Typical behaviors of children at this stage may include playing make-believe with one or more peers where the story plot makes sense and has multiple parts (e.g., playing school may entail leaving the house, getting on a bus, doing work, eating lunch, and then returning home), explaining their behavior (e.g., "Why do you want to go in your room?" "To get my toy"), and having conversations with adults with multiple back-and-forth exchanges.

The Bayley-III also incorporates an assessment of sensory processing in addition to its social-emotional focus. The inclusion of sensory processing in a measure of social-emotional functioning is logical in that sensory processing and social-emotional functioning have a reciprocal relationship – each influences the other's development and expression. For example, a child who displays a sensory processing disorder is likely to experience problems in social-emotional responses and expressions. Thus, an understanding of a child's sensory processing is likely to inform an understanding of the child's social and emotional status. Additionally, the provision of services to a child who feels overwhelmed by certain sensory experiences may enable him or her to use emotions to indicate feelings and needs, and thus help the child better negotiate his or her environment and relationships with others. Thus, the Bayley-III Social-Emotional Scale provides a brief description of selected sensory processing patterns, along with items that assess sensory processing (Bayley, 2006a).

ADMINISTRATION AND SCORING

The next three sections provide a step by step guide for administering and scoring the Bayley-III Social-Emotional Scale, as well as basic interpretation of the scores. Readers who are first learning to administer, score, and interpret this scale will benefit from having the Bayley-III record form and administration manual open while reading these sections.

Administration

The Bayley-III Social-Emotional Scale is intended for use with parents and primary caregivers (i.e., respondents) in a checklist or questionnaire format. The scale does not require the use of an interview. However, the evaluator should remain available while the respondent completes the questionnaire to clarify items and answer questions, if needed. Furthermore, if the respondent is unable to read and rate items, or seems overly anxious or unsure of the assessment method, the examiner may read each item aloud to the respondent and ask for verbal responses. Steps for administering the scale by reading the items to respondents are available on page 174 of the *Bayley-III Administration Manual*.

Respondents should know the child well enough to provide meaningful and accurate information regarding the required items. Thus, respondents should have in-depth knowledge of the child, and the ability to provide meaningful insight into the child's social-emotional functioning. Possible respondents therefore include parents or other primary caregivers. If such a respondent is not available, the examiner should use caution when interpreting responses on the scale because the scores may not accurately represent the child's actual behaviors. Nevertheless, their information may be of some use by suggesting whether a further evaluation is necessary (Bayley, 2006b). Furthermore, examiners often are concerned when primary caregivers are unable to provide answers to a number of questions. This may warrant a more comprehensive evaluation (Bayley, 2006b). Overall, the scale is intended to be completed by primary caregivers who are sufficiently familiar with the child so as to complete all required items, typically in less than 10–15 minutes.

Respondents often complete the scale on their own. When doing so, the examiner should provide the respondent with both the scale and a pencil with an eraser, as well as a chair and a writing surface (e.g., a table or clipboard). The scale should be completed in a setting that is free from distractions. Prior to presenting the questionnaire to the parent or caregiver, the administrator should complete its cover page and identify the appropriate start and stop points for the sections and skill areas. When calculating the child's chronological age, the examiner does not round days upward to the nearest month. Chronological age may be adjusted for children who were premature. Age in months is used to determine appropriate stop points.

Once presented with the scale, the caregiver should be instructed to always start with Item 1, regardless of a child's age, and proceed to the stop point determined by the child's chronological age in months (and highlighted by the examiner). The scale's 35 items provide declarative statements to which the caregiver should respond by selecting the frequency a behavior is displayed: $0 = can't\ tell$; $1 = none\ of\ the\ time$; $2 = some\ of\ the\ time$; $3 = half\ of\ the\ time$; $4 = most\ of\ the\ time$; and $5 = all\ of\ the\ time$. For example, the caregiver should circle 1 (*none of the time*) if a child has not exhibited the specific behavior identified in an item, and should circle 5 (*all of the time*) if a child exhibits the behavior almost always. All items are completed until the child's age-appropriate stop point has been reached.

As noted previously, the scale is divided into sections based on the corresponding stages of functional emotional milestones and their corresponding ages. Thus, caregivers should not complete items beyond the child's current age range. For example, if a child is 4 months, 15 days old, the caregiver should stop at Item 13, which is the stop point for children aged 4 to 5 months of age. If the child was premature, the appropriate stop point should be determined by using the adjusted age in months.

The examiner should review the completed checklist immediately after the respondent completes it, to ensure that all items have been rated. In the event that an item has been overlooked or unrated, the examiner should ask the respondent to rate the item, reminding the respondent that they may circle 0 (*can't tell*) if necessary, or providing additional examples of a specific behavior for clarification of an item. Note that it is crucial that all items within an age band be completed. Raw score totals and subsequent norm-referenced scores cannot be calculated if one or more items have not been completed.

Scoring

Score the Social-Emotional Scale by first adding the responses on each of the items to determine the total raw score. Record this total raw score in the box titled *Social-Emotional Total Raw Score (Items 1–35)* on page 3 of the Bayley-III record form, as well as in the first box in the row marked *Social-Emotional (SE)* on page 1 of the record form. Convert this total raw score into the corresponding scaled scores by turning to Table A.2 on page 190 in the *Bayley-III Administration Manual*. Locate the appropriate column with the child's age in months (without rounding days of age upward to the nearest month), then locate the total raw score in the age-appropriate column and scan across to the corresponding scaled score. Record this scaled score in the corresponding box in the *Social-Emotional (SE)* row on page 1 of the record form.

Next, turn to Table A.5 on page 199 of the manual. It provides corresponding percentile ranks and confidence intervals (at the 90 and 95 percent levels). Thus, using the information found in Table A.5, record the composite score, percentile rank, and confidence interval corresponding to the child's scaled score in the *Social-Emotional (SE)* row on page 1 of the record form. The conversion of raw scores to scaled scores and later to composite scores or composite score equivalents allows test administrators to compare scores across the various Bayley-III Scales and determine intra-individual discrepancies (see the *Interpretation* section of this chapter for further information regarding discrepancy comparisons).

Thus, scaled scores and composite scores or equivalents for all scales can be plotted on the corresponding graphs on page 2 of the record form (i.e., on the *Scaled Score Profile* and *Composite Score Profile* graphs), thus facilitating a comparison of intra-individual scores across scales. Scores are plotted by marking the point on the graph that corresponds to the appropriate scale (e.g., the Social-Emotional Scale) and the value of the scaled score and composite score or equivalent. Lines may be drawn on each graph, connecting the scaled scores and composite scores or equivalents, to aid further in understanding the profile of scores. Furthermore, horizontal lines may be used to mark the confidence intervals for each scale on the *Composite Score Profile* graph.

In addition to the scores derived from the Social-Emotional Scale, possible sensory processing deficits can also be determined. To do this, first add raw scores on the first eight items on the Social-Emotional Scale to yield the Sensory Processing score. Record this score in two locations: on page 2 of the Social-Emotional Scale in the appropriately labeled box beneath Item 8, and on page 13 in the *Total Sensory Processing Score* box. Then turn to Table B.5 on page 218 of the manual. Convert the Total Sensory Processing score to one of the three age-appropriate categories: Full Mastery, Emerging Mastery, or Possible Challenges. Do this by locating the appropriate age band in the left column of the table. Remember to use the adjusted age if the child's birth was premature. Then locate the child's Sensory Processing score range in the columns to the right. The child's age-appropriate category will be determined based on the column under which his or her Sensory Processing score falls according to his or her age. For example, a child aged 16 months with a Sensory Processing score of 25 falls in the Emerging Mastery category. Record this information on page 13 of the Social-Emotional Scale in the *Supplemental Analysis* table by checking the appropriate category of mastery.

While on page 13, record in the *Highest Stage Mastered* column the highest stage in which the respondent circled scores of 4 or 5 for all preceding items on the Social-Emotional Scale. Then plot the highest stage mastered on the Social-Emotional Growth Chart on page 13. The child's age range in months is provided along the horizontal axis of the chart, and the emotional stages are provided along the vertical axis of the chart. Therefore, locate the child's highest emotional stage mastered along the vertical axis of the chart. Then scan across to the child's age range in months using the horizontal axis, marking the appropriate point where the child's age and highest emotional stage meet on the chart.

Interpretation

Percentile Ranks, Composite Scores, and Confidence Intervals

The Bayley-III Social-Emotional Scale is a norm-referenced test based upon the standardization sample and norms provided by the Greenspan Social-Emotional Growth Chart, which reflect the abilities of 456 infants and toddlers ages 16 days to 43 months. The scaled scores, composites, or equivalents from one child are compared with same-age children included in the normative sample. These norm-referenced interpretations are commonly done.

Percentile ranks are provided to assist in these norm-referenced comparisons. For example, a child with a scaled score of 9 on the Social-Emotional Scale of the Bayley-III has a composite score equivalent of 95 and a percentile rank of 37. Thus, this child is exhibiting social-emotional functioning at the 37th percentile. That is, compared to his or her age mates included in the normative sample, this child's scores fall at or above 37 percent of other children of the same age, and at or below 63 percent of other children of the same age.

Similarly, a composite score equivalent of 95 on the Social-Emotional Scale falls within the Average classification range according to the qualitative descriptors of composite scores and composite score equivalents provided on page 114 of the *Bayley-III Technical Manual* (Bayley, 2006a). These qualitative descriptors range through Extremely Low (designating composite score or equivalent of 69 or below), Borderline (designating composite score or equivalent of 70–79), Low Average (designating composite score or equivalent of 80–89), Average (designating composite score or equivalent of 90–109), High Average (designating composite score or equivalent of 110–119), Superior (designating composite score or equivalent of 120–129), and Very Superior (designating composite score or equivalent of 130 and above). Such qualitative descriptors provide a convenient and easily understandable way to describe and interpret a child's functioning compared to the normative sample of the Bayley-III.

In addition to percentile ranks and composite scores, confidence intervals also are provided for the Bayley-III Social-Emotional Scale at the 90 and 95 percent confidence levels. Confidence intervals simply indicate, given a child's obtained score, the range within which a child's true score will fall given a specified level of probability (i.e., confidence level) within the population. In other words, confidence intervals provide a way of expressing the stability and thus the accuracy of scores. Thus, given the example above of a child obtaining a scaled score of 9 and a composite score equivalent of 95 on the Social-Emotional Scale, the confidence interval can be derived at either the 90 percent or 95 percent confidence level. At the 90 percent confidence level, this child's scaled score and composite score equivalent corresponds to a confidence interval of 89–102; at the 95 percent confidence level, this child's scores correspond to a confidence interval of 87–103. Note that the confidence interval at the 95 percent confidence level has a somewhat wider range than that at the 90 percent confidence level. This always occurs when the confidence level is increased. The 95 percent confidence level increases the likelihood that a child's true score falls within the specified range and decreases the chance of error (i.e., that a child's true score does not fall within the specified range). In other words, at the 95 percent confidence level there is only a 5 percent chance that the child's true score does not fall within the range specified by the confidence interval. At the 90 percent confidence level there is a 10 percent chance that the child's true score does not fall within the specified range. Thus, increasing the confidence level decreases the chance of error and leads to a wider confidence interval.

Intra-Individual Discrepancy Comparisons Using Scaled Scores

Intra-individual scores also may be calculated on the Bayley-III in the form of discrepancy comparisons. Such comparisons can be made among the Cognitive, Receptive Communication, Expressive Communication, Fine Motor, and Social-Emotional domains using their corresponding scaled scores (for which the *Scaled Score Profile* graph provides a visual aid). Thus, the administrator can determine significant discrepancies between the scaled score of the Social-Emotional Scale and those from the Cognitive, Receptive Communication, Expressive Communication, Fine Motor, and Gross Motor domains. Discrepancy comparisons also may be made between each of the other domains (e.g., Cognitive vs Receptive domains). However, this chapter discusses only those comparisons involving the Social-Emotional domain.

Determine a discrepancy between the scaled score of the Social-Emotional Scale and the scaled score of another domain by first turning to the *Discrepancy Comparisons* table on page 2 of the record form. Data in this table facilitate these comparisons. Next, locate the rows under the *Subtests* column for which the Social-Emotional Scale is compared to the other domains. The appropriate rows are labeled as follows: *Cognitive vs Social-Emotional, Receptive vs Social-Emotional, Expressive vs Social-Emotional, Fine Motor vs Social-Emotional,* and *Gross Motor vs Social-Emotional.* Once the appropriate rows have been located, record the scaled score for each domain being compared in either the *Scaled Score 1* or *Scaled Score 2* columns of the table. Note that the Social-Emotional scaled score always will be recorded in the *Scaled Score 2* column on the record form (highlighted in blue on the actual form).

Next, calculate the difference between the two scaled scores by subtracting *Scaled Score 2* from *Scaled Score 1*, and record this number in the *Difference* column. Turn to Table B.1 on page 214 of the administration manual. Locate the desired comparison at the preferred confidence level, either 0.15 above the diagonal in Table B.1 or 0.05 below the diagonal in Table B.1. Then identify the difference value between the two-scaled scores needed to achieve statistical significance. Record this number in the *Critical Value* column of the *Discrepancy Comparisons* table on the record form. The desired statistical significance level also should be noted in the small table labeled *Statistical Significance Level* adjacent to the *Discrepancy Comparisons* table on the record form.

After recording the critical value, determine whether the absolute value of the difference between the two scaled scores equals or exceeds this critical value. If it does, record a Y (for yes) in the *Significant Difference* column of the *Discrepancy*

Comparisons table on the Record Form. If the absolute difference value does not equal or exceed the critical value, record an N (for no) in the *Significant Difference* column.

Lastly, locate Table B.2 on page 215 of the manual. This table is necessary when calculating the base rate in the standardization sample for all significant differences. The base rate in the standardization sample indicates the frequency or percentage of children in the standardization sample who obtained the same difference score as the child being evaluated (Bayley, 2006b). Thus, the lower the base rate, the less frequent the child's difference score occurs in the standardization sample. Base rates provide an indication of the rarity of a child's particular difference score.

Note that Table B.2 is divided into separate columns based on the domains/subtests being compared. For example, the column labeled *Cog/SE* corresponds to the base rates of difference scores between the Cognitive and Social-Emotional subtests. Each of these columns is divided further into two sub-columns, based on the direction of the difference between the two domains being compared. For example, the administrator should use the *Cog < SE* sub-column for the Cognitive vs Social-Emotional comparison when the Cognitive scaled score is less than the Social-Emotional scaled score and the *Cog > SE* sub-column when the Cognitive scaled score is greater than the Social-Emotional scaled score. Also note that a column labeled *Discrepancy*, located on both the far left and right sides of the table, provides the same information on either side. This column represents the difference score the child obtained between two subtests or domains.

Obtain the base rate for each significant discrepancy comparison by first locating the difference score under the *Difference* column of the *Discrepancy Comparisons* table on page 2 of the record form. Next, note the absolute value of this difference score and turn to Table B.2 on page 215 of the manual. In the extreme right or left of the table, find the value in the *Discrepancy* column that corresponds to the child's absolute value difference score between two specific domains, then scan across to the appropriate subtest comparison column. For example, scan across to the *Cog/SE* column if the discrepancy comparison is being made between the Cognitive and Social-Emotional domains. After locating this column, select the appropriate sub-column based on the direction of difference between the two subtests or domains being compared. Then, using one finger to scan across from the appropriate value in the *Discrepancy* column and one finger to scroll down the appropriate sub-column, locate the appropriate base rate value. Record this value in the *Base Rate in the Standardization Sample* column of the *Discrepancy Comparisons* table on page 2 of the record form.

Again, this value represents how frequently other children in the standardization sample obtained a particular child's difference score. Base rates (i.e., difference between scores) less than 10 percent of the standardization sample are considered unusual (Bayley, 2006a). Furthermore, given the significant difference scores obtained through the discrepancy compari-sons of domains or subtests, relative personal strengths and weaknesses may be indicated in one domain relative to others. For example, a child with lower scores on the social-emotional domain than on the cognitive domain demonstrates a personal weakness in the social-emotional domain. However, if differ-ences between these scores are not significant, then the child's behaviors in these domains are likely to be comparably devel-oped (Bayley, 2006a).

Using the Social-Emotional Growth Chart

Clinicians also commonly use the Social-Emotional Growth Chart to interpret the child's highest social-emotional stage mastered. Figure 5.1 shows the growth chart. This chart provides a normative growth line that assists in understanding a child's social-emotional functioning by providing a visual trajectory of when certain emotional stages should be reached in light of data from the normative sample. Children whose highest emotional stage mastered falls above the line display higher rates of growth than same-age peers, while those whose highest emotional stage mastered falls below the line display lower rates of growth. If used across multiple assessment periods, the Social-Emotional Growth Chart provides admin-istrators and caregivers with a visual representation of a child's social-emotional progress relative to the trajectory of the normative sample. The case study below provides an excellent example of the value of tracking growth scores over time.

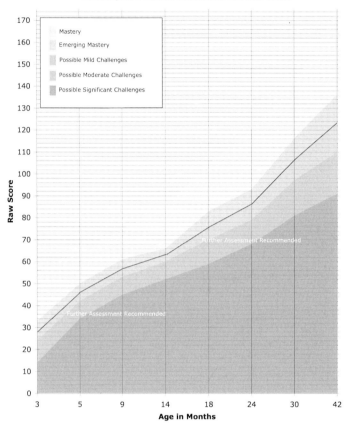

FIGURE 5.1 Greenspan's Social-Emotional Growth Chart. *From*: Bayley Scales of Infant & Toddler Development, Third Edition (Bayley-III). *Copyright © 2006 NCS Pearson, Inc. Reproduced with permission. All rights reserved.* "Bayley Scales of Infant & Toddler Development" and "Bayley-III" *are trademarks, in the US and/or other countries, of Pearson Education, Inc. or its affiliate(s).*

STANDARDIZATION, RELIABILITY, AND VALIDITY

As previously indicated, the standardization sample of the Greenspan Social-Emotional Growth Chart was used to calculate norms for the Social-Emotional Scale. This sample consisted of 456 children ages 15 days to 42 months, and representative of the US population consistent with the October 2000 US Census data (Bayley, 2006a). The sample was stratified at each age band according to parent education level, race/ethnicity, and geographic region. When developing item sets, items from the Greenspan Social-Emotional Growth Chart were analyzed to determine their age-appropriateness; an item was considered appropriate for inclusion at a particular age when the most frequent response for that item was 4 ("most of the time") or 5 ("all of the time") (Bayley, 2006a). These norms were used to calculate scaled scores and composite scores for the scale.

Reliability

Evidence of reliability for the Social-Emotional Scale is derived from the Greenspan Social-Emotional Growth Chart. Coefficient alpha was used to calculate internal consistency reliability for both the Social-Emotional Scale and the Sensory Processing items. Coefficients ranged from 0.83 to 0.94 for the Social-Emotional Scale and from 0.76 to 0.91 for the Sensory Processing items, thus reflecting suitable internal consistency (Bayley, 2006a). Preliminary data were collected on test–retest reliability with a sample size of $n = 35$ (Briggs, 2008). The total growth chart scores and growth chart screening categories showed strong correlations between first and second test administrations on the Social Emotional Growth Chart *among the participants*, with interclass correlations of 0.96 and 0.94 ($P < 0.01$). The total Sensory Processing scores and Sensory Processing screening categories were found to be reliable measures, with interclass correlations of 0.73 and 0.75 ($P < 0.01$).

Validity

Validity for the Social-Emotional Scale is seen, in part, in the discussion of item development for the Greenspan Social-Emotional Growth Chart. Evidence of content validity (i.e., evidence that the items seemingly reflect the trait being measured) is provided in two forms: (1) the items composing the scale are based on three or more decades of research and clinical expertise; and (2) the social-emotional constructs included in the Social-Emotional Scale reflect assessment and intervention guidelines provided by the Interdisciplinary Council on Developmental and Learning Disorders (2000) (Bayley, 2006a).

Empirical evidence of validity, based on estimates of its internal structure, is also provided by the Bayley-III. Intercorrelations between the Social-Emotional Scale and other subtests on the Bayley-III range between 0.18 and 0.25. Intercorrelations between the Language Scale and others are the highest, especially as age increases (Bayley, 2006a). The latter reflects the increasing importance of language on social-emotional development as children become older.

Empirical validity also is seen in the relationships between the Bayley-III and the following external measures: the Bayley Scales of Infant Development, Second Edition (BSID-II), the Wechsler Preschool and Primary Scale of Intelligence, Third Edition (WPPSI-III), the Preschool Language Scale, Fourth Edition (PLS-4), the Peabody Developmental Motor Scales, Second Edition (PDMS-2), and the Adaptive Behavior Assessment System, Second Edition (ABAS-II). Correlations between the Social-Emotional Scale and the BSID-II ranged from 0.24 to 0.38, with a moderate correlation between the scale and the BSID-II Behavior Rating Scale (Bayley, 2006b). Correlations between the scale and the WPPSI-III ranged from 0.27 to 0.53, with a moderate correlation between the scale and the verbal IQ, further indicating the interconnectedness between interpersonal communication skills and social-emotional functioning (Bayley, 2006a). Correlations between the scale and the PLS-4 ranged from 0.20 to 0.23, whereas correlations between the scale and the PDMS-II ranged from 0.06 to 0.33. Correlations between the scale and the ABAS-II ranged from 0.02 to 0.15.

Clinical Validity and Utility

Studies involving special needs children also were included in the validation of the Bayley-III Social-Emotional Scale. These included young children deemed at risk, premature, and small for gestational age, and those with pervasive developmental disorder (PDD), Down syndrome, language impairment, asphyxia, cerebral palsy, or fetal alcohol syndrome/fetal alcohol effects. Data from these special group studies provide evidence of the scale's clinical utility. In other words, such special group studies provide evidence that the Bayley-III Social-Emotional Scale can be used to differentiate the development of infants and young children who do and do not display special needs (e.g., the scale can adequately differentiate typically developing and non-typically developing children). For example, approximately 67 percent of children diagnosed as displaying pervasive developmental disorders obtained scaled scores of ≤ 4 (i.e., 2 or more standard deviations below the mean) on the Social-Emotional Scale, and 0 percent of children in the matched control group had comparable score values (Bayley, 2006a). Thus, the Social-Emotional Scale scores for children with special needs tend to be lower than those of the matched control groups. As such, the Social-Emotional Scale demonstrates clinical utility in that data support its ability to discriminate across various clinical populations when studied in relation to matched control groups. Analysis of these data indicated that, with the scaled score of 6 or less, the Social-Emotional Scale has a sensitivity of 86.6 percent, correctly identifying about 87 percent of children with special needs, and a specificity of 90.2 percent, correctly identifying about 90 percent of all typically developing children (Breinbauer & Casenhiser, 2008).

STRENGTHS AND CONCERNS

The Social-Emotional Scale's ease of administration may be its most notable strength. It provides a straightforward and quick assessment of qualities generally relevant to clinicians, childcare specialists, and parents of infants and toddlers. The scale's built-in interpretation aids are helpful, including its Social-Emotional Growth Chart. Persons new to the scale are likely to find its administration, scoring, and interpretation features can be acquired somewhat quickly and thereafter used efficiently.

The scale's focus on birth to 42 months of age constitutes another strength, thus enabling professionals and caregivers to assess and monitor growth in social-emotional development and functioning from very young ages. Therefore, the Social-Emotional Growth Chart can be an excellent surveillance instrument because it helps clinicians move from observing just one domain of development at a time to observing the inter-action and engagement between the child and caregiver, allowing for observation of child development over a short time period (Breinbauer & Casenhiser, 2008). Other measures of social-emotional functioning generally do not provide assess-ments for such young ages.

The availability of the Sensory Processing score underscores the importance of the reciprocal relationship between sensory processing and social-emotional skills. The inclusion of a sensory processing component within the Social-Emotional Scale is a strength by enabling administrators to more clearly define areas of concern and potential interventions for children who experience problems related to social-emotional func-tioning. Thus, professionals working with a child who displays delayed social-emotional functioning and sensory processing limitations are likely to consider tailoring interventions that address the overlay between social-emotional functioning and sensory processing, noting that a sensory processing disorder may interfere with his or her social-emotional functioning. As such, the impact of the child's sensory processing on the child's social-emotional functioning may be addressed more appropriately.

The scale also has reasonable reliability for a measure that targets an area of development that historically has been diffi-cult to measure objectively at such young ages. As previously indicated, internal consistency reliability coefficients range from 0.83 to 0.94 for the Social-Emotional Scale, and 0.76 to 0.91 for the Sensory Processing score.

USE IN CLINICAL POPULATIONS

The American Academy of Pediatrics (AAP) recommends developmental surveillance at every well-child preventative care visit (Council on Children with Disabilities, 2006; Johnson *et al.*, 2007). The Bayley-III Social-Emotional Scale, also known as the Social-Emotional Growth Chart, can be used as an autism screening instrument as well as a surveillance tool within the clinical population of infants and young children. Developmental surveillance includes "eliciting and attending to the parents' concerns; maintaining a developmental history; making accurate and informed observations of the child; identifying the presence of risk and protective factors; and documenting the process and findings" (Council on Children with Disabilities, 2006: 408). However, according to Edward Schor (2004: 212), "...pediatricians cannot squeeze more into the limited time they have available for each well-child visit."

A review of recent brain development research, evidence, and child development expert consensus can help us identify how pediatricians can use the well-child visit time more efficiently by focusing on the essential developmental processes that are vital for healthy functioning. New findings show that language and cognition emerge from, and are inextricably tied to, increasingly complex affect gesturing between a child and his or her caregiver (Shanker & Greenspan, 2007). There is consensus among child development experts that self-regulation and attention, engagement and attachment, social interaction, reciprocity, social problem-solving, and meaningful use of language and ideas are vital for healthy functioning, and often are impaired in children with various types of challenges (CDC-ICDL Collaboration Report, 2006).

Unlike other child development assessments that include items on each domain measured (e.g., language, fine motor, gross motor, cognition), this developmental scale uses items to assess the six functional emotional milestones consistent with the DIR/Floortime model (see "Content") as the theoretical framework. Each of these milestones or stages can be progressively evaluated at each well-child visit. Table 5.1 shows the functional milestones evaluated at each of the six developmental stages, and the

TABLE 5.1 Social-Emotional Growth Chart Conceptual Framework, Domains and Number of Items

Functional emotional milestones		Age	Well-child visit	Number of questions
Stage 1	Self-regulation and interest in the world	0–3 months	1+2 months	11
Stage 2	Engages in relationships	4–5 months	4 months	13
Stage 3	Uses emotions in interactive, purposeful manner	6–9 months	6+9 months	15
Stage 4a	Uses series of interactive emotional signals or gestures to communicate	10–14 months	12 months	17
Stage 4b	Uses series of interactive emotional signals or gestures to solve problems	15–18 months	15+18 months	21
Stage 5a	Uses symbols or ideas to convey intentions or feelings	19–24 months	18–24 months	24
Stage 5b	Uses symbols or ideas to express more than basic needs	25–30 months	30 months	28
Stage 6	Creates logical bridges between emotions and ideas	31–24	3+4 years	35

months at which well-baby check-ups are recommended. In this sense, the scale involves a paradigm shift from observing the individual child's skills within the classical domains to observing the child's interaction and engagement with the caregiver through a developmental approach (Breinbauer & Casenhiser, 2008). Furthermore, this scale allows pediatricians to conduct a developmental surveillance within 20 minutes during the well-child visit, including "eliciting and attending to parent concerns, making accurate and informed observations of the child, maintaining a developmental history, identifying the presence of risk and protective factors, and documenting the process and findings" (Council on Children with Disabilities, 2006: 408).

The brief developmental questionnaire can be easily completed by parents or caregivers within 5–10 minutes while they are waiting to be seen by the pediatrician. Administration time depends on the number of items to be completed according to the child's age. Table 5.1 also shows the number of items administered at each age and stage. The process of completing the questionnaire also serves to prompt parents/caregivers to ask the pediatrician other questions they may have about their child's development. A nurse or other trained personnel can score the results of the questionnaire. If the questionnaire was completed at a previous well-baby check, the nurse can also chart the child's developmental progress on the growth chart compared to the normative growth line (see Figure 5.1 above). The completed growth chart showing the child's scores then can be viewed by the pediatrician, who can contrast the parent report with his or her own observations of the child's interactions with the parent. This observation can be done while the parent gets the child ready for the examination. At this time, the pediatrician can elicit any parent concerns about the child's development, and provide recommendations according to the scale results and his or her observations. If the scores show the child has "emerging mastery" of the items for his or her age range, then the pediatrician can reassure the parent/caregiver that the child is on track developmentally. The pediatrician can also encourage the parent/caregiver to spend at least 1 hour a day playing interactively with the child while helping him or her to continue to master the age-expected milestones. If the child's scores show possible challenges, the pediatrician can provide a handout with suggestions for a home program that could include more intensive Floortime sessions (Greenspan & Wieder, 1998, 2008), as well as possibly a referral to a specialist for further evaluation.

The use of the scale as a surveillance instrument allows clinicians and caregivers to follow the child's social emotional measures of growth from an early age and continue through time, allowing the monitoring of the child's rate of progress or any developmental growth changes while using interventions.

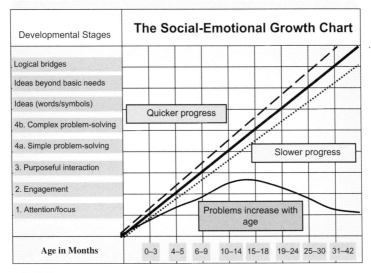

FIGURE 5.2 Quicker Progress, Slower Progress, and Problems increase with age growth lines (Greenspan, 1999).

Figure 5.2 shows examples of three different types of outcomes; quicker progress than expected, slower progress than expected, and problems increasing with age. In the case of Autism Spectrum Disorders (ASDs), the growth chart may also assist in identifying some children who show regression or early onset of developmental disorders. Figure 5.3 shows an example of regression in functioning, and an example of early onset of symptoms, which are patterns sometimes observed in ASD. Thus, the scale in combination with the growth chart is a very effective surveillance instrument for the monitoring of a child's social and emotional development (Breinbauer & Casenhiser, 2008).

The scale also can be used as a valid and reliable screening instrument at the ages recommended by the AAP (ages 9, 18, 24, and 30 months). As shown in Table 5.2, the original 2004 version of the scale identifies children as having possible developmental challenges in social and emotional functioning when they obtain scaled scores under 4. However, further research by Breinbauer & Casenhiser (2008) has determined that when

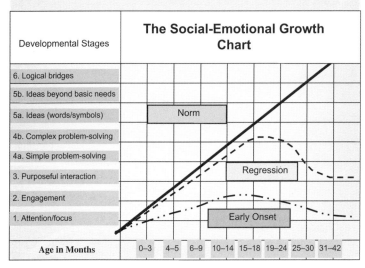

FIGURE 5.3   Norm, Regression and Early Onset growth lines (Greenspan, 1999).

TABLE 5.2   Corresponding Categories when using Scaled Score of 4 as Cut-off Score between Emerging Mastery and Challenges

Age bands	Possible challenges	Emerging mastery	Full mastery
0–3 months	0–14	15–33	34–55
4–5 months	0–33	34–50	51–65
6–9 months	0–44	45–61	62–75
10–14 months	0–52	53–66	67–85
15–18 months	0–60	61–84	85–105
19–24 months	0–68	69–93	94–120
25–30 months	0–84	85–119	120–140
31–42 months	0–96	97–141	142–175
Scaled scores	**1–3**	**4–7**	**8–18**
Corresponding categories	**Possible challenges**	**Emerging mastery**	**Full mastery**

TABLE 5.3 Corresponding Categories when using Scaled Score of 6 as Cut-off Score between Emerging Mastery and Challenges

Age bands	Possible challenges: start early intervention			Emerging mastery	Full mastery
0–3 months	0–14	15–24	25–28	29–33	34–55
4–5 months	0–34	35–42	43–46	47–50	51–65
6–9 months	0–45	46–53	54–57	58–61	62–75
10–14 months	0–52	53–60	61–63	64–66	67–85
15–18 months	0–59	60–70	71–76	77–83	84–105
19–24 months	0–68	69–79	80–86	87–93	94–120
25–30 months	0–81	82–97	98–106	107–116	117–140
31–42 months	0–91	92–110	111–124	125–136	137–175
Scaled scores	1–3	4–5	6	7	8–19
Corresponding categories	Possible challenges: significant	Possible challenges: moderate	Possible challenges: mild	Emerging mastery	Full mastery

using the total growth chart scaled score of 6 or less as the cut-off, the Bayley-III Social-Emotional Scale yields a specificity of 90.2 percent and a sensitivity of 86.6 percent in correctly identifying children with ASDs when used as a screening tool. Table 5.3 shows the newly recommended categories that emerge when using a scaled score 6 as a cut-off score to differentiate different levels of functioning and risk for ASD.

CASE STUDY: STEVEN

A family with a 7-year-old boy diagnosed with Autism Spectrum Disorder (ASD) and his 3-year-old brother illustrates how the Bayley-III Social-Emotional Scale, also known as The Social-Emotional Growth Chart, was used as a surveillance instrument to follow up on the 3-year-old child's development from the time of his birth.

The 7-year-old, Steven, was diagnosed with ASD at age 2 years. After the diagnosis the parents consulted a psychiatrist specializing in child development, who became the case manager for the family, helping them develop a home program based on the DIR/Floortime Model (ICDL, 2000) and coordinate the different therapies needed according to the child's individual processing profile. After a year of intervention Steven was showing good progress, including better self-regulation when visiting crowded places like supermarkets and malls, increased joint attention, engagement and two-way communication when playing with parents, and emerging language abilities to express his own intentions. At this time, the mother became pregnant, and both parents started showing increased anxiety and fear that the new baby would share the same diagnosis as his brother. The clinician observed this increased anxiety when the parents brought Steven for the next follow-up session. He immediately developed a plan with the parents to monitor the new baby's development from birth. He also gave recommendations to both parents on how to use self-regulatory techniques to reduce their anxiety during the pregnancy (e.g., enjoying activities together that were calming and soothing). Both parents are musicians. They started spending time together composing music and sharing new melodies with their son and unborn baby.

The family came for follow-up when the new baby, Peter, was 3 months old. The baby was irritable most of the time during the session. The clinician reviewed with the parents the eight items of the "sensory processing" component of the scale and the three items for Stage 1 (Items 9–11). Peter scored 21 points on the Sensory Processing section and 22 points on Stage 1. For example, parents reported that only some of the time would the baby show attention to sounds or visual objects, enjoy different sensations, or be able to calm down with their help. The scores placed Peter on the category of possible moderate challenges for Stage 1. The clinician recommended they play the "Look and Listen Game" described in the Caregiver Report of the Greenspan Social-Emotional Growth Chart, and suggested doing several floortime sessions per day with both children using ideas from the *Engaging Autism* book (Greenspan & Wieder, 2008) for Steven, and the *Building Healthy*

Minds book (Greenspan, 1999) for Peter. He also recommended follow-up with him when Peter was 6, 9, 12, 15, 18, and 24 months old, bringing a completed questionnaire from the Greenspan Social-Emotional Growth Chart to each visit. At

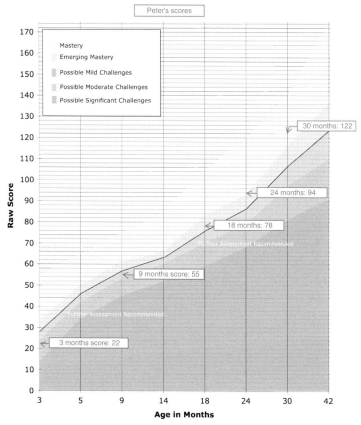

FIGURE 5.4   Greenspan's Social-Emotional Growth Chart: Peter's scores.

every follow-up visit the clinician gave the parents guidelines of how to strengthen each stage through an intensive home-based program built on the DIR/Floortime Model (ICDL, 2000).

Figure 5.4 shows Peter's progress as plotted on the growth chart. As shown in the figure, Peter's scores gradually improved throughout the follow-up period from possible "moderate challenges" at 3 months of age, to "mild challenges" at 9 months, to "emerging mastery" at 18 months, and, finally, "typical functioning" at 24 months of age.

Monitoring Peter's development through the Social-Emotional Growth Chart and future visits with the clinician proved to be very effective, as indicated by the child's increased mastery of social-emotional milestones and re-confirmed by increased scores on the Social-Emotional Growth Chart. The clinician was able to use this tool as a quick and easy assessment of the child's developmental mastery, as well as a surveillance instrument that helped this at-risk child keep on track and derail any further challenges from deepening.

References

Bagdi, A., & Vacca, J. (2005). Supporting early childhood social-emotional well being: The building blocks for early learning and school success. *Early Childhood Education Journal, 33,* 145–150.

Bayley, N. (2006a). *Bayley Scales of Infant and Toddler Development* (3rd ed.). Administration Manual. San Antonio, TX: Pearson.

Bayley, N. (2006b). *Bayley Scales of Infant and Toddler Development* (3rd ed.). Technical Manual. San Antonio, TX: Pearson.

Breinbauer, C. & Casenhiser, D. M. (2008). *Greenspan Social-Emotional Growth Chart.* ICDL 12th Annual International Conference, November 7, 2008. Tysons Corner, VA.

Briggs, A. (2008). *Test–retest reliability of the Greenspan Social-Emotional Growth Chart: An autism screening questionnaire for infants and toddlers.* Washington, DC: School of Public Health and Health Services, The George Washington University.

Briggs-Gowan, M. J., & Carter, A. S. (2008). Social-emotional screening status in early childhood predicts elementary school outcomes. *Pediatrics, 121,* 957–962.

Briggs-Gowan, M. J., Carter, A. S., Bosson-Heenan, J., Guyer, A. E., & Horwitz, S. M. (2006). Are infant-toddler social-emotional and behavioral problems transient? *Journal of the American Academy of Child & Adolescent Psychiatry, 45,* 849–858.

CDC/ICDL Collaboration Report. (2006). *Framework for early identification and preventive intervention of emotional and developmental challenges.* Centers for

Disease Control/Interdisciplinary Council on Developmental and Learning Disorders. (http://www.icdl.com/bookstore/catalog/documents/CDC-ICDLCollaborationReport.pdf, accessed December 4, 2009).

Council on Children With Disabilities. (2006). Identifying infants and young children with developmental disorders in the medical home: An algorithm for developmental surveillance and screening. *Pediatrics, 118*(1), 405–420.

First Signs (2009). *Screening: Making Observations* (http://www.firstsigns.org/screening/index.htm, accessed August 15, 2009).

Greenspan, S. I. (1999). *Building Healthy Minds: The Six Experiences that Create Intelligence and Emotional Growth in Babies and Young Children.* Cambridge, MA: Perseus Books.

Greenspan, S. I. (2004). *Greenspan Social-emotional Growth Chart: A Screening Questionnaire for Infants and Young Children.* San Antonio, TX: Harcourt Assessment.

Greenspan, S. I., & Wieder, S. (1998). *The Child with Special Needs. Encouraging Intellectual and Emotional Growth.* Reading, MA: Perseus Publishing.

Greenspan, S. I., & Wieder, S. (2008). *Engaging Autism: The Floortime Approach to Helping Children Relate, Communicate, and Think.* Reading, MA: DaCapo Press.

ICDL. (2000). *Clinical Practice Guidelines. Redefining the Standards of Care For Infants, Children, and Families with Special Needs.* Interdisciplinary Council on Developmental and Learning Disorders, Bethesda, Maryland.

Johnson, C. P., Myers, S. M., & Council on Children With Disabilities. (2007). Identification and evaluation of children with autism spectrum disorders. *Pediatrics, 120*(5), 1183–1215.

Lavigne, J. V., Binns, H. J., Christoffel, K. K., Rosenbaum, D., Arend, R., Smith, K., Hayford, J. R., & McGuire, P. A. (1993). Behavioral and emotional problems among preschool children in pediatric primary care: Prevalence and pediatricians' recognition. *Pediatrics, 91*, 649–655.

National Research Council and Institute of Medicine. (2000). Acquiring self-regulation. In J. Shonkoff, & D. Phillips (Eds.), *From Neurons to Neighborhoods: The Science of Early Childhood Development* (pp. 93–123). Washington, DC: National Academy Press.

NECTAC. (2008). *Developmental Screening and Assessment Instruments with an Emphasis on Social and Emotional Development for Young Children Ages Birth through Five.* Chapel Hill, NC: The National Early Childhood Technical Assistance Center (NECTAC).

Salvia, J., Ysseldyke, J. E., & Bolt, S. (2007). Assessment of infants, toddlers, and preschoolers. In S. Pulvermacher-Alt, J. Giannotti, & B. Greiner (Eds.), *Assessment in Special and Inclusive Education* (10th ed.). Boston, MA: Houghton Mifflin.

Schor, E. (2004). Rethinking well-child care. *Pediatrics, 114*(1), 210–216.

Shanker, S., & Greenspan, S. I. (2007). The developmental pathways to pattern recognition, joint attention, language and cognition. *New Ideas in Psychology, 25*(1).

The Bayley-III Adaptive Behavior Scale

Jennifer L. Harman[1] and
Tina M. Smith-Bonahue[2]

[1] *Yale University Child Study Center, New Haven, CT*
[2] *University of Florida, Gainesville, FL*

INTRODUCTION

The 1986 amendment to Public Law 99-457, the Education of Handicapped Children Act, and its subsequent iterations require assessments of infants and young children at risk for disabilities to be comprehensive, multidisciplinary, and focus on functional abilities. Therefore, understanding the adaptive skills present in early childhood is essential in any assessment of young children. Adaptive behavior encompasses the key functional developmental tasks accomplished during the first years of life. In many ways these tasks are critical to a child's survival, and include activities such as communicating basic needs, learning to feed oneself, crawling, walking, and toileting.

This chapter provides an overview of adaptive behavior in young children, and briefly discusses theory related to adaptive skills in infants, toddlers, and preschoolers. The content, administration, scoring, and interpretation of the Adaptive Behavior Scale of the Bayley-III are discussed, including its strengths and concerns regarding the use of this scale. Next, the use of the Adaptive Behavior Scale with clinical populations is discussed. A case study illustrates an evaluation of a 21-month-old child with the use of the Bayley-III.

ADAPTIVE BEHAVIOR IN YOUNG CHILDREN

A child's adaptive behavior encompasses the ability to manage the demands of the environment and the ability to meet daily needs. These behaviors change significantly as young children develop in form, intensity, sophistication, and precision. Their adaptive skills are tied inextricably to other developmental domains and abilities. The growth and development of young children leads to advancements in various skills, including communication, social, motor, health and safety, home living, self-care, leisure, community use, functional preacademics, leisure, and self-direction.

For example, newborns rely on reflexes (e.g., crying, rooting, sucking) to inform their parents they need to eat. Although older babies may continue to cry, they add new learned behaviors, such as pointing or whining for desired food items. The emergence of language enables toddlers to point to an object or say "eat" to inform their caregivers they are hungry. They no longer have to rely on crying as their primary means of communication. As language continues to develop, toddlers become increasingly explicit about expressing their eating and other preferences.

As their motor skills develop, toddlers increasingly are able to obtain food for themselves – a hallmark of adaptive skills. An infant's motor functions progressively become more complex until they are able to "toddle" around. For example, infants first learn to roll over. They then may be able to roll to desired objects. Later, they learn to crawl to get to desired locations. Eventually, they pull themselves up and begin to cruise along furniture. Before too long infants are able to walk on their own and, later, to run, jump, and skip. Likewise, toddlers and preschoolers learn self-care skills such as washing their hands and brushing their teeth. These adaptive skills were not in their repertoire as infants.

Similarly, as young children develop, so do their adaptive leisure skills. For example, an infant may progress from being able to play with a single toy or game for less than a minute to being able to do so for several minutes. They may progress from looking at pictures in a book or magazine to asking to be read to from a favorite book. Likewise, their self-direction skills steadily increase. For example, an infant may progress from being able to sit quietly without demanding attention for only a short time (e.g., 1 minute) to being able to do so for longer time periods (e.g., more than 5 minutes). Children also progress from being able to move only a few feet away from a parent when in a new situation, to wanting to work independently and asking for help only when needed.

Attachment theory as well as synactive theory of development are well-known theories of early development. They contribute to our understanding of adaptive skill development during the early childhood years. Each of these theories is described in the following paragraphs.

Attachment Theory

In the context of attachment theory, the word "attachment" describes the natural tendency for a child to bond with caregivers or a few special adults (Bowlby, 1958; Grossman & Grossman, 2005). "Attachments are the natural pre-requisite for becoming emotionally and socially acculturated" (Grossman & Grossman, 2005: 10). Thus, attachment theory underscores the paramount importance of social acculturation for survival and adaptation. Social acculturation utilizes social adaptive skills. For example, social acculturation requires an individual first to be able to interact socially with others and later to be responsive to the needs of others – again, a hallmark of adaptive skills. Each of these is a quintessential component of social adaptive behavior development.

Additional adaptive functions also are served by the instinct to form an attachment with one's caregiver. The formation of attachment, when examined from an evolutionary perspective, highlights its role as essential to help ensure newborns have access to emotional, social, and physical resources needed for survival. Therefore, the skills required to form attachments should be considered among the most important early adaptive skills infants must possess. Forming and maintaining secure attachments helps children obtain necessary survival resources and thus foster both their mental and physical health (Grossman & Grossman, 2005).

Therapists, clinicians, developmentalists, pediatricians, psychologists, and other professionals often focus on the importance of directly observable abilities and behaviors of an infant, toddler, or preschooler when assessing adaptive skills. Using attachment theory as a framework, the following three questions may be addressed during the observable assessment of adaptive behaviors in young children:

1. How successful are young children at establishing attachment(s) to caregiver(s)?
2. How successful are young children at maintaining attachment(s)?
3. What primary role does a young child play in the formation of attachments?

In other words, what does the child do to foster the formation and maintenance of the attachment?

Most children begin life with several instinctual drives that assist in the initiation, development, and maintenance of attachment(s). For example, normal healthy newborns are able to suck, cling, cry, and smile. The expression of each of these behaviors helps in the formation and maintenance of attachment (Bowlby, 1958). For example, infants may become calm when in their mothers' arms, or may cry when their mother leaves the room. Likewise, infants smile when approached by important caregivers, thus helping promote a secure attachment with them – again, qualities essential to an infant's survival (Bowlby, 1958). The Adaptive Behavior Scale of the Bayley-III asks parents to rate how often their infant or toddler displays a special closeness or relationship to a parent, and runs to greet special family members and friends, and how their child responds differently to familiar and unfamiliar people. Each of these items assesses the young child's adaptive behaviors related to critical aspects of attachment with special adults in the child's life.

Synactive Theory of Development

The synactive theory of development, like attachment theory, assumes that instinctive abilities must be present at birth for early adaptive functioning to flourish. However, whereas attachment theory focuses primarily on an infant's social pattern, the synactive theory of development focuses primarily on infants' developmental capacity to respond to their environment (Als, 1982). Thus, an infant's primary responsibility is to adapt to life outside the womb and to develop neurobehavioral competence. Specifically, the newborn is charged with gaining control over his or her physiological system, including breathing, heart rate, and temperature control. Next, the newborn must establish organization and differentiation of his or her motor system. Newborns learn to affect the range, smoothness, and complexity of their movements (Brazleton, 2000; Robertson, Bacher, & Huntington, 2001). Newborns also attain organization and later control of their states of consciousness, including deep sleep, light sleep, indeterminate drowsy, wide-awake alert, fussy alert, and crying. Infants achieve control over the transitions between states of consciousness as they develop their adaptive skills.

Within the synactive theory of development, an infants' neurobehavioral competencies and organization (e.g., sleep–wake cycles, crying, attention, self-regulation) are understood through the following five subsystems that guide an infant's interaction with his or her environment: the autonomic system, the motor system, the state-organizational system, the attention and interaction system, and a self-regulatory balancing system that integrates and organizes the other subsystems. According to this theory, these subsystems interact with one another during each stage of development. The purpose of the self-regulatory subsystem is to synthesize the actions of the other four subsystems.

Autonomic System

The autonomic system includes the regulation of bodily functions. The adaptive behaviors related to the autonomic system (e.g., cardiopulmonary activity, bowel movements, blood flow, etc.) are assessed typically by pediatric specialists, and are not addressed in the Adaptive Behavior Scale of the Bayley-III. The autonomic system is the most basic of the systems described by the synactive theory. Infants who fail to attain control of it tend to remain dependent on medical equipment (e.g., respirators). Therefore, assessment of the autonomic system is specialized, and is addressed by measures such as the APGAR at birth and the Neonatal Behavioral Assessment Scale (Brazelton, 1973). The reader is directed to Chapter 7 of this book for more information on the autonomic system as described by the synactive theory of development (see also Als, 1982, and Brazleton, 1990a).

Motor System

The motor system includes posture, movement abilities, and muscle tone (Als, 1982). Items on the Adaptive Behavior Scale of the Bayley-III that are related to this subsystem assess an infant's movement and posture abilities. For example, items progress from an infant's ability to follow a moving object by moving his or her head, to lifting the head to look around, and rolling over, through the ability to manipulate materials such as shaking toys, reaching for objects, and ultimately using objects as tools.

Similarly, infants' gross motor skills progress from gaining basic trunk and head control, moving to and maintaining a sitting position, standing with and without support, and progressing through a series of complex gross motor activities required to accomplish other functional tasks (e.g., squatting to lift a desired object, balancing and then hopping on one foot, running, and skipping). The synactive theory underscores the importance of assessing motor abilities when examining the adaptive behavior of young children, as these motor abilities enable young children to achieve other important functional and social tasks. One strength of the Adaptive Behavior Scale of the Bayley-III is its attention to the assessment of the adaptive behaviors supported by the motor system.

State-organizational System

The synactive theory of development describes the state-organizational system as one that addresses the ability to cycle between quiet sleep, active sleep, active–quiet transitional sleep, sleep–wake transition, and wakefulness – including crying. One of an infant's the most important tasks is "learning to control alert states and maintain habituated states in sleep" (Brazleton, 1990a: 1662). A primary role of an infant's caretaker (s) is to help the infant obtain and maintain the skills necessary to adapt to sleep schedules that meet both the infant's and the family's needs (Brazleton, 1990a, 2000). Therefore, estimating the state control and effective sleep states of the newborn is an essential goal of an assessment of the neonate (Thoman & McDowell, 1989; Brazleton, 1990a, 2000). Accordingly, the Adaptive Behavior Scale of the Bayley-III asks caregivers how often infants and toddlers sleep through most of the night. Although the Adaptive Behavior Scale of the Bayley-III does attend to the state-organizational system, it is important to note that detailed information regarding a young child's progression through various stages is not obtained through the use of this scale.

Attention and Interaction System

An infant's ability to attain and maintain an alert and attentive state is addressed by the attention and interaction system, as described by the synactive theory of development. Specifically, differentiation, or the shifting and internal organization to the attentional-interactive system, is a primary developmental task of neonates. Newborns must rely on the assistance of primary caregivers when working toward this adaptive skill, again highlighting the importance of attachment in acquiring adaptive skills (Als, 1982; Als, Butler, Kosta, & McAnulty, 2005). The attentional-interactive system also addresses the adaptive functions of crying. Shortly after birth, the adaptive purposes of cries often are apparent – for example, infants commonly cry when hungry or uncomfortable. These cries inform the infant's primary caretaker that the infant is in need of something (Brazleton, 1990b). The presence of crying to communicate physiological needs is an adaptive skill. Therefore, the Adaptive Behavior Scale of the Bayley-III asks caregivers if infants are able to raise and lower voices to express different feelings and to cry to communicate. Again, although the Adaptive Behavior Scale of the Bayley-III adequately addresses this system, detailed information regarding this system is not rendered only through the use of this tool.

Self-regulatory System

The self-regulatory system is synonymous to a conductor of a symphony. Each of the systems described thus far is easily able to be described independently. However, it is the process of each of the four systems described previously (i.e., autonomic, motor, state-organizational, and attention and interaction systems) interacting with one another, as well as with the infant's environment, that the synactive theory of development eloquently describes. The job of the fifth system, the self-regulatory system, is to ensure that the previous four systems are interacting with one another (Als, 1982; Als *et al.*, 2005). Self-regulation is described further in Chapter 5 of this book.

THE ADAPTIVE BEHAVIOR SCALE

The assessment of adaptive behavior is necessary when evaluating young children, especially if a child is suspected of having a developmental delay. An assessment of adaptive behavior development differs from many other assessments of developmental abilities, in part, because the examiner needs to know what a child typically does, not what a child is capable of doing. Thus, third-party informants, usually a caretaker of the young child, are utilized when assessing adaptive behavior. Individuals who spend multiple hours a day with children are the best informants to utilize when assessing a child's adaptive skills. These individuals are often well-informed respondents about the child's typical behaviors in various settings. Information from two or more respondents may be acquired. For example, information from a daycare provider who is responsible for a child during weekdays may be useful to supplement information from a parent who is unable to be with the child during the day while working.

The Bayley-III utilizes the Parent/Primary Caregiver Form of the *Adaptive Behavior Assessment Scale – Second Edition* (ABAS-II; Harrison & Oakland, 2003) as its Adaptive Behavior Scale. Thus, the items included on the Parent/Primary Caregiver Form of the ABAS-II are identical to those included on the Adaptive Behavior Scale of the Bayley-III.

Adaptive Behavior Assessment Scale – Second Edition (ABAS-II) and the Adaptive Behavior Scale

The ABAS-II measures the adaptive behavior of individuals from birth through age 89. Five forms are provided: Parent/ Primary Caregiver Form (for ages 0–5), Teacher/Day Care Provider Form (for ages 2–5), Parent Form (for ages 5–21), Teacher Form (for ages 5–21), and an Adult Form (for ages 16–89). Its standardization sample is congruent with the 1999–2000 United States census data in reference to gender, race/ethnicity, parental education, and proportion of individuals with disabilities.

The ABAS-II, and thus the Adaptive Behavior Scale of the Bayley-III, is consistent with models advocated by the American Association on Intellectual and Developmental Disabilities (AAIDD, 1992, 2002). Ten skill area scores combine to produce standard scores in three broader domains: (1) conceptual (communication, functional academics, and self-direction skills); (2) social (social and leisure skills); and (3) practical (self-care, home or school living, community use, health and safety). Motor skills are also assessed; however, they do not contribute to any of the three domains. A general adaptive composite also is derived from the skill scores.

As previously mentioned, the Adaptive Behavior Scale of the Bayley-III is derived from items for children, ages birth through 5, on the ABAS-II. The Bayley-III manual notes this scale is based on (1) a concept of adaptive behavior promoted by the American Association on Intellectual and Developmental Disabilities; (2) legal and professional standards applicable to disability classifications, special education classifications, the *Diagnostic and Statistical Manual of Mental Disorders – Fourth Edition, Text Revision*, and federal (i.e., the *Individuals with Disabilities Education Act*) and state special education regulations; and (3) diagnostic, classification, and intervention research conducted to investigate the skills of people with various disabilities (Bayley, 2006).

Purposes

The functional skills necessary for young children to become increasingly more independent are evaluated using parents' and/or caregivers' reports of observable behaviors on the Adaptive Behavior Scale of the Bayley-III. Respondents are asked to base their ratings of the child's adaptive behavior based on their previous observations of the child. Respondents report whether a child is not able to display the desired behavior, is able to perform it but never or almost never performs it, performs it sometimes when needed, or performs it almost always when needed. To receive credit, all behaviors must be performed without assistance from others. Caregivers' thoughts on what a child may be able to do if provided with the appropriate opportunity may be elicited, yet are not considered when scoring the Adaptive Behavior Scale (Bayley, 2006).

Definition of Adaptive Behavior

The AAIDD states that adaptive behavior is "the collection of conceptual, social, and practical skills that have been learned by people in order to function in their everyday lives" (AAIDD, 2002: 41). The ABAS-II and the Adaptive Behavior Scale of the Bayley-III define the adaptive skills measured as practical, social, and conceptual skills necessary for children to be able to function and meet environmental demands (Harrison & Oakland, 2003).

Content

The Adaptive Behavior Composite of the Bayley-III is comprised of 241 items. When assessing infants from birth through 11 months, the following skill areas are addressed: communication (e.g., speech, non-verbal communication, and listening), health and safety (e.g., skills related to being cautious and keeping out of physical danger), leisure (e.g., skills related to playing, engaging in games at home, and following rules), self-care (e.g., eating, toileting, cleaning self, and bathing), self-direction (e.g., making independent choices, following directions, and utilizing self-control), social (e.g., getting along with others, using manners, assisting others, and recognizing emotions), and motor (e.g., moving, and manipulating of the environment). Adaptive behaviors related to an infant's autonomic system are not addressed by the Adaptive Behavior Scale of the Bayley-III. As previously mentioned, pediatric specialists commonly are responsible for assessing these adaptive skills, and the reader again is referred to information on the Bayley Infant Neurodevelopmental Screener in Chapter 7 of this book.

For toddlers and preschoolers ages 12 through 42 months, the seven above-mentioned skill areas are addressed as well as the following: functional pre-academics (e.g., letter recognition, counting, and drawing shapes), community use (e.g., interest in activities outside the home and recognition of different facilities), and home living (e.g. helping adults with household tasks and taking care of personal possessions).

Regardless of the age of the young child being assessed, data from each assessed skill area (i.e., the seven areas for children under the age of 11 months, and the ten areas for children 12 through 42 months) are used to compute the Adaptive Behavior Scale composite, which is the total score for this scale. Scores for three domains (i.e., conceptual, practical, and social) and for each of the seven or ten skill areas assessed also are able to be obtained. Skill areas comprising each of the three adaptive domains are outlined in Table 6.1.

TABLE 6.1   Skill Areas Comprising Adaptive Domains for the Adaptive Behavior Composite

Adaptive domain	Birth–11 months	1–3.5 years
Conceptual	Communication	Communication
	Self-direction	Functional pre-academics
		Self-direction
Social	Leisure	Leisure
	Social	Social
Practical		Self-care
		Home living
		Health & safety
		Community use

Adapted from Harrison & Oakland (2003).

Administration

The Adaptive Behavior Scale should be completed by the child's primary caregiver in a setting free from distractions. The examiner should introduce the scale, inform the respondent of what it measures, why this information is important, and how it may be used. A questionnaire and pencil should be provided to the primary caregiver. The caregiver should be informed how to complete the questionnaire by reading and discussing the instructions. The caregiver is instructed to read and respond to all items within required item sets, and rate the adaptive skills of his or her child. Caregivers are told they should rate the extent to which their child performs the adaptive skill when needed. Ratings include the following options: 0 = not able to do it, 1 = able yet never does it when needed, 2 = does it sometimes when needed, and 3 = does it always or almost always when needed. Additionally, caregivers are allowed to guess if they are unsure whether a behavior has been displayed. They check a box next to the item indicating the response was a guess. The examiner and respondent should discuss guessed items in an attempt to assign a number to these items (Bayley, 2006).

The Adaptive Behavior Scale also allows for the examiner to read items to respondents. In doing this, the examiner first completes the required demographic information. The following is stated: "I will read the items to you. For each item, select one of the following ratings and tell me your rating. I will circle your rating in the questionnaire. If your answer is based on a guess, tell me you guessed." Next, the examiner is asked to provide an extra questionnaire to the caregiver for him or her to follow along. Finally, each item is read verbatim, and the caregiver is asked to tell the examiner (or point to) the rating chosen (Bayley, 2006).

Scoring and Interpretation

After the Adaptive Behavior Scale of the Bayley-III has been completed by a caregiver, or by the examiner and the caregiver together, the examiner adds the raw scores to obtain a total raw score for each skill area. The examiner then determines the number of items were checked as "guess". As noted previously, the behaviors reflected in the guessed items should be discussed, with the goal being to remove the guess and assign a number to these items. If, after these efforts, the total number of guessed responses for any skill area is four or more, the examiner decides whether to score the area. A high number of guesses suggests the need for information from additional respondents. An examiner is urged to report the higher-than-average guessed responses if he or she continues to score the area. Next, the examiner either derives scores by entering the total scores for each skill area into a computer scoring program, or consults tables found in the appendix of the *Bayley-III Administration Manual*. Both norm-referenced scaled scores for skill areas (mean = 10, standard deviation = 3) and standard scores for the three domains and the composite (mean = 100, standard deviation = 15) then are obtained. If the computer option is utilized, a graph of the data is provided. Specifically, the computer scoring program provides information on the development of all skill areas and compares their development. This allows the examiner to identify a child's clinically and statistically significant strengths and weaknesses easily – information that should be utilized when presenting the results (Bayley, 2006).

Psychometric Properties

Internal consistency

The reliability of the Adaptive Behavior Scale is obtained by utilizing data on the ABAS-II's internal consistency (Bayley, 2006). Ten age-groups of children were used to obtain the internal consistency of the Adaptive Behavior Scale of the Bayley-III: 0–3 months, 4–7 months, 8–11 months, 12–15 months, 16–19 months, 20–23 months, 24–29 months, 30–35 months, 36–41 months, and 42–47 months. Internal consistency estimates ranged from 0.86 to 0.98 for the Composite score, from 0.90 to 0.92 for the three adaptive domains, and 0.79 to 0.92 for the skill areas (Bayley, 2006).

Test–retest Reliability

Two hundred and seven parents of young children were asked to complete the ABAS-II on two different days 2–5 weeks apart in order to determine the test–retest reliability. The test–retest reliability for the composite score ranged from 0.86 to 0.92 for the following three age groups: birth to 11 months, 12–23 months, and 24–35 months. The vast majority of test–retest reliabilities were above 0.80 for the three adaptive domains and above 0.70 for each skill area.

Content Validity

The theory and constructs of the ABAS-II (and consequently those items used for the Bayley-III Adaptive Behavior Scale) rely heavily on the AAIDD's definition of adaptive behavior; legal and professional standards regarding disability classification; the *Diagnostic and Statistical Manual of Mental Disorders – Fourth Edition, Text Revision*: the Individuals with Disabilities Act; and intervention research. Readers are encouraged to see Harrison and Oakland (2003, 2008) and Ditterline, Banner, Oakland, and Becton (2008) for a more complete discussion of the test's reliability and validity.

CASE STUDY: ROCHELLE

Rochelle, a 26-month-old toddler, was referred for a developmental evaluation by her parents, Marguerite and Javier Ramirez. Mr and Mrs Ramirez were concerned about the possible neurotoxic effects of Rochelle's lead exposure. The parents also reported concerns regarding Rochelle's gross motor skills. The evaluation was sought for a baseline measure of functioning; to better understand Rochelle's needs, strengths, and weaknesses; and to obtain appropriate recommendations for interventions.

Background Information

Mrs Ramirez provided the following information on Rochelle. She is the biological child of Marguerite and Javier Ramirez. She resides with her mother, father, and 4-year-old sister, Marissa, in a downtown area of working-class homes in a large northeastern city. The family's apartment is one of four, all part of a large house built in the 1920s and divided into apartments in the late 1960s. Mr Ramirez is a custodian in a downtown apartment building. Mrs Ramirez works part time, in the late afternoon after Mr Ramirez returns from work, in a neighborhood convenience store. Marissa attends Head Start for half a day; Rochelle is cared for only by her parents and her maternal grandparents, who live nearby.

PREGNANCY AND BIRTH

Mrs Ramirez reported her planned pregnancy with Rochelle was unremarkable. Rochelle was born full-term with no peri- or postnatal complications, and weighed 7 pounds, 3 ounces. Rochelle went home with Mrs Ramirez after an overnight stay in the hospital.

DEVELOPMENTAL HISTORY

As an infant, Rochelle was easy going and displayed no sleeping or eating problems. Rochelle was breast-fed until approximately 14 or 15 months of age.

Rochelle's development was typical until approximately 11 months of age. Specifically, Rochelle smiled by 2 months, responded to her name by 4 months, and sat unsupported by around 6 months of age. Rochelle had more than 50 words by the time she was 15 months old, and was also speaking in short phrases by 15 months. At the time of this evaluation, Rochelle was not toilet trained; however, Mrs Ramirez reported they have begun to speak about toilet training with Rochelle.

Around 11 months of age, Rochelle's development began to slow. Specifically, Mrs Ramirez noted concerns with Rochelle's motor development. Rochelle did not walk by herself until she was 16 months old, and continues to walk with an awkward gait. At age 2, Rochelle began to try to run. However, Rochelle's running was described as "looking funny, like she's about to fall." Mrs Ramirez attributes this lag in Rochelle's development to lead poisoning.

In terms of temperament and behavior, Rochelle is described as a loving child with family, and somewhat unfriendly and slow to warm up with unfamiliar adults. Rochelle cries easily, experiences mood swings, and can get very angry. Rochelle may display anger more often and easier than others her age. Although she is interested in other children and engages in parallel play when around them, she often gets very upset when they try to take her toys. For example, Rochelle commonly yells or cries when another child tries to take something of hers. Rochelle also will scream at her parents when she dislikes what they are telling her or when they ask her not to yell.

MEDICAL HISTORY

Rochelle was diagnosed with lead poisoning 6 months ago as the result of routine screening during a pediatric well-child check-up. The source of her lead exposure is unknown, but suspected to be a result of lead-based paint in the Ramirez's apartment. At the time of her diagnosis, her lead level was 20 µg/dl with a ZPP of 79. Rochelle's mother hypothesizes that the lead poisoning actually began when Rochelle was approximately 11 months of age. At this point, her appetite drastically decreased, and she started to drop below normal growth rates on the growth-chart. Rochelle dropped from right below the 50th percentile to the 8th percentile in a matter of months. Rochelle's appetite returned recently.

Prior to being diagnosed with lead poisoning, Rochelle had an ear infection which led to a perforation. Other than this incident and her lead poisoning, no documented medical problems have occurred.

Tests Administered

Bayley Scales of Infant and Toddler Development, Third Edition (Bayley-III).

Clinical Observation of Behavior

Rochelle presented as a sweet child who initially clung to her mother and eventually established rapport with the examiner. However, she was quite distractible, very active, and demonstrated a low frustration tolerance. Specifically, if she was unable to do something on the first attempt, Rochelle commonly asked her mom for help, or would say "can't do it." Moreover, Rochelle displayed some opposition to following directions from adults, including examiner requests. Her play and interactions with materials were much more self-directed, and she showed little desire to engage in some of the activities presented to her.

Despite these difficulties, Rochelle appeared at ease with the examiner and the testing situation. Moreover, Rochelle appeared to enjoy playing with the examiner and the testing materials. Each of Rochelle's parents were competent and nurturing in their interactions with Rochelle. Both her mother and her father encouraged Rochelle to continue trying when items were difficult, telling her what a good job she was doing when she was appropriately following the lead of the examiner.

The Bayley-III was administered over three 1-hour sessions, as Rochelle's behavior and distractibility warranted frequent breaks and opportunities for self-directed play to complete the tasks. The administration was not rushed, allowing Rochelle to engage in self-directed activities throughout the course of the evaluation. Thus, the results of this assessment are thought to demonstrate a valid report of Rochelle's developmental capabilities and difficulties.

Evaluation Results

DEVELOPMENTAL ASSESSMENT

The Bayley Scales of Infant and Toddler Development, Third Edition (Bayley-III), is an individually administered instrument whose primary purposes are to identify children with developmental delay and to provide information for intervention planning. The Bayley-III assesses infant and toddler development across five domains: Cognitive, Language (Receptive & Expressive), Motor (Gross & Fine), Social-Emotional and Adaptive. Assessment of the former three scales is conducted using items administered to the child. Assessment of the latter two scales relies on primary caregiver responses to a questionnaire. The results from this scale are summarized in Table 6.2.

The Cognitive Scale includes items that assess sensorimotor development, exploration and manipulation, object relatedness, concept formation, memory and other aspects of cognitive processing. Rochelle's cognitive abilities as measured by the Bayley-III are in the average range (Cognitive standard score = 95; 37th percentile) and consistent with a child her age.

TABLE 6.2   Bayley-III Data for Rochelle Case Study

Domain	Composite score (mean = 100, SD = 15)	Scaled score (mean = 10, SD = 3)	Percentile rank
Language	129		97
Receptive Language		15	
Expressive Language		15	
Motor	88		21
Fine Motor		10	
Gross Motor		6	
Social-Emotional	105	11	63
Adaptive Behavior	60		0.4
Communication		4	
Community Use		5	
Functional Pre-Academics		7	
Home Living		5	
Health & Safety		4	
Leisure		4	
Self-Care		3	
Self-Direction		5	
Social		4	
Motor		6	

Rochelle had difficulty when asked to complete timed items. Specifically, Rochelle was more interested in exploring objects and self-directing her interactions with the objects than following the examiner's lead. Rochelle may be able to display behaviors assessed by some of the items for which she did not get credit; however, she was unable to receive credit for these items because she was unable to demonstrate this capacity during the standardized administration of items. Conversely, Rochelle was able to engage in game-like, problem-solving items with ease. For example, she was easily able to find hidden objects and correctly place shapes on a form-board. Rochelle also used representational play with ease. She pretended to mix up food and feed it to a teddy bear, then she fed herself and placed the bear down for a nap and covered it.

The Language Scale is composed of receptive and expression communication items that form two distinct subtests. Rochelle's overall language composite score on the Bayley-III was the same as or better than 97 percent of her same-age peers (Language standard score = 129, 97th percentile).

The Receptive Communication subtest of the Bayley-III includes items that assess preverbal behaviors; vocabulary development related to objects and pictures, social referencing, and verbal comprehension. Rochelle's receptive communication skills as measured by the Bayley-III are in the superior range, and above what is expected for a child her age (Receptive Communication scaled score = 15). Rochelle was able to point to various actions, including waving, sleeping, eating, drinking, reading, and riding. Additionally, Rochelle demonstrated an understanding of possessives when she was able to identify a boy's car and a cat's ball. However, she experienced more difficulty discriminating between the possessive pronouns his, hers, him, me, my, you, and your.

The Expressive Communication subtest includes items that assess preverbal communication such as babbling, gesturing, joint referencing, and turn taking, and vocabulary development such as naming objects and pictures. Rochelle's expressive communication skills as measured by the Bayley-III also are superior and above what is expected for a child her age (Expressive Communication scaled score = 15). She utilizes multiple word questions and uses different word combinations when expressing her needs, wants, and ideas. However, Rochelle experiences more difficulty responding verbally to questions that begin with "what" and "where," using plurals, and naming colors.

Rochelle's overall motor skill development as assessed by the Motor Scale of the Bayley-III is at the low end of the average range (Motor standard score = 88, 21st percentile). The Motor Scale of the Bayley-III is divided into a Fine Motor and a Gross Motor subtest. Rochelle's use of small muscle groups (i.e., her fine motor ability) was significantly better developed than her use of larger muscle groups (i.e., her gross motor ability).

When interviewed about Rochelle's adaptive motor skills, Mr Ramirez also reported Rochelle has more difficulty with gross motor skills than fine motor skills. Specifically, Rochelle's fine motor skills are average (Fine Motor scaled score = 10) and consistent with those expected of a child her age. She held a pencil and a crayon in a transitional grasp and made purposeful markings on paper. However, she did not use her hand to hold the paper in place. Rochelle also was unable to imitate strokes in various directions.

Rochelle experienced the most difficulty when asked to engage in gross motor activities (Gross Motor scaled score = 6). She was able to walk up stairs with support using both feet on each step; however, she was unable to walk down stairs the same way. Rochelle also was unable to balance on either foot, walk sideways, or kick a ball.

The adaptive behavior scale assesses daily functional skills. The areas measured include communication, community use, health & safety, leisure, self-care, self-direction, home living, and social and motor. The General Adaptive Composite (GAC) provides a general estimate of adaptive development. Mrs Ramirez was the respondent for this scale. Mrs Ramirez's responses on the adaptive scale suggest Rochelle demonstrates significant adaptive behavior delays. With few exceptions, Rochelle's development in all skill areas are low and indicative of delays. Within functional communication, although Rochelle has many words in her repertoire, she often does not use them to obtain what she wants. Instead, Rochelle will scream until her mother or father figures out what she wants. Additionally, although Rochelle is capable of following a two-step direction as evidenced by performance during the testing, Rochelle rarely follows simple commands at home. In regards to home living, Rochelle will assist others while putting away toys and will occasionally pick up and throw away her trash. She does not run simple errands (e.g., get a towel for a spill), and does not refrain from kicking or hitting the furniture.

In the area of health & safety, Rochelle only sometimes follows an adult direction to "stop" when in danger. She does not avoid getting too near the stove, and does not test hot food before eating it. Rochelle does not look at pictures in books with an adult, and is not consistent in her ability to find something to do for 5 minutes without demanding attention. She also does not typically obey an adult request to "quiet down" or "behave." Additionally, Rochelle does not share toys willingly or when told to do so. However, she does consistently respond differently to familiar and unfamiliar people.

The Social-Emotional Scale assesses acquisition of social and emotional milestones. Items assess mastery of functional emotional skills, such as self-regulation and interest in the world; communicating needs; engaging others and establishing relationships; using emotions in a purposeful manner; and using emotional signals to solve problems. Additionally, her overall social-emotional functioning, as assessed by caregiver report on the Bayley-III, is in the average range. This finding is somewhat inconsistent with direct behavioral observations and information collected during the initial parent interview. Although Rochelle has a very close relationship with her parents, she also demonstrated difficulty following the lead of adults. Moreover, Rochelle displays difficulty self-soothing when she does not get her way.

Summary and Case Discussion

Rochelle was referred for evaluation by her parents after learning of her toxic lead level. She received a developmental evaluation that included administration of the Bayley-III. Results indicate her cognitive abilities are average and her language abilities are superior. Rochelle demonstrated very strong receptive and expressive language abilities. Rochelle's fine motor skills are consistent with those expected for her age; however, her gross motor skills are slightly below those expected for her age. In contrast, her adaptive behaviors are significantly delayed. Moreover, Rochelle's mother reported her behavior is difficult to manage at times. This is consistent with the parent report of Rochelle's difficulty interacting with others, playing, and following the direction of others. Rochelle also presented with a low frustration tolerance, which could result in the presentation of difficult behaviors. To some degree, these are developmentally normal characteristics of toddlers of Rochelle's age; she is entering the stage commonly referred to as "the terrible twos." Thus, her parents may benefit from implementing interventions that target and help manage these challenging behaviors, such as Parent–Child Interaction. Additionally, early intervention services that focus on improving Rochelle's adaptive functioning are essential.

Reflections on Rochelle's Assessment

Rochelle's developmental delays demonstrate the power the physical environment may have on disrupting the development of the most basic functional skills in young children. Rochelle's cognitive and language skills are intact, and some are above average. However, her motor ability and emotional development are slightly delayed. Her daily adaptive functioning is significantly impaired. As a result, Rochelle is in need of intensive early intervention services to address her daily living skills.

The Adaptive Behavior Scale is quite useful with various populations, as it provides information on what the child typically does, not what he or she is capable of doing. This information, when used alone or in conjunction with other direct measures of behavior, proves useful when identifying where to target intervention efforts. For example, as demonstrated in the case study above, a child may have well-developed expressive and receptive language skills when assessed using direct measures of each of these constructs; however, her use of functional communication skills may be inadequate. In the example above, Rochelle had an extremely low frustration tolerance. Additionally, although she had many words in her repertoire, and she was able to form short sentences and speak quite comprehensibly, she rarely used these skills when trying to communicate her needs. Instead, she reverted to infantile behaviors and screamed until her parents discovered, sometimes by pure luck, what she wanted. An intervention aimed at teaching her new words likely would not lessen the screaming, nor would it increase her use of functional communication skills. Instead, a behavioral approach where instances of appropriate functional communication were attended to and instances of screaming to get her needs met were ignored might be tried. Additionally, given Rochelle's average cognitive abilities and superior receptive language skills, her parents should continue to strive to explain to her why they are not responding to her screaming and how she could better get her needs met using the skills she has in her repertoire (i.e., asking for things she needs instead of screaming).

Without information on Rochelle's daily use of adaptive behaviors, she likely would not qualify for intervention services. However, as illustrated previously, this child and her family are in grave need of interventions to improve her adaptive behavior. Differences often exist between what a child can do under optimal conditions, what a child does do when directly assessed, and what a child typically does on a day to day basis. Therefore, parents and caregivers should be invited to be active members in any developmental assessment of young children. Caregivers' input regarding the typicality of a child's responses, typicality of certain behaviors, and the capacity to perform other behaviors is imperative to any developmental evaluation.

References

Als, H. (1982). Toward a synactive theory of development: Promise for the assessment and support of infant individuality. *Infant Mental Health Journal, 3*(4), 229–243.

Als, H., Butler, S., Kosta, S., & McAnulty, G. (2005). The assessment of preterm infants' behavior (APIB): Furthering the understanding and measurement of neurodevelopmental competence in preterm and full-term infants. *Mental Retardation and Developmental Disabilities, 11*, 94–102.

American Association on Intellectual and Developmental Disability. (1992). *Mental Retardation: Definitions, Classifications, and Systems of Supports* (9th ed.). Washington, DC: Author.

American Association on Intellectual and Developmental Disability. (2002). *Mental Retardation: Definition, Classification, and Systems of Support* (10th ed.). Washington, DC: Author.

Bayley, N. (2006). *Bayley Scales of Infant and Toddler Development* (3rd ed.). Technical Manual. San Antonio, TX: Harcourt Assessment Inc.

Bowlby, J. (1958). The nature of the child's tie to his mother. *International Journal of Psychoanalysis, 39*, 350–373.

Brazelton, T. (1973). *Neonatal Behavioral Assessment Scale*. Philadelphia, PA: Lippincott.

Brazelton, T. B. (1990a). Saving the bathwater. *Child Development, 61*, 1661–1671.

Brazelton, T. B. (1990b). Crying and colic. *Infant Mental Health Journal, 11*(4), 349–356.

Brazleton, T. B. (2000). In response to Louis Sander's challenging paper. *Infant Mental Health Journal, 21*(1–2), 52–62.

Ditterline, J., Banner, D., Oakland, T., & Becton, D. (2008). Adaptive behavior profiles of students with disabilities. *Journal of Applied School Psychology, 24* (2), 191–208.

Grossman, K. E., & Grossman, K. (2005). *Universality of Human Social Attachment as an Adaptive Process.* Regensburg, Germany: Institut für Psychologie, Universität Regensburg.

Harrison, P., & Oakland, T. (2003). *Adaptive Behavior Assessment System* (2nd ed.). San Antonio, TX: Harcourt Assessment.

Harrison, P., & Oakland, T. (2008). *ABAS-II Interpretative Report.* San Antonio, TX: Harcourt Assessment.

Robertson, S. S., Bacher, L. F., & Huntington, N. L. (2001). The integration of body movement and attention in young infants. *Psychological Sciences, 12*(6), 523–526.

Thoman, E. B., & McDowell, K. (1989). Sleep cyclicity in infants during the earliest postnatal weeks. *Physiology and Behavior, 45*(3), 517–522.

7

The Bayley Infant Neurodevelopmental Screener (BINS):
Different Test and Different Purpose

Glen P. Aylward

Division of Developmental–Behavioral Pediatrics/Psychology,
Southern Illinois University School of Medicine, Springfield, IL

BACKGROUND

The Bayley Infant Neurodevelopmental Screener (BINS; Aylward, 1995) is a developmental screening instrument applicable for ages 3–24 months. The BINS was developed contemporaneously with the Bayley Scales of Infant Development – Second Edition (BSID-II; Bayley, 1993), and incorporated some similar items and test materials. However, the BINS is distinct and is not a "mini-Bayley." Rather, it is a screening tool used to identify infants who are at risk for neurodevelopmental problems and who require further more detailed evaluation with an instrument such as the Bayley Scales of Infant and Toddler Development – Third Edition (Bayley-III; Bayley, 2006). The BINS evolved as the product of two converging influences: infant and early childhood neuropsychology, and the increasing emphasis on the need for developmental screening and assessment. The importance of screening and assessment has been underscored recently by the American Academy of Pediatrics (2006). These influences will be discussed subsequently.

Setting the Stage I: Infant and Early Childhood Neuropsychology

Infant and early childhood neuropsychology (Aylward, 1997a, 2009a) is a multidisciplinary hybrid, drawing from the fields of pediatric, clinical child and developmental psychology; child neurology; developmental/behavioral pediatrics; and occupational therapy/physical therapy. The terms *neuropsychological*, *neurodevelopmental*, and *neurobehavioral* often are used interchangeably in the infant and early childhood age range because all involve brain–behavior relationships and combine neurological and developmental approaches (Aylward, 1997a, 2010).

Twenty years ago, neuropsychological assessment of infants and young children was considered a fledgling area (Aylward, 1988, 1994). At that time the field was referred to as *early developmental neuropsychology*, which was defined as "the assessment of brain–behavior relationships in the context of developmental change and maturation" (Aylward, 1988: 226). Neuropsychological assessment of infants and young children was considered unique because it occurred against a backdrop of qualitative and quantitative developmental, behavioral, and neuroanatomic changes. Distinct assessment challenges evolved because of expanding behavioral repertoires of infants and young children and the corresponding divergence of neurological, motor/sensorimotor, and cognitive functions into more distinctive areas of development (Aylward, 1997a, 2010).

Increased interest in this area parallels increases in the number of infants and young children at biologic risk who now survive early central nervous system insults (e.g., preterm infants) and their need for earlier evaluation and serial assessment, greater awareness of the effects of identified intrauterine drug exposure and other toxicants, and better identification of genetic disorders and their neurodevelopmental sequelae.

The age range for infant and early childhood neuropsychology extends from the neonatal period (first 30 days of life) through infancy and culminates at the toddler/preschool period (5 years). The importance of assessments of neurological, developmental, and intellectual functions and their relationships for children within this age range has gained increased recognition. In the neonatal period, neurological/ neurobehavioral functioning typically is assessed. During infancy, assessment of developmental (cognitive and motor/ sensorimotor) and neurodevelopmental functions is underscored. From approximately 3 years onward, assessment emphasizes intelligence and specific cognitive functions (Aylward, 2009).

A basic conceptual scheme for infant and early childhood neuropsychologic assessment was introduced in earlier publications (Aylward, 1988, 1997a). This scheme includes the following five clusters.

1. *Basic Neurological function/intactness.* This cluster includes measurement of neurological and functional intactness, and affords general determination of the integrity of the child's central nervous system (CNS). Component items include early reflexes, muscle tone, asymmetries, head control, presence of protective reactions (in response to change in body orientation in space), and absence of abnormal indicators (e.g., motor overflow, stereotyped movements, excessive drooling).

2. *Receptive functions.* This cluster involves the entry of information into the central processing system through sensation and perception. Visual, auditory, and tactile inputs are involved, with greater emphasis placed on the first two modalities. The complexity of receptive functions increases over time, and includes verbal receptive behaviors.

3. *Expressive functions.* Expressive functions are behaviors produced by the infant or child that are observable during testing. Three primary functional areas are involved: fine motor (prehension, reaching, midline behaviors, eye–hand coordination), oral motor (vocalizations, verbalizations), and gross motor (crawling, sitting, standing, ambulating, running, jumping).

4. *Cognitive processing.* Cognitive processing includes two components: memory/learning, and thinking/reasoning. Cognitive processing involves higher-order functions such as habituation, object permanency, imitation, and problem-solving skills. This area includes coordination of a variety of skills and functions, involves interrelated neural networks,

and is considered a good prognostic indicator of a young child's later potential (Aylward, 2009).

5. *Mental activity.* This cluster includes goal directedness, attentional activities, and activity level. Motor functions also include behavioral states and related executive functions. These components generally are assessed using qualitative methods, and require good observational skills and familiarity with age-appropriate behavior. Understanding the integration of various brain functions becomes increasingly important.

Setting the Stage II: Screening

The American Academy of Pediatrics (AAP) and the Commonwealth Fund (www.cmwf.org) emphasize the need for early identification of developmental problems through surveillance during every well-child visit. Early identification of delayed or disordered development (*vis-à-vis* screening) is presumed to lead to further evaluation (e.g., the use of the BSID-III), convergence of information to produce a diagnosis, and appropriate intervention (American Academy of Pediatrics, 2006; Sices, 2007). The AAP also recommends that standardized developmental screening tests be administered routinely at the 9-, 18- , 24/30- and 48-month well-child visits, or when parents or clinicians raise concerns. Similar screening also is mandated under the Individuals with Disabilities Education Act (IDEA) of 2004 (P.L. 108-446). The AAP also distinguishes three terms: surveillance, screening, and evaluation. *Surveillance* involves the more informal, flexible, continuous process of monitoring the child's development over time, including parental concerns, developmental history, observations, and identification of risk and protective factors. *Screening* involves the use of brief standardized tests completed by parents or professionals to identify delays. *Evaluation* (also referred to as assessment) refers to a more complex and definitive process that leads to a diagnosis. The AAP (2006) acknowledges wide variation in the focus of screening instruments, and recommends all should address a variety of areas, including fine and gross motor skills, language, problem-solving/adaptive behavior, and personal–social skills.

Early Neuropsychologic Optimality Rating Scales

Very few tests are designed specifically to evaluate neuropsychological functions in infants. However, most developmentally-oriented measures allow professionals to extrapolate information regarding a young child's neuro-psychological functions (Aylward, 1997a). This situation led the author to develop the Early Neuropsychologic Optimality Rating Scales (ENORS; Aylward, 1988, 1991a, 1991b, 1994; Aylward, Verhulst & Bell, 1988a, 1988b, 1992) – an early prototype of the Bayley Infant Neurodevelopmental Screener (BINS). Six versions of the ENORS have been developed, applicable to the key ages of 3, 6, 9, 12, 18, and 24 months of age (corrected age in the case of preterm infants). A more detailed description of the ENORS is found in Appendix A.

BAYLEY INFANT NEURODEVELOPMENTAL SCREENER

The Bayley Infant Neurodevelopmental Screener (BINS; Aylward, 1995) is an outgrowth of the Early Neuro-psychological Optimality Rating Scales. The ENORS item sets provided items for the BINS try-out version (Aylward, 1995). The BINS enables assessment of posture, tone, movement, developmental status, and basic neurological intactness in infants from 3 to 24 months (corrected age in the case of preterm infants). There are six item sets: 3–4, 5–6, 7–10, 11–15, 16–20, and 21–24 months. Each contains 11–13 items that comprise four conceptual areas: Basic neurological function/intactness (N), Receptive functions (R), Expressive functions (E), and Cognitive processes (C) (combined cognitive processes and mental activity groupings from the ENORS). The conceptual clusters are not orthogonal. Thus, the abilities assessed by any one item in one cluster also may involve abilities from other clusters. A brief description follows.

- *Basic neurological functions/intactness (N)*: Items assess neurological intactness of the developing central nervous system. Evaluation includes muscle tone (hypo- or hypertonia), head control, asymmetries in movement, and abnormal indicators (motor overflow, excessive drooling).

- *Receptive functions (R)*: Items assess the reception of information into the central processing system – more specifically, sensation and perception. Visual and auditory input are involved. Assessment of higher-order verbal processing becomes more important at later ages.
- *Expressive functions (E)*: Items assess overt behaviors in three areas: (1) fine motor (prehension, manipulating object with fingers, eye–hand coordination), (2) oral motor (vocalizations, verbalizations), and (3) gross motor (sitting, crawling, ambulating). Assessment also includes verbal-cognitive functions.
- *Cognitive processes (C)*: Items assess higher-order functions such as memory/learning, and thinking/reasoning, including object permanence, goal-directedness, attention, and problem-solving. These items assess a young child's coordination and integration of various cognitive processes and brain functions thought to be useful prognostically, not simply reflections of canalized behaviors (Aylward, 2009b). Canalized behaviors are simple, fixed behavior patterns (e.g., smiling, babbling, reaching, hand-to-mouth activity) that are species-specific, "pre-wired," and present early in development. Canalized behaviors are less affected by mild adverse circumstances.

The BINS can be administered in approximately 10 minutes. Caregiver reports are allowed only on certain items. Although the administration may rely on information from two informed reports, only one caregiver report is allowed for any conceptual grouping.

Until somewhat recently, scoring of measures of infant development focused on complications. Thus, points were awarded for the presence of risk factors. The BINS uses a different method to score infant assessment; namely, methods consistent with the aforementioned *optimality concept*. Importantly, we can predict positive outcomes more accurately by signs of early optimal development, while our predictions of negative outcomes by early non-optimal findings often are less accurate. This belief is widely held by specialists in early neuropsychological assessment. The greater prominence of optimal behaviors is believed to indicate better integrity of the underlying central nervous system, and the potential for recovery from adverse events.

Therefore, similar to the ENORS, the basic premise of Prechtl's (1980) optimality framework was employed to score the BINS. The optimality approach emphasizes optimal or desired responses based on *a priori* decision rules. Professionals are not required to classify responses as normal or abnormal. Each individual item is scored as optimal (1) or non-optimal (0), and the number of optimal responses is summed (Aylward, 1995).

For each age, three cut-off scores were established to identify infants' level of risk for likelihood of developmental delay or neurodevelopmental impairment. Two of the cut scores form three risk categories: low risk, moderate risk, and high risk. The third cut score (indicated by a dashed line on the scoring form) represents the score at which specificity and sensitivity (clinical versus non-clinical samples) are best matched (see Figure 7.1).

Because the BINS is used to screen infants, no comprehensive norms tables are needed. Rather, empirically based cut scores are used in place of norms tables that have raw-to-standard score conversions (Wilson, 2000). Comparison of an infant's performance on items in the four conceptual clusters provides the opportunity to determine whether the problems are either global or specific, and to define areas of function that need more detailed evaluation. The BINS also assists the examiner in determining whether the dysfunction is more restricted to neurological findings (e.g., increased tone), developmental milestones (walking, transferring at midline), or both areas. The use of serial evaluations enables examiners to determine whether dysfunction is static or progressive. If static, dysfunction should remain unchanged. If progressive, dysfunction should increase over time.

The BINS is not a short form of the Bayley Scales. The BINS differs from other developmental screening tests due to an increased emphasis on neurodevelopmental functions. It is applicable to clinical and research settings. It was developed using a high-risk follow-up clinical sample in addition to a larger, non-clinical group, and thus is particularly well suited to use with biologically at-risk populations. It can also be used

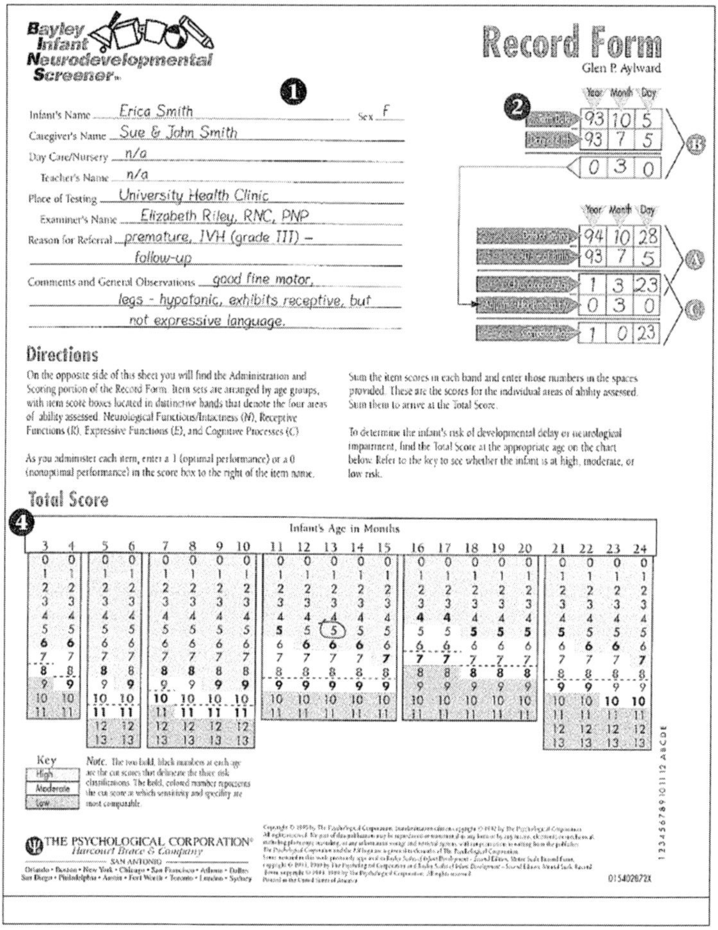

Bayley Infant Neurodevelopmental Screener.

Record Form
Glen P. Aylward

Infant's Name __Erica Smith__ Sex _F_
Caregiver's Name __Sue & John Smith__
Day Care/Nursery __n/a__
Teacher's Name __n/a__
Place of Testing __University Health Clinic__
Examiner's Name __Elizabeth Riley, RNC, PNP__
Reason for Referral __premature, IVH (grade III) –__
__follow-up__
Comments and General Observations __good fine motor,__
__legs - hypotonic, exhibits receptive, but__
__not expressive language.__

Directions

On the opposite side of this sheet you will find the Administration and Scoring portion of the Record Form. Item sets are arranged by age groups, with item score boxes located in distinctive bands that denote the four areas of ability assessed: Neurological Functions/Intactness (N), Receptive Functions (R), Expressive Functions (E), and Cognitive Processes (C).

As you administer each item, enter a 1 (optimal performance) or a 0 (nonoptimal performance) in the score box to the right of the item name.

Sum the item scores in each band and enter those numbers in the spaces provided. These are the scores for the individual areas of ability assessed. Sum them to arrive at the Total Score.

To determine the infant's risk of developmental delay or neurological impairment, find the Total Score at the appropriate age on the chart below. Refer to the key to see whether the infant is at high, moderate, or low risk.

Total Score

THE PSYCHOLOGICAL CORPORATION®
Harcourt Brace & Company
SAN ANTONIO
Orlando • Boston • New York • Chicago • San Francisco • Atlanta • Dallas
San Diego • Philadelphia • Austin • Fort Worth • Toronto • London • Sydney

FIGURE 7.1 Example of BINS scoring form. Bayley Infant Neurodevelopmental Screener (BINS). *Copyright © 1995 NCS Pearson, Inc. Reproduced with permission. All rights reserved. "Bayley Infant Neurodevelopmental Screener" and "BINS" are trademarks, in the US and/or other countries, of Pearson Education, Inc. or its affiliate(s).*

as a hands-on screener in general screening or pediatric practices. The brevity of the instrument makes it suitable for use in high-volume settings.

The scale's administration requires a process approach; one that considers *how* the ability is expressed, not simply whether the ability is expressed (see also Aylward, 2004). Examiners should be well versed in infant development, and experienced in handling infants. Psychologists may have less difficulty than professionals from other disciplines when administering specific items that are of a developmental nature. Conversely, they may have more difficulty assessing muscle tone and detecting subtle neurological indicators. Qualified examiners include psychologists, developmental pediatricians, general pediatricians, pediatric nurse practitioners, neurodevelopmental pediatricians, occupational and physical therapists, and early childhood specialists.

Standardization sample

The BINS standardization sample consisted of 600 cases, 100 at each of six ages: 3, 6, 9, 12, 18, and 24 months. Infants were tested at ± 1 week conceptional age (age corrected for prematurity) for 3-month-old, ± 2 weeks for 6-, 9-, 12- and 18-month-old, and ± 3 weeks for 24-month-old infants. The sample consisted of 50 males and 50 females at each age, and all infants were full-term, and had no prenatal, perinatal, or neonatal medical complications. The sample was stratified based on 1988 US Bureau of the Census data with regard to age, gender, race/ethnicity, geographic region, and parent education level.

The clinical sample consisted of 303 infants tested at 3 months ($n = 50$), 6 months ($n = 66$), 9 months ($n = 48$), 12 months ($n = 50$), 18 months ($n = 37$), and 24 months ($n = 52$) of age. Medical complications in these infants included prematurity/low birth weight, respiratory distress syndrome/mechanical ventilation, apnea, prenatal drug exposure, intraventricular hemorrhage, patent ductus arteriosis, seizures/asphyxia, being small-for-gestational-age, and HIV positive status. Most infants had more than one medical condition.

Final item sets

BINS item sets were selected based on three criteria. Items had to discriminate infants who had no complications, and those who had various degrees of medical involvement. Items had to be consistent with the predetermined conceptual groupings listed above. The number of items had to be limited because the BINS is a screening instrument. Items also were assessed for gender and racial/ethnic bias. The selected items were vertically scaled using the Rasch model, thus providing simultaneous estimates of the infant's ability and item difficulty.

A cumulative total test score distribution was generated for the non-clinical and clinical samples for the age groups tested (see above for age groups tested). For those ages not tested, the difference between the mean ability of the untested age group (interpolated) and the mean ability of the closest tested age group was computed.

Cut Scores

In general, cut scores delineate the low, moderate, and high-risk groupings (e.g., those who are at risk for developmental delay or neurological impairment). A score falling in the high-risk category was obtained by approximately 50 percent of the clinical group, and 8–18 percent of the non-clinical sample. The percentage from the non-clinical sample was expected because 16 percent of the normative population score 1 standard deviation below the mean. Referring to Figure 7.1, at 6 months a cut score of 9 demarcates moderate and high risk, with 93 percent of the non-clinical sample and 61 percent of the clinical group scoring ≥ 9 (see Table 5.14 in BINS manual, pp. 68–69). A cut score of 11 is the highest value for the moderate-risk grouping, and hence delineates moderate- and low-risk groups, with 72 percent of the non-clinical and 38 percent of the clinical group scoring ≥ 11.

At 12 months, a score of 6 (moderate/high-risk determination) or above would be obtained by 94 percent of the non-clinical sample and 64 percent of the clinical sample. A score of 9 (moderate/high-risk cut point) would be obtained by 62 percent of the non-clinical sample and 30 percent of the clinical sample.

At 24 months, the high/moderate-risk cut score of above 7 would be obtained by 92 percent of the non-clinical sample and 56 percent of the clinical sample. The moderate/low-risk score of above 10 would be obtained by 69 percent of the non-clinical sample and 20 percent of the clinical sample. Not all children from the normative (non-clinical) sample would necessarily be "normal," nor would all children from the clinical group be "abnormal." Instead, the likelihood of normality or abnormality in each group is greater.

Reliability

Internal consistency for the BINS clinical and non-clinical samples (Cronbach's alpha) ranges from 0.73 to 0.85 (Aylward, 1995). Most values are above 0.80, with the exceptions of 3- and 12-month item sets. This is not unexpected, given the limited number of items at each age. Test–retest reliability at 3, 9, and 18 months ($n = 100$ for each age group) is 0.71, 0.83, and 0.84, respectively. Greatest change was found at 3 months – a period that may reflect accelerated developmental change. With respect to risk categorization, 150 infants at 3, 9, and 18 months of age were followed, for whom classification consistencies were 72 percent, 68 percent, and 78 percent, respectively. Most misclassifications were due to infants who had a score in the moderate-risk range on the first testing and in the low-risk range on the second testing, as well as infants who had a score in the high-risk range on the first testing and in the moderate-risk range on the second testing. Interrater reliability at 6, 12, and 24 months ($n = 30$ for each age group) was 0.79, 0.91, and 0.96, respectively.

Validity

Convergent validity with the Bayley Scales of Infant Development – Second Edition (BSID-II) was reported in the BINS manual (Aylward, 1995) using the BSID-II standardization sample of 50 children at 3 months, 50 at 6 months, 49 at 18 months, and 50 at 24 months. The BSID-II cut-off score for mildly delayed/significantly delayed was 1 standard deviation below the mean. Three BINS cut scores were used: (1) high–moderate (value at the delineation of high- and moderate-risk groups), (2) middle cut score (value immediately below the dashed line that indicates best delineation of clinical/non-clinical groups), and (3) low–moderate (value at delineation of moderate- and low-risk groups). Percent agreement was highest when the lowest cut score for the BINS was used, next highest when the middle cut score was employed, and lowest when the highest cut score was used. The use of the highest cut score tended to over-identify infants (18–37 percent).

Pearson correlations among the 3-, 6-, 18- and 24-month BINS and the BSID-II Mental Developmental Index (MDI) ranged from 0.43 to 0.82, and for the Psychomotor Developmental Index (PDI) from 0.39 to 0.58. The highest correlations were found at 24 months (Aylward, 1995). Correlations with the Battelle, using 30 children at 12 months, were 0.50, 0.51, and 0.50 for the Communication, Cognitive, and Motor Scales, respectively. Correlations between the measures, with 30 children evaluated at 18 months, were 0.31, 0.43, and −0.16 for the Communication, Cognitive and Motor Scales, respectively.

DESCRIPTION OF BINS ITEM SETS

3- to 4-month Item Set

This set consists of 11 items that primarily fall into the Neurological functions/intactness cluster, with several items from Expressive functions and Receptive functions – visual clusters. *Holds Head Erect and Steady* (N) and *Regards Pellet* (R) were items frequently found to be non-optimal in the clinical standardization group (Aylward, 1995). Among another high-risk group of nursery children ($n = 52$), 46 percent received a non-optimal score on *Reach for a Suspended Ring* (E), 40 percent had non-optimal *Lower Muscle Tone* (N) and 40 percent did not *Sit with Slight Support for 10 Seconds* (E) (Aylward, unpublished data). The BINS Technical Update (Psychological Corporation, 1996) indicated that the *Vocalizes Two Different Sounds* and *Fingers Hands in Play* items can be scored by caretaker report. The *Coordinated Movement of Extremities* item enables examiners to score overall quality of motor coordination, posture, and motor modulation, essentially enabling quantification of more "qualitative findings."

Two items can be specifically scored by simple observation over the course of the exam (*Fingers Hands in Play; Demonstrates Coordinated Movement of Extremities*).

5- to 6-month Item Set

This item set contains 13 items. The three that assess cognitive processes are thought to reflect higher-order processes and involve integrative and associative neural networks. Infants with medical complications had a decreased likelihood of optimal scores on the *Regards Pellet* (Receptive functions – visual), *Bangs in Play* (Cognitive processes), *Uses Partial Thumb Apposition* (Expressive functions – fine motor) and *Vocalizes One Vowel Sound* (Expressive functions – oral motor) (Aylward, 1995). Among a high-risk clinical sample ($n = 1,027$), 47 percent did not *Look for Fallen Spoon* (C), 75 percent did not *Move Forward Using Prewalking Methods* (E), and 39 percent did not display optimal *Muscle Tone of the Lower Extremities* (N) or *Imitate Others* (C) (Aylward, unpublished data). Caretaker report is acceptable for the *Bangs in Play, Vocalizes One Vowel Sound*, and *Imitates Others* items (Psychological Corporation, 1996). Care must be taken regarding accuracy of the last item, as parents often misinterpret true imitation. Two items can be scored by observation over the course of the screening (*Coordinated Movements, Imitates Others*).

A pairwise principal components factor analysis with varimax rotation was employed with data from a sample of 569 infants evaluated at 6 months (Aylward, 2004). This approach was selected because the four original BINS conceptual areas were developed in an *a priori* fashion and were not orthogonal. At this age, a three-factor solution accounted for 52 percent of the variance: cognitive/fine motor had seven items, neuromotor four items, and gross motor two items. Only two items (i.e., *Look for Fallen Spoon* and *Sits with Support*) loaded on more than one factor, indicating minimal communalities (Aylward, 2004).

Stepwise logistic regression (likelihood ratio) was employed to generate clinically meaningful prediction data regarding factor scores and later probability of optimal cognitive and motor outcome. The BINS cognitive/fine motor outcome score had a resultant Odds Ratio (OR) of 3.04. This means that, if the cognitive/fine motor score was 7 ($\geq$ 75th percentile), then the infant was three times more likely to have a normal 3-year outcome than if the score was below the 75th percentile. With respect to 36-month motor outcome, the BINS gross motor factor was predictive (OR $= 7.94$), with a score of 1 being in the top quartile.

When reviewing cut-off scores for risk groups, clinical experience suggests that many infants who receive a score of 11 should be considered low–moderate risk, as many will improve by their 12-month evaluation.

7- to 10-month Item Set

This item set contains 13 items. Among them, three fall into Neurological function/intactness (N), one into Receptive functions (R), six into Expressive functions (E) (the plurality falling into gross motor expressive), and three into Cognitive processes (C). This change in loadings reflects the increase in intentionality and purposeful activity. One item can be scored by observation (*Coordinated Movements*), while *Responds to Spoken Request* and *Vocalizes Three Different Vowel–Consonant Combinations* can be scored by parent report (Psychological Corporation, 1996). Two items, *Lifts Inverted Cup* (Cognitive processes involving goal-directed behavior) and *Responds to Spoken Request* (Receptive functions – verbal) appear to particularly differentiate the non-clinical group from the clinical group with the most medical complications (Aylward, 1995). It has been our experience that the age cut-off of 7 months corrected age is too difficult for infants who have graduated from high-risk nurseries. Therefore, the 5- to 6-month item set also should be used for those infants aged less than 7 months, 16 days. Concern is decreased if the 7- to 10-month item set is moderate or high risk but the 5- to 6-month item set is low risk. A recent analysis of data from 128 infants who were followed up from Neonatal Intensive Care Units and administered the 7- to 10-month item set found that 39 percent of the babies did not *Use Early Stepping Movements* and 56 percent did not *Respond to Spoken Request*. Conversely, 90 percent achieved *Look for Fallen Spoon*, 90 percent showed optimal *Muscle Tone of the Upper Extremities,* and 87 percent could *Sit Alone for 30 Seconds* (Aylward, unpublished data).

11- to 15-month Item Set

At this age, cognitive processes and expressive abilities are more evident and can be assessed. Three items fall into the Neurological functions/intactness (N) grouping, two into Receptive functions (R), three into Expressive functions (E), and three into Cognitive processes (C). Two items can be scored by observation (*Gestures* and *Coordinated Movement*). *Walks Alone* (Expressive functions – gross motor), *Imitates Words* (Expressive functions – verbal), *Responds to Spoken Request* (Receptive functions – verbal) and *Puts Three Cubes in a Cup* (Cognitive processes) are discriminative items (Aylward, 1995). *Imitates Words, Responds to Spoken Request, Listens Selectively to Two Familiar Words,* and *Uses Gestures to Make Wants Known* are items that can be scored by parent report (two maximum in any single administration) (Psychological Corporation, 1996). In a high-risk clinical sample of 801 babies (Aylward, unpublished data), 59 percent did not *Remove Pellet from Bottle*, 46 percent did not *Imitate Crayon Stroke*, 55 percent did not *Walk Alone*, while 42 percent did not *Imitate Words*. Therefore, these items are most likely to be scored non-optimal.

A factor analysis of data from 458 infants (Aylward, 2004) identified a three-factor solution that accounts for 53 percent of the common variance: motor with four items, verbal/language with four items, and cognitive/verbal expressive with three items. One item, *Walks Alone*, loaded on more than one factor. Data from logistic regression modeling for cognitive outcomes found the OR for the verbal/language factor to be 2.51 and the cognitive processes factor to be OR = 2.43. Thus, children who obtained a score ≥ 75th percentile on either factor were 2.5 times more likely to have optimal cognitive outcomes than if the factor score was < 75th percentile. The motor and cognitive processes factors were included in the motor outcome regression model (ORs = 4.0 and 2.14, respectively) (Aylward, 2004). Our clinical experience suggests that children with summary scores of 9 should be considered to be at low–moderate risk, with many of them improving to low risk by 24 months.

16- to 20-month Item Set

This grouping contains 10 items: 1 Neurological functions/intactness (N), 2 Receptive functions (R), 6 Expressive functions (E) (verbal, fine motor and gross motor) and 1 Cognitive processes (C). There is good discrimination between clinical and non-clinical groups on most items. *Places Threes Pieces in Puzzle Board* (C), *Names Three Objects* (E – verbal) and *Points to Three of Doll's Body Parts* (R – verbal) identified infants with the most severe medical complications (Aylward, 1995). Because of the increase in verbal items, examiners should consider environmental influences on performance at this age. *Imitates Two-word Sentence* and *Combines Word and Gesture* can be scored by caregiver report (Psychological Corporation, 1996), while *Combines Word and Gesture* and *Absence of Drooling/Motor Overflow* can be incidentally observed.

Analysis of data from a sample of 69 high-risk infants evaluated at this age (Aylward, unpublished data) found 52 percent did not successfully *Place Three Pieces in Puzzle Board*, 73 percent did not *Name Three Objects*, 78 percent did not receive an optimal score on the *Builds Tower of Six Cubes*, 52 percent did not *Point to Three of Doll's Body Parts*, and 69 percent did not *Imitate a Two-word Sentence*. Although these data are informative, the sample size is relatively small to make generalizations. In addition, given that the follow-up protocol has infants evaluated at 6, 12, 24, and 36 months, selection bias may account for why these infants were evaluated out of cycle at 16–20 months. They tended to be at the younger age range of this item set (i.e., < 18 months). These findings warrant further investigation with larger samples.

21- to 24-month Item Set

The final item set comprises 13 items: 1 Neurological functions/intactness, 2 Receptive functions (verbal), 9 Expressive functions (fine motor, verbal, gross motor), and 1 Cognitive processes. *Places Three Pieces in Puzzle Board* (C), *Builds Tower of Six Cubes* (E – fine motor), *Names Four Pictures*, and *Names Three Objects* (E – verbal) appear most discriminating between clinical and nonclinical samples (Aylward, 1995). *Uses a Two-word Utterance* could be scored by caretaker report, while the items *Speaks Intelligibly* and *Absence of Drooling/Motor Overflow* may be observed incidentally (Aylward, 1995; Psychological Corporation, 1996). Once again, because of the increase in verbal items, consideration must be given to environmental influences.

Analysis of data from a clinical sample of 590 infants in this age range (Aylward, unpublished data) found 45 percent did not receive an optimal score on *Names Four Pictures*, 41 percent did not *Name Three Objects*, 50 percent did not *Jump off the Floor* (with both feet leaving the surface simultaneously), and 56 percent did not receive an optimal score on the *Jumps from Bottom Step* item. Hence, these items can be expected to have the highest probability of failure in at-risk populations.

A factor analysis of data from 358 babies, 21–24 months of age, identified a three-factor solution that accounts for 64 percent of the variance (Aylward, 2004): verbal expressive with four items, motor with five items, and cognitive/verbal receptive with four items. The verbal expressive factor at 21–24 months correlated 0.70 with cognitive outcome at 36 months and 0.60 with cognitive/verbal expressive outcomes at 36 months. The motor factors at 21–24 and 36 months correlated 0.60.

A logistic regression analysis found the verbal expressive OR to be 7.69 and the motor factor OR to be 2.58 with respect to optimal 36-month cognitive outcome. When predicting optimal 36-month motor outcome, the OR for the BINS motor factor top quartile score was 5.78 (Aylward, 2004), indicating that the likelihood of an optimal motor score (< 1 SD below the mean) was almost six times greater when the child scored in the top quartile on the motor factor than when the infant was in a lower quartile.

STUDIES USING THE BINS

Numerous studies employing the BINS have been published, and these are described in more detail in Appendix B. From these studies, several generalizations can be made:

- The BINS is particularly useful in various medical/biological risk populations.

- In general, the greater the degree of biologic risk, the lower the BINS score.
- The BINS is related to later neurologic, motor, and cognitive outcomes.
- Risk can be low, moderate, or high. It also can be binary–that is, the moderate risk category can be subdivided based on the cut score. High–moderate and high-risk categories can be combined into a high-risk grouping, while low–moderate and low-risk categories can be combined into a low-risk grouping.
- The BINS may not be as useful when used with children who only display environmental risk.
- Correlations among the total BINS scores are high across different age groups (i.e., item sets).
- There is continuity in risk classifications over time, particularly with respect to the high- and low-risk groups. Greater variability is found in the moderate-risk group.
- The BINS items can be easily adapted to a caretaker report format with a high (70–83 percent) rate of agreement.

Prediction

Considerable scholarship indicates that sensitivity (co-positivity), specificity (co-negativity), and the positive and negative predictive values (PPV, NPV) of the BINS vary, depending on cut-offs used to indicate risk or delay (Aylward et al., 1992; Macias, Saylor, Greer, Charles, Bell, & Katikaneni, 1998; Aylward & Verhulst, 2000). The BINS appears best suited for use with infants who are at biological risk, and perhaps is most useful when the degree of risk is dichotomized into categories (Aylward & Verhulst, 2000; Aylward & Aylward, 2004). However, the BINS manual emphasizes the importance of clinical judgment and that the purposes of screening need to be considered when weighing the impact of a score that falls in the moderate-risk range (Aylward, 1995).

This issue was investigated further using summary scores for 5–6, 11–15, and 21–24 months, as well as cognitive and motor outcomes at 36 months. The McCarthy Scales, BSID-II, and BSID-III were administered at 36 months, reflecting changes in the follow-up protocol. Outcome data were viewed in a continuous or in a categorical manner (≥ 1 SD below average considered non-optimal), depending on analysis (Aylward, unpublished data). A total of 320 infants were seen at 5–6 and 36 months, 344 at 11–15 and 36 months, and 354 at 21–24 and 36 months. Continuous data were analyzed using ANOVA and Tukey follow-up tests; dichotomous variables were compared using Pearson's Chi square and odds ratios.

Mean 36-month cognitive and motor scores for high-, moderate- and low-risk groups at each of the three ages are found in Table 7.1. All between-groups comparisons were significant ($P < 0.0001$). Follow-up tests revealed that infants in the high-risk group consistently performed more poorly than those in the moderate- or low-risk groups on both cognitive and motor scores ($P < 0.0001$). The moderate- and low-risk groups did not differ significantly except at the 21- to 24-month evaluation (both cognitive and motor, $P < 0.0001$ and $P < 0.002$, respectively). These data indicate that, prior to 24 months, although the moderate- and low-risk groups did not differ significantly, the mean score for the moderate-risk group was below that for the low-risk group.

TABLE 7.1 Bayley Infant Neurodevelopmental Screener Risk Categories and 36-month Cognitive and Motor Outcome Scores

	5- to 6-month item set	11- to 15-month item set	21- to 24-month item set
COGNITIVE OUTCOME			
High risk	79.17	75.90	73.12
Moderate risk	91.79	90.98	89.51
Low risk	94.98	95.61	98.46
MOTOR OUTCOME (T-SCORES)			
High risk	37.73	34.73	34.80
Moderate risk	46.69	45.58	44.90
Low risk	49.05	49.05	50.07

High-risk consistently differed from moderate- and low-risk groups ($P < 0.0001$); moderate and low risk did not differ except at 21–24 months for both cognitive and motor outcome ($P \leq 0.002$).

BINS risk also was considered as a binary variable using the method outlined previously (subdividing the moderate-risk group and combining with either high- or low-risk groups; Aylward & Verhulst, 2000; Aylward & Aylward, 2004). In every comparison, the 36-month cognitive and motor mean outcome scores of the HIGHRISK group were significantly lower than the LOWRISK mean scores (Table 7.2) ($P < 0.0001$ to $P < 0.002$). Scores obtained by infants in the low-risk group fell in the average range, while those of the high-risk group routinely were ≥ 1 SD below average.

Finally, both the BINS at 6, 12, and 24 months, and the 36-month cognitive and motor outcome, were viewed as binary variables, and co-positivity and co-negativity (used in place of sensitivity and specificity, because there is no true gold standard in developmental assessment, and the comparison measure is a reference standard), Positive Predictive Values (PPV) and Negative Predictive Values (NPV) were calculated (Table 7.3). Given that this is lagged prediction, the values are quite acceptable, and indicate that the BINS is predictive of later outcomes. With regard to the odds ratios, compared to those who obtained a non-optimal (high-risk) score at 6 months, children who obtained an optimal (low-risk) score at 6 months will have almost a four times greater likelihood of obtaining an

TABLE 7.2 Comparison of 36-month Cognitive and Motor Outcome by Bayley Infant Neurodevelopmental Screener: HIGHRISK and LOWRISK Binary Risk Classification

	5- to 6-month item set	11- to 15-month item set	21- to 24-month item set
COGNITIVE OUTCOME			
HIGHRISK	82.54	82.20	76.16
LOWRISK	94.90	94.09	96.03
MOTOR OUTCOME (T-SCORES)			
HIGHRISK	40.32	38.92	37.64
LOWRISK	48.74	48.35	48.24

HIGHRISK/LOWRISK comparisons were significant at each comparison (P < 0.002).

TABLE 7.3 Lagged Prediction: Bayley Infant Neurodevelopmental Screener and 36-month Outcome

	Co-positivity/ co-negativity[a]	PPV/NPV[b]	Odds Ratio (95% CI)
COGNITIVE			
5–6 months	0.74/0.57	0.46/0.82	3.87 (2.31–6.48)
11–15 months	0.74/0.58	0.46/0.81	3.73 (2.28–6.10)
21–24 months	0.70/0.77	0.60/0.84	8.12 (4.91–13.42)
MOTOR (T-SCORE)			
5–6 months	0.63/0.76	0.61/0.77	5.26 (3.24–8.53)
11–15 months	0.75/0.61	0.56/0.78	4.59 (2.81–7.49)
21–24 months	0.71/0.58	0.52/0.76	3.47 (2.10–5.71)

[a]Co-positivity is used instead of sensitivity; co-negativity is used in place of specificity.
[b]PPV = positive predictive value; NPV = negative predictive value.

optimal 36-month cognitive outcome (≥ 85). All ORs were significant.

CLINICAL CASES

When engaged in developmental screening, examiners need to consider an evaluation matrix that consists of five components: BINS (or other screening) results, environment, area of function assessed, age of the infant, and the child's medical history (Aylward, 1997b). This approach involves a clinical reasoning process that incorporates weighing and considering interrelationships among these matrix components. Examiners should not blindly use a summary number or score without these considerations. Several clinical principles follow:

• Positive test findings should be viewed in terms of functional significance. For example, does increased tone affect crawling, cruising around furniture, or walking? If not, then the functional significance or impact of increased tone is lessened.

- Experiential factors/environment can affect development. However, these will have more of an impact on language and cognitive processes items than on neurologic or motor items.
- Verbal expressive and receptive functions as well as cognitive processes will be more predictive of later cognitive outcome than will motor or neurologic function (unless these areas are particularly impaired).
- Our ability to screen different developmental areas varies by age because of the natural course of emergence of different skills (e.g., language deficits would be more obvious with increasing age).
- Mild or even moderate neuromotor problems tend to improve with age.
- Deviations in test performance can be due to a variety of causes (e.g., poor performance in the form board could be due to poor prehension skills, fine motor modulation problems, visual-perceptual deficits, an inability to understand the task, lack of persistence, or some combination of these factors). These possibilities need to be considered when describing the results of screening.
- Correction for prematurity should occur over the first 2 years.
- Examiners also should look for congruence between medical events and neurodevelopmental findings. Some examples are provided: Grade III intraventricular hemorrhage often would be associated with neuromotor dysfunction, and severe hypoxic-ischemic encephalopathy (HIE) frequently is associated with cognitive and motor dysfunction. However, Grade II IVH and specific language deficits are not routinely related.

Case Study 1

MS is a 6-month-old male (corrected age), born at 26 weeks gestational age with a birth weight of 720 g. He had a Grade III IVH, was on a ventilator for 21 days, and was hospitalized for 70 days after birth. He resides in a lower socioeconomic status household, and both parents are unemployed. MS is reported to have "tight" muscle tone. On the 5- to 6-month BINS, MS received non-optimal scores on *Transfers Objects* (Item 4), *Looks for Fallen Spoon* (Item 5), *Sits with Slight Support* (Item 6), *Precrawling Movements* (Item 7), *Muscle Tone of the Lower Extremities* (Item 10), and *Coordinated Movements* (Item 12) (see Figure 7.1). His total risk score was 7/13, placing him in the high-risk range.

In this case, most problems cluster in the neurologic functions (N) and expressive motor (E) realms – deficits often associated with events from the infant's medical course (Grade III IVH, extremely low birth weight/prematurity). Given his age and areas of deficit, environment probably does not have much of an impact at this time. Serial screening will be necessary due to the possibility of transient dystonia. Early intervention services (particularly OT/PT) should be instituted.

Case Study 2

LS is a 24-month-old female born at 39 weeks gestational age with a birth weight of 3700 g. Her Apgar score at 5 minutes was 7, the delivery was long, and LS was lethargic for 24 hours after birth. She eventually perked up, and was discharged in 8 days. LS resides in a low socioeconomic status household with a single, adolescent mother with no extended family close by. On the 21–24 BINS item set, LS received non-optimal scores (0) on *Names Four Pictures* (Item 3), *Identifies Four Pictures* (Item 4), *Names Three Objects* (Item 6), *Produces Two-word Utterances* (Item 11), and *Speaks Intelligibly* (Item 12). Her overall score was 8/13, placing her in the moderate-risk range (see Figure 7.1).

In this case, most of the non-optimal scores are in the verbal expressive (E) and, to a lesser degree, verbal receptive (R) areas. Other areas of neurodevelopmental function appear adequate. In general, language skills are more developed by age 2 years, allowing for better detection of problems. Conversely, language is strongly influenced by environment. The specific deficit in the expressive language cluster (and one receptive item) with optimal scores in other areas is not particularly congruent with what may have been mild hypoxic-ischemic encephalopathy. Hence, environment may be a strong factor, and early intervention services in speech/language would be recommended.

SUMMARY

The BINS is a useful screening instrument that is particularly applicable to infants at medical/biological risk. The BINS differs significantly from the BSID-II and BSID-III, both in purpose and emphasis. Nonetheless, the BINS moderately correlates with Bayley cognitive and motor scores, and is predictive of later outcome, using either the three-tier risk classification scheme or a binary approach. The BINS is translatable to caretaker report, and is unique in that the same items can be used for report and hands-on versions. Depending on the purpose of using the BINS, scores falling in the moderate- or high-risk range should be followed by more detailed evaluation with the BSID-III.

APPENDICES

Appendix A: The Early Neuropsychologic Optimality Rating Scales (ENORS)

The BINS has its conceptual, theoretical, and empirical roots in a precursor test known as the Early Neuropsychologic Optimality Rating Scales (ENORS). This appendix describes the derivation of the ENORS and its relation to the BINS, and is intended to document the historical background for serious reviewers.

ENORS consists of multiple versions, and each version contains 16–22 component items grouped into the 5 infant and early neuropsychologic conceptual scheme clusters outlined previously. Items are scored by three methods: observation, elicitation, and caregiver report. The proportion of items scored by each method varies by age, and the infant is placed supine or prone, held upright, seated on the caretaker's lap, or ambulates. The ENORS versions were designed to take approximately 15 minutes to administer (see Aylward, 1994, 1997 for more detailed description of the ENORS items).

Scoring of neurodevelopmental tests such as the ENORS also can be complex, due to differential emphasis of functions at different ages. Weighting items therefore would be difficult, and it is unclear as to how to group scores into a meaningful summary score. An optimality approach (Prechtl, 1980) is probably most applicable; here, factors (or optimal responses on items) are identified that are most likely to produce positive outcomes. Items are given equal variable weights, the assumption being that non-optimal conditions do not occur in isolation and the more serious a given condition, the fewer optimal scores. It is also assumed that a normal neuro-psychologic finding has a higher predictive value for later "normal" functioning than an abnormal sign does for later "abnormal" outcome. Moreover, the so-called "optimum" sometimes is more narrowly defined than is the range of normal (Aylward, 1994). A percentage score (number optimal/(number optimal + number non-optimal)) is calculated, and cut-off values could be employed.

The *Basic neurological function/intactness* item cluster of the ENORS includes the following component items and item parts: primitive reflexes, asymmetries, head control, muscle tone, abnormal indicators, protective reactions and drooling/ motor overflow. *Receptive functions* involve auditory, visual, visual tracking, and verbal receptive skills, as well as under-standing body parts. *Fine motor/oral motor expressive functions* include reaching behavior, hands open/midline behaviors, prehension skills, eye–hand coordination, fine motor control, vocalizations/verbalizations, and naming pictures and objects. The *gross motor expressive functions* category contains such component items and item parts as: elevates self when prone, supports weight, coordinated movement, sitting/rolls over, crawling, ambulation, throwing/kicking, ascends stairs and jumps. *Processing* includes social smile, regards objects, object permanence, imitative abilities, problem-solving, and form boards. *Mental activity* component items involve goal-directed behaviors, attentiveness, activity level, and persistent crying/ irritability. Although component items may be evaluated at several ages, the individual parts and scoring criteria may differ.

In summary, on the ENORS Basic Neurological function/ intactness items are important primarily during the first year, visual receptive items are important throughout infancy, and verbal receptive skills increase in significance from 9 months onward. Mental activity items are emphasized consistently throughout infancy. Although different functions assume differential importance over the six key ENORS ages, each area is evaluated to some degree, underscoring conceptual continuity (Aylward, 1997).

Appendix B: Studies Using the Bayley Infant Neurodevelopmental Screener

This appendix collects the extant research findings related to BINS in one place, and describes each study in detail. It is intended for those who may want to seriously evaluate the empirical support of the BINS prior to selecting the instrument for system-wide adoption by large healthcare systems, or use in large-scale clinical studies, or for scholars interested in conducting further research.

Babakhanyan, Jochai, and Frier-Randall (2008) used the BINS in a sample of 76 children with craniofacial abnormalities. Infants were evaluated on two occasions, from 3 months to 24 months. Repeated measures ANOVAs indicated improvement in level of risk from time 1 to time 2. However, in the abstract, the specific ages at each time period were not specified. Talkukder, Ferdousy, Parveen, and Khan (2004) utilized the BINS in Bangladesh to assess 70 infants, aged 3–24 months, who were treated for acute bacterial meningitis. Both the BINS and a neurological assessment were administered, and a low-risk/high-risk and an impaired/not impaired classification were given for each, respectively. On the BINS 46 percent of the infants were low risk while 54 percent were high risk; on the neurological exam 60 percent did not have neurological sequelae (not impaired) while 40 percent had neurological problems. Using the neurological assessment as the reference standard, the BINS had high sensitivity (82 percent) and moderate specificity (64 percent). The authors recommended the BINS as a useful bedside screener. However, the article was not clear with respect to ages of BINS administration or how the three BINS risk groups were translated into a dichotomous risk variable.

Constantinou, Adamson-Macedo, Mirmiran, Ariagno and Fleisher (2005) administered: (1) the Neurobehavioral

Assessment of the Preterm Infant (NAPI) to 113 extremely low birth weight (ELBW) and very low birth weight (VLBW) infants at 36 weeks post-menstrual age; (2) the BINS at 12 months corrected age; and (3) the BSID-II at 18 and 30 months (the last evaluation given at the child's chronological age). ELBW infants scored significantly lower than VLBW babies on the 12-month BINS and later BSID-II scores, as did children with the diagnosis of cerebral palsy (CP) versus those without CP. The NAPI orientation score significantly correlated with the BINS total score ($r = 0.31$). In an earlier, related study (Constantinou, Adamson-Macedo, Korner, & Fleisher, 2000), 47 children < 1,250 g and < 30 weeks gestation age were given the NAPI at 36 weeks and the BINS at 4 and 12 months. There was no significant correlations between the NAPI clusters and BINS total score at 4 months (mean BINS score was 8.63, indicating moderate risk). However, there were significant correlations between the NAPI motor cluster (0.40), alertness and orientation cluster (0.30), and scarf sign (0.30) and the 12 months BINS summary score (mean = 5.73, high risk). The authors indicated that at 4 months early reflexes are suppressed by higher cortical function; at 12 months voluntary motor behavior becomes operational. Therefore, at 4 months, emerging developmental problems are possibly masked. This makes short-term prediction less reliable than long-term prediction. The authors also suggest discontinuity in development.

Gucuyener *et al.* (2006) applied the BINS to 122 Turkish infants born at 26–37 weeks. Infants were grouped in by gestational age at birth: 26–29 weeks, 30–32 weeks, and 33–37 weeks. At 3–4 months, those born 30–32 weeks had significantly lower BINS summary scores than the 33- to 37-week group. At 7–10 months, total BINS scores in those born at 26–29 weeks were lower than in both older groups (particularly expressive and cognitive items), while at 16–20 months, infants born at 26–29 weeks gestational age had scores lower than those born at 33–37 weeks (expressive items in particular).

Macias *et al.* (1998) compared the BINS to the Clinical Adaptive Test/Clinical Linguistic Auditory Milestone Scale (CAT/CLAMS) in 78 high-risk infants, ages 6–24 months (mean age 12.9 months). The BSID-II MDI was the reference standard, and was administered at the same visit. Both screening tests correlated with the BSID-II MDI, and the BINS had optimal sensitivity (90 percent) when referred for a high- or moderate-risk categorization. The middle cut score (dashed line on the scoring form) yielded 70 percent sensitivity and 71 percent specificity. BINS risk scores correlated with the MDI ($r = -0.51$). The authors indicate that the BINS was significantly related to the BSID-II, regardless of cut-off method used: (1) high risk versus moderate or low risk, (2) high or moderate risk versus low risk, or (3) middle cut score, producing a high- and low-risk group. They go on to say that if emphasis is on maximum identification of infants with potential delays, a child receiving a BINS score in the high- or moderate-risk range should be referred for additional assessment. In clinical groups with a higher likelihood of risk, a screening test with higher sensitivity for identification of infants with developmental delays is preferred because under-referral is a critical factor.

Hess, Papas, and Black (2004) applied the BINS to 106 infants born to low-income African-American adolescent mothers. The BSID-II was given at 24 months, and a score < 85 was considered to be indicative of delayed development. The BINS was found to have low sensitivity but high specificity; the positive predictive value was better when the BSID-II cut-off was < 90. The authors suggested that the low predictive validity in this population highlights difficulty inherent in developmental screening of infants who are at environmental but not biological risk. They also inferred that the BINS may be better suited to biologically at-risk infants.

Leonard, Piecuch, and Cooper (2001) administered the BINS at a mean age of 6.8 months and the BSID-II at 12.9 months to a sample of 133 preterm infants born at $< 1,500$ g. The 6-month BINS total score significantly correlated with the BSID-II MDI ($r = 0.40$) and PDI ($r = 0.35$); predictive validity was an acceptable 67–76 percent for identifying lower functioning infants, given that the likely base rate of abnormality was estimated to be 20–40 percent. The authors also recommended subdividing the moderate-risk category and using low–moderate and high–moderate cut scores, based on the dashed cut score found on the BINS scoring form.

Aylward and Verhulst (2000) gave the BINS and McCarthy Scales of Children's Abilities (MSCA) to 92 children at 6 and

36 months, 105 at 12 and 36 months, and 118 at 24 and 36 months of age. BINS scores were inter-correlated for 190 infants at 6 and 12 months, 125 at 6 and 24 months, and 140 at 12 and 24 months. BINS total scores, standard risk groupings (low, moderate, high), and a binary alternative risk group scheme (HIGHRISK, LOWRISK; Aylward, 1998) were employed. The binary grouping scheme was developed by subdividing the moderate-risk group based on the cut score in the BINS manual that offered the best measures of sensitivity and specificity (dashed line). Those with moderate-risk scores falling between the cut-off point and the BINS high-risk category were combined into a moderate/high-risk group (HIGHRISK); Moderate-risk scores falling between the cut-off point and the BINS low-risk category were combined with the low-risk category to form a LOWRISK group.

Correlations among total scores for 6 and 12 months were $r = 0.72$; 6 and 24 months, $r = 0.62$; 12 and 24 months, $r = 0.68$. Risk score correlations ranged from 0.46 to 0.54 (the lowest being from 6–24 months). Correlations between the BINS-6 and the MSCA General Cognitive Index at 36 months were $r = 0.51$, BINS-12 and GCI $r = 0.38$ (0.52 with the MSCA Perceptual-Performance Index), and BINS-24 with the GCI, $r = 0.69$ (0.57 for the Verbal Index to 0.77 for the Perceptual Performance Index). With regard to motor outcome, the correlation between the BINS at 6 months and 36 months was $r = 0.34$, 12 and 36 months, $r = 0.59$, and 24-month BINS and MSCA motor outcome, $r = 0.66$.

Of those infants who were high risk at 6 months, 68 percent were high risk at 12 months and 79 percent were high risk at 24 months; 83 percent of those who were high risk at 12 months were also high risk at 24 months. Using the BINS HIGHRISK and LOWRISK dichotomous groupings (discussed above) at 6 months, the mean GCI was 77 and 95, respectively; at 12 months, 80 and 90, and at 24 months, the HIGHRISK mean GCI was 73 and the LOWRISK GCI was 94. There was a minimum 10-point difference between groups on the Motor Index at each age comparison, favoring the LOWRISK group.

Aylward and Verhulst (2008) administered a caretaker-completed Neurodevelopmental Prescreening Questionnaire (NPQ) and the BINS to a high-risk sample of infants aged from

6 to 24 months. The sample consisted of 1,436 infants drawn from five academic centers: 471 were evaluated at 6 months corrected age, 376 at 12 months, and 244 at 24 months (corrected for prematurity). Caretakers completed the NPQ (based on the BINS) while watching a video depicting infants successfully completing items. For example, the BINS item *Puts Three Cubes in Cup* was translated into "my baby can put at least three small blocks into a cup if she is asked or shown how to do so." An actual sized drawing of the cube is also included on the response form, and performance of the item was portrayed on the video. Scoring is on a Likert scale: scores of 1–3 (rarely/ never to some of the time) were considered non-optimal (0) while options 4 and 5 (usually/always) were considered optimal (1), based on previous analyses (Aylward & Aylward, 2004). The BINS was subsequently administered by examiners blinded to the results of the NPQ. Sensitivity (co-positivity) ranged from 80 to 91 percent (using the BINS as the reference standard), while specificity (co-negativity) ranged from 57 to 82 percent. Overall agreement was 70 to 83 percent, depending on age. Correlations between the NPQ and BINS summary scores were: 5–6 months $r = 0.66$, 12–15 months $r = 0.65$, and 21–24 months $r = 0.85$. Mean NPQ summary scores were routinely lower than the BINS, by 0.52, 0.87, and 0.67 points at 5–6 months, 12–15 months, and 21–24 months, respectively. Agreement varied depending on the infants' risk status, being best in those falling in the high-risk group, next in those with low risk, and poorest in the moderate-risk group. This finding was most apparent in the first two age groups; by 24 months, race (a marker for SES) was influential.

These data indicate that the BINS can be translated into a caretaker report instrument that is clinically useful. Sensitivity ratings indicated that the vast majority of infants whose neurodevelopmental status is compromised will be identified. Negative predictive values are adequate. NPQ factors derived from previous BINS analyses (Aylward, 2004) were found to correlate with 36-month outcome: at 6 months the cognitive/ fine motor factor predicted 36-month cognitive outcome ($r = 0.43$); at 12 months the verbal and cognitive factors were predictive ($r = 0.42$ and 0.35, respectively); at 24 months the cognitive and verbal receptive factors were most strongly related (r = 0.70 and 0.60, respectively) to 36-month cognitive outcome. However, in the Aylward and Verhulst study (2008), items loading on these factors had the highest percent of disagreement between the NPQ and BINS, and most had to be elicited. Finally, since parents tend to underestimate their infant's abilities when the child falls in the moderate-risk range (Aylward & Verhulst, 2008), the likelihood of false negatives is reduced. In clinical practice, if the caretaker report is non-optimal for a given item, the clinician can administer that specific item for verification.

Taken together, these studies support the reliability and validity of the BNS for clinical use in large healthcare systems, and as part of research projects with infants.

References

American Academy of Pediatrics. (2006). Identifying infants and young children with developmental disorders in the medical home: An algorithm for developmental surveillance and screening. *Pediatrics, 118*, 405–420.

Aylward, G. P. (1988). Infant and early childhood assessment. In M. Tramontana, & S. Hooper (Eds.), *Assessment Issues in Child Neuropsychology* (pp. 225–248). New York, NY: Plenum Press.

Aylward, G. P. (1991a). Predictive utility of the six- and 12-month Early Neuropsychologic Optimality Rating Scales (ENORS). *Developmental Medicine and Child Neurology, 33*(9, Suppl. 64), 22.

Aylward, G. P. (1991b, August). *Six and 12-month Early Neuropsychologic Optimality Rating Scales*. Washington, DC: Paper presented at the convention of the American Psychological Association.

Aylward, G. P. (1994). Update on early developmental neuropsychologic assessment: The Early Neuropsychologic Optimality Rating Scales (ENORS). In M. G. Tramontana, & S. R. Hooper (Eds.), *Advances in Child Neuropsychology, Vol. 2* (pp. 172–200). Berlin: Springer-Verlag.

Aylward, G. P. (1995). *The Bayley Infant Neurodevelopmental Screener Manual*. San Antonio, TX: Psychological Corporation.

Aylward, G. P. (1997a). *Infant and Early Childhood Neuropsychology*. New York, NY: Plenum Press.

Aylward, G. P. (1997b). Conceptual issues in developmental screening and assessment. *Journal of Developmental and Behavioral Pediatrics, 18*, 340–349.

Aylward, G. P. (1998). Alternative risk grouping method for the Bayley Infant Neurodevelopmental Screener (BINS) in prediction of later dysfunction. *Journal of Developmental and Behavioral Pediatrics, 19*, 386–387.

Aylward, G. P. (2004). Prediction of function from infancy to early childhood: Implications for pediatric psychology. *Journal of Pediatric Psychology, 29*, 555–564.

Aylward, G. P. (2009). Developmental screening and assessment: What are we thinking? *Journal of Developmental and Behavioral Pediatrics, 30*, 169–173.

Aylward, G. P. (2010). Neuropsychological assessment of newborns, infants and toddlers. In A. Davis (Ed.), *Handbook of Pediatric Neuropsychology.* New York, NY: Springer.

Aylward, G. P., & Verhulst, S. J. (2000). Predictive utility of the Bayley Infant Neurodevelopmental Screener (BINS) risk status classifications: Clinical interpretation and application. *Developmental Medicine and Child Neurology, 42*, 25–31.

Aylward, G. P., & Aylward, B. S. (2004). Accuracy of developmental pre-screening in biologically at-risk infants. *Developmental Medicine and Child Neurology,* (Suppl. 46), 26.

Aylward, G. P., & Verhulst, S. J. (2008). Comparison of caretaker report and hands-on neurodevelopmental screening in high-risk infants. *Developmental Neuropsychology, 33*, 124–136.

Aylward, G. P., Verhulst, S. J., & Bell, S. (1988a). The early neuro-psychologic optimality rating scale (ENORS-9): A new developmental follow-up technique. *Journal of Developmental and Behavioral Pediatrics, 9*, 140–146.

Aylward, G. P., Verhulst, S. J., & Bell, S. (1988b). The 18-month Early Neuro-psychologic Optimality Rating Scale (ENORS-18): A predictive assessment instrument. *Developmental Neuropsychology, 4*, 47–61.

Aylward, G. P., Verhulst, S. J., & Bell, S. (1992). Predictive utility of the 24-month Early Neuropsychologic Optimality Rating Scale. *Developmental Medicine and Child Neurology, 34*(9, Suppl. 66), 33–34.

Babakhanyan, I., Jochai, D., & Freier-Randall, K. (2008). Children with craniofacial anomalies: Developmental risk over time. Abstract presented at the MCH Infant and Child Health Poster Session. American Public Health Association 136th Annual Meeting, October 25–29, San Diego, CA.

Bayley, N. (1993). *Bayley Scales of Infant Development* (2nd ed.). San Antonio, TX: The Psychological Corporation.

Bayley, N. (2006). *Bayley Scales of Infant and Toddler Development* (3rd ed.). San Antonio, TX: Psychological Corporation.

Constantinou, J. C., Adamson-Macedo, E. N., Korner, A. F., & Fleisher, B. E. (2000). Prediction of the neurobehavioral assessment of the preterm infant to the Bayley Infant Neurodevelopmental Screener. Presented at the International Society of Infant Studies, Brighton, UK, July, 2000.

Constantinou, J. C., Adamson-Macedo, E., Mirmiran, M., Ariagno, R. L., & Fleisher, B. E. (2005). Neurobehavioral assessment predicts differential outcome between VLBW and ELBW preterm infants. *Journal of Perinatology, 25*, 788–793.

Gucuyener, K., Ergenekon, E., Soysal, A. S., Aktas, A., Derinoz, O., Loc, E., & Atalay, Y. (2006). Use of the Bayley Infant Neurodevelopmental Screener with premature infants. *Brain & Development, 28*, 104–108.

Hess, C. R., Papas, M. A., & Black, M. M. (2004). Use of the Bayley Infant Neurodevelopmental Screener with an environmental risk group. *Journal of Pediatric Psychology, 29*, 321–330.

Leonard, C. H., Piecuch, R. E., & Cooper, B. A. (2001). Use of the Bayley Infant Neurodevelopmental Screener with low birth weight infants. *Journal of Pediatric Psychology, 26*, 33–40.

Macias, M. M., Saylor, C. F., Greer, M. K., Charles, J. M., Bell, N., & Katikaneni, L. D. (1998). Infant screening: the usefulness of the Bayley Infant Neurodevelopmental Screener and the Clinical Adaptive Test/ Clinical Linguistic Auditory Milestone Scale. *Journal of Developmental and Behavioral Pediatrics, 19*, 155–161.

Prechtl, H. F. R. (1980). The optimality concept. *Early Human Development, 4*, 201–205.

Psychological Corporation. (1996). *Bayley Infant Neurodevelopmental Screener. Technical Update.* San Antonio, TX: Psychological Corporation.

Sices, L. (2007). *Developmental Screening in Primary Care: The Effectiveness of Current Practice and Recommendations for Improvement.* New York, NY: Commonwealth Fund.

Talkukder, M. R., Ferdousy, R., Parveen, M., & Khan, N. Z. (2004). The use of the Bayley Infant Neurodevelopmental Screener (BINS) in identifying neurodevelopmental sequelae in acute bacterial meningitis. *Bangladesh Journal of Child Health, 28*, 51–54.

Wilson, P. L. (2000). Book Review: Bayley Infant Neurodevelopmental Screener. *Journal of Psychoeducational Assessment, 18*, 82–89.

Index